GREAT TEACHERS

ON

GREAT SINGING

By Robin Rice

In every block of marble, I see a statue as plain as though it stood before me, shaped and perfect in attitude and action. I have only to hew away the rough walls that imprison the lovely apparition to reveal it to the other eyes as mine see it.
Michelangelo

Inside View Press

Great Teachers on Great Singing

By Robin Rice

Edited for concision, clarity, and continuity by Katherine Osborne and Scott McCoy

Transcripts of singing lessons observed by the author are available to view at www.voxped.com/GTOGS

ISBN: 978-0-9910876-2-4

Printed in the United States of America
Inside View Press
Gahanna, Ohio

www.VoxPed.com

To the greatest parents I could ever hope for,
Bill and Rachel Rice.
Without your love and support, I would be nothing.
You are my heroes.

Acknowledgements

I am very grateful to the following colleagues, friends and former students for their help and advice in planning this book: Justin T. Swain, who spent a great deal of time notating all the musical examples, Edward Bak, Josh Cook, Laura Pederson, Dr. Stephanie Adrian, Dr. Daniel Hunter-Holly, Dr. Jonathan Retzlaff, Kerri Marcinko, Taylor Stayton, Michele Angelini, Maureen McKay, Emily Holsclaw, Mark and Sadie Rucker, Charles Wilburn, and Carisa Danielle Allen, my audio transcriber.

My eternal thanks to my good friend and colleague, Dr. Scott McCoy who has helped me realize this project, and to Dr. Katherine Osborne for her insightful editorial assistance.

To my lovely wife, Dr. Yung-Wei Sun and my beautiful daughters, Reagan and Raina Rice, who saw me hunched over the computer for many nights and understood.

Finally, my deepest thanks to all of my students, past, present and future: I learn from you every day. I am eternally grateful for our work and your trust.

GREAT TEACHERS ON GREAT SINGING

Robin Rice

TABLE OF CONTENTS

THE INTERVIEWS

Editorial Principles

When I first received the approximately 1500 pages of audio transcripts from the interviews and lessons observed by Robin Rice that are the basis of this volume, I was presented with a significant dilemma: how can this wealth of information be distilled and organized most usefully for the reader, while preserving each teacher's personality and distinctive approach? The transcript of *any* voice lesson would be filled with irregular sentence structure, conversational fillers, broken syntax, colloquialisms, and the efficiently abbreviated language that develops synergistically as a teacher and student build a working relationship. Few of us speak in formal, complete prose as we formulate a pedagogic explanation or directive. And yet, simply presenting verbatim selections from the transcripts would have been difficult to read and contextualize in the absence of audio or visual references.

Excellent voice teachers dynamically respond to changes in body positioning, tone production, language, and phrasing with an ever-shifting combination of multisensory teaching techniques and cognitive learning strategies that cannot be fully captured in a book. However, I think readers will intuit many of these instructional layers as they read and consider this text. For those who wish to quickly identify the major pedagogic messages conveyed to students during these sessions, I excerpted statements about fundamental singing and interpretational issues that are characteristic of each teacher's philosophy and technique, which are presented under the heading *Lesson Highlights* in each chapter. Many of the vocalises and exercises used during the observed lessons are also included, along with directives given to individual students to optimize their application. Although we cannot hear or see the student singing these exercises, which would help us more fully understand what the teachers were particularly addressing in each situation, the specificity of these directions is instructive in itself to lifelong students of the art of teaching. More detail can be found in the full transcripts online for those who want to delve further into these ideas in the fuller context (www.voxped.com/GTOGS).

These editorial decisions also were guided by my desire to give the reader the experience of witnessing spirited conversations between master teachers. More formal language was prioritized for explanations involving complex pedagogic, dramatic, and musical ideas, or scientific concepts. In an effort to avoid turning these exchanges into something resembling an article in an academic journal, a more casual, conversational style was preserved whenever possible. Statements were streamlined, when appropriate, in pursuit of greater clarity. However, the characteristics and personality of each teacher should easily be recognizable to readers and bring smiles to the faces of those who already know them as friends, colleagues, and teachers.

My hope is that the information presented in these chapters will provide inspiration to teachers and singers as they digest the contrasting teaching styles, technical aesthetics, and pedagogic methods described within. Great teachers evolve and respond to the aesthetics of their time and the students who seek their guidance. Robin Rice's encounters with these educators is somewhat akin to anthropology fieldwork in the voice community, providing us with detailed "snapshots" of their teaching careers and creating a temporal record of the days he spent with them. This collection of snapshots presents a compelling portrait about what it means to teach operatic singing in our time, and the dedication of those who daily expend their energies to preserve the art of acoustic singing in the Twenty-first century.

Katherine Osborne, 2017

Publisher's Foreword

I am delighted to introduce *Great Teachers on Great Singing*, by my colleague and friend, Robin Rice. The subtitle for this book might read: *Interviews with some of the finest singing teachers in America, based on observations of their lessons*. These master teachers present a broad range of technical approaches to vocal excellence and artistry, proving once again that there is more than one way to "skin the cat."

Rice's book follows in the footsteps of Jerome Hines' masterpiece, *Great Singers on Great Singing* (1982), but with a twist. Hines interviewed singers with whom he worked on the great opera stages of the world, and with medical experts who attended to their health. In the process, he revealed a huge diversity of opinions and techniques, along with some significant misconceptions about physiology and resonance maintained by the top echelon of professionals. By contrast, Rice explores the diverse techniques used by highly successful teachers—people who enable the beautiful singing we love to hear.

Over the past twenty years or so, I've written articles and books, and given presentations at conferences around the world addressing the acoustic and physiologic variables among singers and how they impact the manner in which we play our instrument—the voice. Given our rich pedagogic history, which can be traced through the monumental works of Tosi, Mancini, Garcia, Lamperti, Doscher, and Miller, and the contemporary scientific foundations of singing revealed by Vennard, Sundberg and Titze, we might expect to have arrived at a universal singing technique that is uniformly effective for everyone. But all we need do is observe our colleagues, their students, or professionals on the opera stage to realize the folly of any such idea.

In the not-too-distant past, I participated in a panel discussion at an international congress that focused on current and future trends in voice research. During this session, each panelist was asked to think outside the box in terms of future research that might have direct implications for better teaching and singing. My response was to propose a massive dataset consisting of voice and physiometric measures that could be correlated with information about a singer's technique, as compiled through interview and observation. If that sounds horribly complicated, it really is not. Let's look at a possible example.

Imagine you are teaching your first heldentenor. He is six feet three inches tall, weighs 230 pounds, has a forty-eight-inch chest, a long waist, long neck, large jaw that easily drops three inches, a large larynx, a high-domed hard palate, and a generally robust physiognomy. With a large enough dataset, we could see what approaches to breathing, resonance, registration, and phonation tend to be most successful for singers with matching physical characteristics, thus minimizing the inevitable trial-and-error inherent in the teaching process. While it is true that singers approach these technical aspects in a huge variety of ways, it actually could turn out that people with similar physiognomy and voice type might have quite a lot in common with each other. Our teaching process, therefore, could be guided by what we know tends to work better for people of a given size, shape, and gender.

This idea, however, immediately was shot down by another person in attendance, who presented research demonstrating a specific breathing method that was effective for more than eighty-five percent of all singers. There was no need to explore alternatives, because this method was optimal for virtually everyone. As evidence, data were presented showing that singers using this breathing method reduced or eliminated their vibrato. I don't know about you, but I have little faith that Leontyne Price or Luciano Pavarotti would have sounded even better without vibrato. But this counter-position helps illustrate not just the diversity of technique, but also the variety of aesthetic preferences we have.

Ultimately, I remain firm in my belief that there is no possibility of developing a unified technical approach to singing. As teachers, it is our responsibility to explore the optimal technique for each individual instrument and singer. And since no two of us—with the possible exception of identical twins—have precisely the same body, it is logical that we each play our instrument in the manner best suited to our individuality. In short, we must be flexible, not dogmatic. If a student is unsuccessful with the breathing method we are teaching, it is the method, not the student, that has failed.

The teachers who were interviewed and observed for this book provide extraordinary examples of this flexibility in teaching. Not only do we see a great variety of general approaches, but also variations within each teacher's approach as necessitated by the needs of individual students. As you read, I suspect you will find many ideas and techniques you currently employ in your own teaching. You also might find a few items that leave you scratching your head in wonder, or that you want to steal immediately for use with your students. But I hope you also will come to realize there is no such thing as a miracle vocalise that is guaranteed to produce a specific result. Indeed, the examples provided in this book show that almost any pattern of pitches and rhythms can lead to excellent singing—provided the exercise is backed up by the skilled ears of a teacher who is able to motivate students to their best vocalism.

As the publisher of this book and an advocate for fact-based singing pedagogy, I must take a moment to address an elephant in the room: alternative facts (statements that are inconsistent with established physiologic and acoustic principles). Inside View Press also publishes *Fundamentals of Great Vocal Technique*. While there are important pedagogic ideas and practical concepts in that book, it is rooted in experiential observations that often run contrary to scientific evidence. Please do not misunderstand me: I wholeheartedly believe that teachers should use any idea or language that inspires beautiful singing. And excellent teaching often is best supported by language, concepts, or images that have no factual basis. But from my perspective, we encounter a pedagogic dilemma when teachers conflate their personal perception (or misperception) of physiology and acoustics with reality.

For example, I have no issue with teachers citing Newton's *Third Law of Motion* (for every action, there is an equal and opposite reaction) to trigger a response. But in reality, there is nothing in that law that suggests palate elevation is related to the descent of the diaphragm. Yes, the diaphragm moves down and the palate moves up, but that is a coincidental, rather than causal relationship. And if one breathes through the nose, the palate cannot be lifted while the diaphragm contracts. Other physiologic, and therefore pedagogic confusion results from the misidentification of body parts, their function, and location, as often happens in discussions about the diaphragm. The location and number of resonating chambers, the location and function of the tongue, the cause of velar closure, the relationship between facial muscles, palate, jaw, and larynx, glottal configurations for different voice registers and registrations, and basic vocal tract acoustics—including the dreaded *f-word* (formant)— too often are described through conjecture masquerading as science.

There is a line in a song by Ani di Franco that helps us confront another issue. "My father, he told me the story, and it was true for his time. But now the story's different, maybe I should tell him mine."[1] Pedagogic and scientific understanding of singing grows and continues to evolve over time. The *Bernoulli Effect* provides a prime example. When voice science first became a serious avenue of inquiry, researchers and pedagogues theorized that the *Bernoulli Effect* (the inverse relationship between pressure and velocity as fluid moves through a system) was the primary factor in maintaining vocal fold oscillation, and hence phonation. This was wonderful news for singing teachers, as it meant that the only thing singers ever needed to worry about was providing an adequate and appropriate supply of air; if breathing was correct, all other elements of singing automatically would fall into place. But more recent scientific evidence demonstrates that *Bernoulli* plays a much smaller role. We now know that vocal fold oscillation is maintained through the coordinated contributions of aerodynamics (including pressure variation resulting from the *Bernoulli Effect* and from turbulence in the air above the glottis), elasticity and the natural oscillation rates of vocal fold tissue, inertive reactance in the air column above the glottis, and acoustic resonance. A full discussion of these elements is well beyond the scope of this brief foreword, but interested readers might visit the website of the National Center for Voice and Speech for more details (www.NCVS.org). Because science clearly has demonstrated that production of a beautiful singing tone requires quite a bit more than well-controlled breathing, all of this information has significant implications for singers and their teachers.

You will see the *Bernoulli Effect* referenced by several teachers interviewed for this book, as well as a number of other things that might fall into the category of alternative or preterite reality. My dilemma as publisher and editor-in-chief lies in how the matter should be addressed. On one level, people who understand the factual underpinnings of acoustics and physiology are likely to view any misinformation as a pedagogic tool or an expedient means to an end. It is more problematic for readers who cannot identify inaccuracies. I hope they do not become teachers who inadvertently pass along these alternative facts to future generations of singers and teachers, as many of our own beloved mentors did with us.

I fully realize that I'm asking a lot of our current and future teachers. In reality, there is more information than anyone possibly can learn in a lifetime. Given everything we must know about repertoire (I suspect there only are a few people on the planet who thoroughly know every Schubert song or Donizetti opera), language and diction, performance etiquette and dramatic expression, musicality and musicianship, expecting singing teachers also to be up to date on voice acoustics and physiology could be viewed as the proverbial straw

---

[1] Excerpt from the song *The Story*, written and recorded by Ani di Franco. © 1989

that breaks the camel's back. But I think not. Employing a fact-based pedagogy that has its roots in science *and* artistry makes our teaching more efficient, allowing us to reach that ultimate goal of beautiful singing with fewer detours along the road. It's a bit like learning a new language: if you aren't willing to immerse yourself in French and risk making errors, you never will become fluent. Likewise, I hope that our struggles with fact-based pedagogy and pedagogic language never stifles the conversation about singing and teaching.

Finally, I suspect that some of you will disagree with the selection of people included in this book. Others may wonder why their idolized master teacher is not present. *Great Teachers on Great Singing* provides examples of teachers in our current generation who have proven records of successful students. There is no suggestion that these are the *only* teachers who merit inclusion, or that they are the *best* teachers in America. But they do serve as examples of practitioners of the teaching art who have achieved consistently fine results. We all should aspire to be so effective with our students.

Scott McCoy, 2017

Author's Foreword

"In every block of marble, I see a statue as plain as though it stood before me, shaped and perfect in attitude and action. I have only to hew away the rough walls that imprison the lovely apparition to reveal it to the other eyes as mine see it."
Michelangelo

One of the first things any teacher learns the truth in Michelangelo's words. But students are unique, and they learn in different ways; therefore, teachers can't rely on a fixed methodology, most especially when it comes to teaching singing. Successful teachers quickly learn they must be creative. And as their teaching of the art evolves, teaching becomes an art in its own right. In short, their skill and wisdom is guided by experience.

Having a compilation of ideas and techniques from some of the brightest and best voice teachers in our country has always been an exciting prospect to me, and is one of the biggest reasons that I wanted to write this book. I chose my subjects from both inside and outside academia not only for their successes, but for the uniqueness of their approaches. In talking with them and observing them in action, I discovered that while each has his or her individual style of teaching and strong ideas about what works and what doesn't, they all have one very important thing in common: their end game is all the same. They want to take their students to the highest attainable level of the art. This book highlights how they go about moving toward that goal as they do their best to simplify the process and demystify singing technique.

When I began this journey, I had a list of questions I planned to ask every teacher during the interview. In the spirit of this being a learning process for me as well, I quickly discovered that asking direct questions did not always lead me to the best answer. Observation of them in their "realm" as they taught, and comfortable, relaxed conversation often revealed their strengths on their own.

I was fortunate to spend quite a bit of time with these great teachers, some of whom were so busy that I was lucky just to get what little time they could spare! With that said, I want to be sure to clarify that although some chapters may be quite a bit longer than others, it's definitely not a reflection of a teacher's relative importance. Every person who graciously made time for me in his or her busy schedule deserves accolades, and I hope that I've expressed how much they are appreciated. This book was written to call attention to the work of some of the finest teachers in the country and was not meant to be negative in any respect. This is one aspect that I would ask each reader to keep in mind; there is nothing in this book that should be viewed in a negative light. I can assure you that everything that was said and every instruction given by each teacher was effective for the student with whom they were working.

I'd like to thank each of the teachers I've interviewed, as well as the students who so willingly allowed me to observe their learning process. There are many more great teachers out there and I've already compiled a list of those I hope to interview for my next book.

My life has been enriched greatly by this experience, and I have learned so much from these teachers who were so willing to share their time, techniques, and ideas with me. My own teaching skills have become much more effective based on the knowledge and skills I have gained, and I hope to use those skills to set my students on the best possible path toward achieving their goals.

Finally, I'd like to say to everyone I've met during this journey from an idea to a book in print that I wish you all the best in your endeavors to achieve success in this wonderful art that we have chosen.

My Methodology

I began compiling the list of teachers based on my own knowledge and through the recommendations of other teachers and singers. Some of the teachers I contacted did not want to participate, and I did have a few who began the process but subsequently withdrew for personal reasons. I conducted each live interview at the teacher's chosen location. Almost every teacher in this book teaches at several venues, so they stay very busy. Ultimately, I was able to observe at least two lessons for each teacher.

A brief summary of my study about the art of teaching voice

The first question one might ask is, "Why are these teachers so effective?" The overarching reason is that the personalities of students and teachers were strongly compatible, and that the teachers' technical approaches matched the needs of their students. I noticed a respect between everyone in the studio at all times. It was a wonderful mix of business, hard work, and the love of the art, and I will again say that at no time did I see anything that could be perceived as negative.

As Dr. Joyce Farwell said, "Singing is basically about four things: breath, space, vowel and the resulting resonance." The teachers I interviewed for this book exhibited how quickly they could get the student to learn each technical move, or maximize each vowel and resonance. But they also were expertly adept in getting their students to the end result of releasing the voice. This is what matters, and is what creates the indescribable, almost mystical, and wonderfully beautiful art of singing.

The art of singing is one of the most natural human activities. It is evident that all of these teachers have built their philosophies on making the process simpler and more natural, in a sense, unlearning overproduction or misconceptions.

Some thoughts about vocal technique

Barbara Doscher told me once that her view of vocal technique was simple, "Eighty percent was negative knowledge; knowing what not to do. The other twenty percent was left up to the taste of the teacher and singer." I believe that this is one of the most intriguing and accurate statements about teaching singing.

Another Barbara, Barbara Honn told me, "You know Robin, all you have to do is to decide what kind of sound you want from a singer and then work on your vocabulary to get it."

Technique is not a set of mystical ideas that you must chase in frustration for many, many years; it merely is an understanding of the process that provides the best approach for every voice. Therefore, it is important for singers to clarify their ideas and the directions they give to themselves while singing. One to two very general but specific ideas are good. This helps keep the mind clear and allows the body able to remain flexible and available for any unplanned changes, such as a faster tempo taken by a conductor or pianist. Too many directions to the body will slow down the thinking process, causing the body to become static or stuck as it tries to do too many things. So, singers must work out those details in the practice room and then quickly turn those ideas into how they do business. In other words; macro, not micro. The singer ultimately is responsible for the process, which has a direct influence on the product. All of the teachers in this book were masters at simplifying the whole process. They all worked on proficiency of movement and economy of work. Be effective, not perfect.

The difficulty and the beauty of singing are found simply in the duality of opposing forces. Balance is the central word for all things we consider as singers and teachers. We are constantly thinking of competing ideas as we sing or teach: feel the breath lower in the body as pitch rises; the palate must continue to be lifted during a descending scale; and the ever-present balance of bright and dark in a *chiaroscuro* tone. This constant sense of balance is especially important in working with the breath gesture during singing. Newton's Third Law of Motion is in play constantly: *for every action, there is an equal and opposite reaction.* Each force must exist with the other in balance, not overtaking the other, thus creating a functional paradox. There is nothing that is perfect. This balance of opposing forces is constantly moving and elusive—it is never static. Gridlock and dormancy are archenemies. It was of particular interest to me that each teacher was quick to add a counterbalance when giving a specific directive. Relaxation is somewhat of an oxymoron: it is not passivity, but rather is the understanding of which muscle groups to energize, while allowing other muscle groups to find a point of energetic stasis. The analogy here is watching football players run: certain parts of their bodies are used to generate massive amounts of quick energy, while other parts remain less active. Some singers must work to find a more energetic body language, while others must learn to release an overabundance of energy or thrust with the breath. Every singer at one point or another will experience too much movement or not enough movement of the body and breath during singing. It is important for each singer to find the way that works best for him or herself. I believe that Scott McCoy's foreword to this book frames this argument very well.

My teacher in the early 1980's was Richard Hughes. He was a wonderful man who helped me to understand my voice and what I needed to do to make it more efficient. Mr. Hughes worked with many great singers at the time, yet he was patient with me and answered a lot of questions that I had. I specifically remember our discussion about the breath and how that related to the space. He said, “If the space is free, then the breath is free." He paused and smiled and then said, “If the breath is free, then the space is free." After all these years, he is still correct. Mr. Hughes actually focused more on freeing the space, while other teachers more specifically work toward freeing the breath. And many teachers are like me, working simultaneously in both areas.

So, singers must love to work on their craft. They also must love to be intellectually curious about how to improve their work or mechanics, and to find their own efficiency of movement. Teachers must guard against trying to go too fast or down a road that leads to frustration and backtracking. When singers are introduced to new thoughts and ideas, they must decide if those things are going to be good for them. Some may not be. Therefore, singers must distinguish whether or not if the new work will lead their voices to a more natural ease, opulence, and power, or if it will not be effective for them. It is my firm belief that singers always should keep in mind the rule of Occam's Razor, which is "the idea that, in trying to understand something, getting unnecessary information out of the way is the fastest way to the truth or to the best explanation," and that "one consequence of this methodology is the idea that the simplest or most obvious explanation of several competing ones is the one that should be preferred until it is proven wrong."[2] In other words, stay on the paved road in your thought and direction to the voice. Singers basically are working with mechanics, sequencing and timing. Knowing what to do, the order in which each skill must be done, and the timing within each phrase will lead to the most natural and opulent vocalism.

Singing is like many sports where intricacies and strategies are involved; conversations and arguments are continuous over which strategies are best in the short and long term for every player and team—just listen to people talk about baseball. One of the great movies from the late 1980's was *Bull Durham*. In the story, Crash (Kevin Costner) is an aging minor league ball player, brought up from another team to help a young pitcher, Nuke (Tim Robbins). Nuke has tremendous potential, but is plagued by inconsistency. Ultimately, Crash tells him, “A good friend of mine used to say, ‘This is a very simple game. You throw the ball, you catch the ball, you hit the ball. Sometimes you win, sometimes you lose, sometimes it rains.”[3] The art of singing is pretty much the same.

Robin Rice, 2017

[2] http://whatis.techtarget.com/

[3] http://imdb.com

Great Teachers on Great Singing

By Robin Rice

Penelope Bitzas

Penelope Bitzas, mezzo soprano, is an Associate Professor of Music and former chairman of the voice department at Boston University College of Fine Arts School of Music. She came to BU with a bachelor of music degree from Ithaca College where she graduated magna cum laude, and a master of music degree from the New England Conservatory of Music.

Ms. Bitzas has performed in a wide variety of musical genres, including opera, contemporary music, solo recital, orchestral performances, and Greek music. She has appeared as a soloist under such notable conductors as Kurt Masur, Seiji Ozawa, Gustav Meier, Luciano Berio, and Richard Westenburg. She has concertized in the United States, Germany, Cyprus, Greece, Turkey, and Venezuela. As a frequent performer of new music and Greek music, she has been heard at Alice Tully Hall, Merkin Hall, Jordan Hall, and other venues in concerts and world premieres of this repertoire. In the New England area, Ms. Bitzas has been a soloist with the Bangor Symphony Orchestra, ALEA III, Back Bay Chorale, Just in Time Players, the MIT Chorale and Orchestra, First Monday Concerts, and Time's Arrow.

Ms. Bitzas was National Semi-Finalist in the Metropolitan Opera National Council Auditions, and a member of the Minnesota Opera Studio, The New Music Ensemble at the Banff Centre, and the Blossom Music Festival. She was also a recipient of two fellowships to the Tanglewood Music Center. Her students have been winners and finalists of numerous competitions, including the Metropolitan Opera National Auditions, Joy in Singing, Opera Index, George London, Jensen Foundation, Reyfuss, Poulenc, Gerdna Lissner, Loren Zachary, NATS and NATSAA competitions, and the MacAllister Awards. Her students have performed roles with the New York City Opera, Florida Grand Opera, Santa Fe Opera, Des Moines Opera, Nashville Opera, Virginia Opera, Opera Theater of St. Louis, Sarasota Opera, Opera Colorado, Boston Lyric, Michigan Opera Theater, Lake George Opera, and Opera Boston. Her students have participated in opera apprenticeships at the Santa Fe Opera, Opera Theater of St. Louis, Wolf Trap, Opera North, Brevard Music Festival, Cincinnati Opera, Des Moines Metro Opera, Seattle Opera, Lake George, Utah Festival Opera, Virginia Opera, Glimmerglass Opera, Merola, and Anchorage Opera.

The Interview

RR: *I noticed that you have your students place their hand on their clavicle?*

PB: Yes.

RR: *And that is for…?*

PB: It depends; some people put their hands on their clavicle and it helps them to keep their larynx down without talking about it.

RR: *Really? Okay.*

PB: I picked that up somewhere. But for Jane[4], I put it there because I think she sings off her voice too much. So, by putting it here I think she keeps a little more chest registration in it without me having to talk about it. It also keeps her from lifting up off her voice so much. So, usually, the more we do that, the better it gets. That's why I do that.

RR: *What do you look for in a singer? What are the main things that you're looking for when someone comes to sings for you or you go to auditions?*

PB: You mean about the voice, or about everything?

RR: *About everything.*

PB: I want to see that they have a sense of what music is about—a sense of what a phrase is. For me, it's about timbre. Some people just like those high, light girls and want to teach them. I have a couple of them, but for me it's usually their artistry and the color of their voices that interests me. I can hear it even if she is a mess. And I think, "I want to fix that to get it where I think it's supposed to be." So that's how I hear it.

RR: *Now what about the voice specifically? Anything?*

---

[4] Names of students cited in the text have been altered to ensure anonymity

PB: Well, I like it to be clear. I like it round, not too wide and spread. I like it more *chiaroscuro* than just favoring one side or the other. I really like an Italianate sound, but I like an "oo-ey" top. So, I look for those things I can hear. When people sing, I'm usually thinking, "Oh, their tongue is getting in the way." Not everyone will gravitate to some voices that interest me, because I can hear under the clutter and can tell I can fix the clutter. I'm a sound person. I like sounds when I find them interesting, different, or intriguingly colored, or I hear where I think they can go with time and development. I really like a mix of things, because I like to hear a good chest connection but "dome-y" at the same time. That's how I go at it.

RR: *So you talk about the chest connection with your females?*

PB: I do a little bit. I try to do it in a way that cultivates a head voice mix. I speak of it as a register, not a voice, so you can sing your chest register and not sing throaty. It's when they do it in the musical theater way that it's throaty—I talk to them about it that way. I say, "Go into chest, but round it, so it's rounded forward instead of going, 'Ah!' like that, into your throat." That's how I tend to approach it with them.

RR: *Do you have any specific exercises that you do with females?*

PB: To work on the chest register? If it's weak, I do a little bit of /ae/ to /a/ sometimes from E-flat or E natural downward. I also do that exercise [singing][5], where you crescendo down to the "ah" and relax into that lower, fatter cord. I do that a lot. If I really feel like their vocal folds aren't coming together, I'll do a lot of /ɛ/ and staccato and then move from the staccato into a sustained phrase. I also use talky exercises and phrases a lot.

RR: *I've noticed with both of these singers you spend a lot of time working from that B to F-sharp. It's always about that area.*

PB: It's about that area, yes. My journey was tricky with that B^4 to F-sharp^5 area. It's different for everybody. [Her student] Jane was way too wide and really heavy today. She tends to be too wide anyway. So, I like it to be more 'oo-ey.' I use /u/ a lot from B^4 to F-sharp^5.[6] I don't like to talk about lightening up so much. I don't usually use that terminology, because I think it closes down some people and causes them to start hiking. But I also talk a lot about taking more head voice up there, so that's why I try to use more rounded vowels. I talk about tallness. Occasionally, I talk about the center of the hourglass, but not too often, because it doesn't work for a lot of singers I have. I say instead, "Let it feel thinner. Let it feel taller. Let it feel more 'oo-ey,' more head voice." That's how I usually approach it.

RR: *Mezzos are similar, just in a different way?*

---

[5] Throughout this text, words or phrases in [brackets] are editorial additions to aid in clarity

[6] Pitch designations used in the text are inserted by the editors for clarity and follow the international standard where the lowest C-natural on the piano keyboard is C^1 and Middle-C is C^4. Octave designations run C to C, with the lowest pitch on the piano being A^0

PB: Yes. I do tend to talk about where their flip is. I talk about the flip a lot, only because it helped me find my top better once I understood that a little bit.

RR: *Where would you say your flip is/was?*

PB: Well, it was taught to me as being F-sharp^5 or G^5.

RR: *Well, then that's soprano, isn't it?*

PB: Yes, but that wasn't where it was for me, and E-flat^5 and E-natural^5 were always terrible. One of my teachers talked about the hourglass, which didn't work for me. And she said, "Well, can you think this?" No. None of it worked for me, because I'm not a soprano. Anyway, I talk about turn, and sometimes I talk about vowel modification because I always had a really big chest voice as a kid. Even when I was little, I talked really, really low, so everybody was always trying to get my speaking and singing voice up higher. Some of that was right, and some of that was wrong. Even if I'm singing something that's sort of lyric and sitting in that upper middle, I have to sing so my *passaggio* starts at B-flat^3 so that the E-flat^4 and E-natural^4 feel comfortable and stay in a lower laryngeal position. I talk to the mezzos about rounding the vowel, more toward /o/, and more toward /a/ when they go up from there, and to start thinking about making the adjustment lower. And, even with the sopranos, depending on what their issues are, I'll sometimes talk about thinking head voice a little bit lower.

RR: *And guys? Do you teach…?*

PB: Yes, I teach a bunch of guys. Yes. I do the same things. Especially for the tenors, I try to figure out where their turn is, whether it's F^4 or F-sharp^4. But even with them sometimes I tell them to do it lower. With the tenors, I like from B-flat^3 to F^4 to be more closed. I get a lot of "ah-ey" tenors, so I do more /u/ with them than the other way around. So, I do /u/ with them and then I say, "Then go 'ah' all you want." With the baritones, it's more like the mezzo kind of thing, not having D-natural^4 covered.

RR: *So, a singer comes to you. What do you think that you normally help people do?*

PB: You mean a regular lesson, or a consultation kind?

RR: *Over the span of two years.*

PB: Well, I try to see where they are. I try to make an assessment of what I think I need to fix, and then I usually tell them what I think that assessment is, for better or worse. But I tend to be fairly nice about it, because I find that people are unbelievably fragile and can't take the bad news like in the days when we were in school. They wouldn't last five minutes. Not five minutes! And you probably have the same thing where you are teaching too. So, I always work on breath a lot and they never get it. It drives me crazy. I talk about *appoggio*. I talk about leaning out so they don't overblow. I do usually teach them how to do tongue out trills, because I want to see if they can do them or not. I think if there's something going on, they can't do the tongue out trills.

RR: *Something more with the breath or with the tongue?*

PB: With the voice, with the vocal folds. So, I try to do that first. Then I usually start with /o/, go to /u/ and /i/, and then proceed from that to other vowels—usually

54321 [sol fa mi re do] descending and variations. I do triplets down, because most of the people I get need that kind of work as opposed to the forward-focused kind of work. I get people who tend to be kind of "ah-ey" or too "ae-ey" [very high and very spread] so I'm always correcting that. I tend to start there and do octave glides and things like that to see if they can sing them without their larynx going up to their eyeballs. I get a lot of people who sing with a really high larynx, so I have to do work like that a lot. I like to use upward leaps and lots of scales. If they get pretty advanced, I'll do something from the Marchesi book. I have a doctoral soprano now who is in her third or fourth year, so now we do Marchesi.

RR: *Are there any other method books that you use?*

PB: Yes, sometimes I use Vaccai and Liebling exercises because I know them and use them myself. I've worked with Garcia and Lamperti exercises too. Those are the ones I play around with. I like to do descending onsets so the high notes and low notes feel the same. I often use closed-to-open and open-to-closed vowel combinations, and then move into more expansive kinds of exercises. That's generally what I do. Two years is just not enough time for some of them to get it going, and I usually have to do a lot of work on tongue tension and things like that. I believe the tongue should be up and out of the throat, with a little height and no pressing. I get a lot of people who retract the back of their tongues. I talk about the tongue all the time. I call it "fluffy tongue," like a humpbacked whale, not like a spoon. I talk about not retracting the back. I talk to them about tongue positions for vowels a lot.

I sometimes do the straw [phonation—semi-occluded vocal tract] with people if they're too fat with their singing. I tend to use that more as a therapeutic exercise rather than a regular exercise.

RR: *That's the exercise created by Ingo Titze?*

PB: Yes. I use that with them when they're fatigued. It helps them. I talk about the surprise breath, but without lifting up. I talk about a hint of a yawn but not the full yawn.

RR: *Can you give me your basic three high points of how you talk about breathing?*

PB: I talk about a feeling of suspension—feeling the back and front expansion with some abdominal release. I'm not one of those people who believes in letting your lower abdomen relax out and looking like you're having a baby. It doesn't work for me. I know a lot of people teach that, but I don't teach that way. I believe in low support underneath the breath.

Appoggio. I want them to feel that sensation of suspending and trying to resist the inevitable collapse. That's how I talk about it. I don't feel any abdominal pulling or tucking in at all, but some people have to. So, if I sense that they have to, I'll tell them, "You know, at the end of the breath, you may feel that right below your belly button is going to come in and up a little bit. If that's what you need to do, so be it." But I don't want anybody to actively pull the breath out. I don't believe in that. Less is more for me. Most people overblow, and I like to talk about compressed air, compressed by *appoggio*. I talk with them about imagining their torso sitting on their hips and their hips being their center of balance. That's where their support is.

I differentiate between breath flow and the breath support underneath it. They are connected, but not really the same thing. When they think, "My breath is my support," the tone doesn't spin. I try to talk about breathing as two different but related concepts. I have them do things like lift the piano and stand on one foot so they feel their core [muscles] once in a while. I don't do a lot of those things. I'm not that kind of teacher.

RR: *But that's what I love about your teaching. I remember talking with you and some of the people who worked with you in Italy. Your teaching is very tangible. It's not smoke and mirrors and tricks. It's not bumper sticker psychology that will get your through the day but not the next day when it doesn't work anymore.*

PB: Well, sometimes I use short-term tricks, but I usually don't keep that a secret. I'll say, "Okay, in the short term you can get away with that. In the long run, you have *do* this, period."

RR: *Yes, tell your body what to do, and then do it.*

PB: Yes.

RR: *I noticed your student Jane's jaw wiggles a bit.*

PB: Yes, it does.

RR: *What do you do for that?*

PB: I hold her jaw and put my hand and finger between her teeth and make sure her jaw's not pushing forward. I occasionally use a chewing exercise. I haven't done this with Jane. I usually talk to her about her jaw coming too far forward. I talk about the jaw hinge. I get students to feel that spot right in front of the ear where the hinge is, and encourage them to open from there all of the time. So, it's not going to be fully open for everything, but it has to be a little open. I talk to them about how the inhalation opens everything. You must open before you start to sing and be able to articulate constantly.

RR: *But then when they would take that space in, you would correct them not to [demonstrates] and then immediately compress out.*

PB: I want it to suspend there.

RR: *So you want it to blossom up and over.*

PB: Up and over. I mean, Jane is different, because up and over doesn't always work for her. She pulls her palate down.

RR: *She goes back in her head.*

PB: For her, I have to say, "Rounded forward," and that's when it releases. I tend to talk about "in," "up," and "over" all the time. I tend to talk about the upward backspace a lot, so that the vowel is more forward and the tongue is really high at the top of the vocal tract. I also talk about the vocal tract sometimes—just singing at the top of the column and things like that.

RR: *So, you tailor it to where each student is and what they need.*

PB: Yes. When I have a studio class, I'll say, "Now see how she's doing that. That's what you do." Or I'll say, "Now this person has nothing to do with anything that anybody else in this room does." Because I get some people who are too "oo-ey" and narrow. So, I tend to be a bit more individualized with my instructions.

RR: *How do you go about choosing repertoire for the singers?*

PB: I would have to have a really clear picture of where I think the voice is going, and most of the time I do. So, for me, it's about where the spin is, and what I think the size of the voice is. Jane is a tricky one, because she has a really hard time with the top, but she has that color.

RR: *The color is really interesting.*

PB: It's really interesting, and I think it lends itself to different repertoire. She was singing Pamina [*Magic Flute*], and she's okay as Pamina, but I'm not sure anybody's ever going to hire her to sing the role. She has all the color in the voice, which is why she's really good as Elvira [*Don Giovanni*]. The temperament of that character and vocal color works for her. That's the first time I heard sing the Mimi [*La Bohème*] aria: I think that will really be good for her, so I think she could be singing more Italianate repertoire. I try to decide whether they're really an Italian singer or not. I try to make everybody an Italian singer. That's kind of what I do!

RR: *How do you know if someone is in the wrong Fach?*

PB: I had a tenor come to me a while back. He was singing Pinkerton [*Madama Butterfly*]. I said, "How do you sing this with no top?" I thought, "Well, I'll fix his *passaggio* and then he'll have his top," because I knew his approach to the *passaggio* was wrong. It wasn't narrow enough for a tenor. So, I worked with that and thought, "It doesn't work for his voice at all." We continued to work for a while and finally I decided, "I'm just going to do this *passaggio* a different way and see what happens." So, I directed him to sing through his *passaggio* like a baritone *passaggio* and then he could sing higher. Eventually I told him, "If you are a tenor, you would be a heldentenor and you wouldn't be able to sing for twenty years, because it's not there yet. But I think you're a baritone. You've been singing with a very high larynx." His larynx was really high. He was really off the voice, and he really couldn't turn over. When you helped him to turn over, it was lower. As soon as he turned over lower, and really turned over, then he could sing higher. And it didn't sound like a tenor.

I have another interesting one. She's a really tall soprano. She can sing runs for days, but couldn't sing high! I asked her, "How can you be singing these things as a soprano?" So, she came to study with me, and I said, "You're too vertical." It was so vertical it resembled a pencil. Her jaw was really forward, her high voice couldn't turn over, and her high range just petered out. I told her, "I don't think you're a soprano. Her larynx was high and her palate was down. When she opened that up, it became really plummy, yummy, and more like a mezzo sound. So, I trained her as a mezzo—much better. It is functional, the timbre is rounder, and it's more "spinny." People are interested in her as a singer. So, for me, it's when I hear that something about the color is wrong, or where the flip is. I try to figure out where their *passaggio* is, because I think that's important to identify.

RR: *Are there specific voice types that you like to work with, or think that you work better with?*

PB: Yes. I think I don't do so well with high, light sopranos, except someone like Julie because she has some color in the tone. So, if they are really light, I'm probably the wrong teacher for them. I do really well with big voices, as scary as I find them to be. I like fixing them and making them better.

RR: *What about the culture these days about not liking big bodies, tall people, or heavy people?*

PB: I think they're missing out on a lot of great singers. I mean, I get it, and I understand it, but if they look great and don't sound great, who cares? It's about singing, really. I think it ruins the art form. I think you could also say, "Okay, if they're fat, that ruins the visual of it," and that's true too, but if they're heavy and sound like a million bucks, I don't care as much.

RR: *It's a verbal art. I don't go to watch Brittney Spears sing Verdi or Bellini, and I could cast an opera based on listening to an audio recording, not on watching a movie with no sound.*

PB: It's about the sound and whether or not it thrills you. I think there's a lot of fluffy singing going on—a lot of overly heavy, off the voice, fluffy, European singing. I don't like it.

RR: *How much time should singers practice per day?*

PB: It depends on what their schedule is. I'd like them to do at least an hour minimum. Some people say two hours.

RR: *Every day, seven days, or should they take a day off?*

PB: Well, they can take a day off if they want. I'm not as rigid about that. I have to be careful, because sometimes they are singing way too much. I will tell them, "Okay, you have this incredibly busy singing schedule, way too many hours every single day for weeks on end, so you're going to go home and be quiet and just warm up for ten minutes. That's all you're going do, because you will be singing all day." When they are stretched too thin, I have to watch them.

RR: *Do you tell your singers to warm up? Do you have guidelines for them?*

PB: I talk to them about the difference between warming up and vocalizing. With warming up, I say, "Get your brain, your voice, and your body going, and here are some exercises for that." I give them several things they can do and tell them to be nonjudgmental until they feel like they've gotten the vocal folds going. Then we vocalize five notes up, five notes down. I give them vocalises every week to do and say, "These are the things you should do all the time. Here are the things you can do to fix this problem."

RR: *The things to do all the time?*

PB: Lip trills. I also want them to be able to do tongue trills, because that lets them know how they are doing. Then we do a lot of work with leaps and runs. I recommend taking periodic breaks—every three to four minutes—when they are first starting out. I also recommend a break after twenty minutes, because they're not going to be paying attention after twenty minutes. Their brains will be in another place. They might as well practice piano.

RR: *Then how do they go into their vocalizing?*

PB: Five note exercises. The five note patterns I do are descending and ascending scales using triplet patterns, alternating vowels, and things like that. And then I add on phrases and embellishments so it's all getting bigger and longer.

RR: *As a teacher, what would you say are your major influences?*

PB: Well, I love Lamperti's *Vocal Wisdom*. I think it's great. It's just a broad conceptual book on what singing is about, and that's what I like about it. I've read tons of other things and try to be voice "sciencey" and learn all that material because I find it interesting, but I don't know a hell of a lot about it. I guess I would have to say, and a lot of people would scream to hear this, is that Edson Burr really helped me a lot. He understood my voice—nobody understood my voice.

RR: *What was it about your voice?*

PB: It was low. It was sometimes fuzzy. I'll give you an example: when I was going through my soprano phase, I auditioned for CCM [Cincinnati College Conservatory] as a soprano for the doctoral program. I sang Marenka's [*Bartered Bride*] aria in German and a list of other things. It was fine. Then they asked for Bolcom's "Amor." One of the people at the audition—who was my teacher at the time—said I sang it beautifully in my next lesson. It was really interesting, because the Bolcom was four times louder in the hall than the aria. I asked, "So, do you want to hear me sing a mezzo aria?" She wasn't the first person to try to make me a soprano, but I had no dome tone. I had no dome, and I have a Greek voice, which has a different kind of *chiaroscuro* kind of tone. I probably used too much chest. I've always had chest voice for days. I never had any head voice, and nobody talked about it. And so, I went to Ed Zambara, who was overly simple. He used to say. "Just drink it in, Penny. Just drink it in." And drinking it in worked for me and helped to raise my palate. I found the center of my voice. He understood my voice. So, I was very appreciative of that. My first teacher, Susan Clickner, was very good with me. My last teacher was Dodi Protero.

I worked with Dodi for a long time. She used to say, "Honey, your tongue's too high in back. Will you relax a little?" Because it *was* too high. She would ask, "How's it feel?" "Fuzzy." "It doesn't sound fuzzy, dear." I mean, she just understood me and I could ask her things because I was already teaching. She just guided me more into the center of my voice, because everyone thought that the low that I had was too chest voice dominant. But that's where my voice is, really. It has a lot of chest. It's not fat. I don't have a fat voice. I have a really narrow voice, but still, they didn't get it. My first teacher understood my voice too, but she didn't talk about the palate or anything. So, I think those two, Ed and Dodi, really understood me the best. They knew how to get my voice into the real center of my sound and not try to make it be a different voice than it was, which I think a lot of people do. They hear something and say, "Oh, that can't be right." Maybe that's really what it is.

RR: *When did you start teaching, and why did you start?*

PB: I've always been teaching, even when I was in school. When I was an undergrad, I was telling everybody how to sing. I had no business doing that. I didn't know what I was talking about. I was twenty-four when I finished grad school and started teaching privately. I taught high school kids after school. That's where I started: musical theater, "*Caro mio ben,*" blah blah blah. And I was singing in town here for a couple years, did Minnesota Opera studio, and lucked into a teaching job. I just happened to be at a concert with somebody who was looking for new voice teachers, and they asked, "Have you ever taught?" And I said, "Yes." So, I got this teaching gig at Gustavus Adolphus College, which is south of Minneapolis. It's a liberal arts college with a pretty big music department. I taught a bunch of kids there. They were pretty good. And I became pretty good at teaching. And then I went back to New York.

My old college teacher asked if I would substitute for him when he went on sabbatical, and I said yes. I knew enough to really make a difference in how they were singing, and they all improved. I stayed there for three or four years. But I've always been teaching. My whole family's full of music teachers. It's sort of in the gene pool. Oh, there's one more teacher who helped me: Joan Heller. She taught here for years, and then at SMU. She's a high coloratura. But she was actually the first person that made me start to understand what turning up and over was. She gave me a much better top voice. It was a really big change for me.

Parting Thoughts

I first met Ms. Bitzas years ago when we were teaching in Italy at the Amalfi Coast program. I had heard her students prior to our time together in Italy and had always admired how they sang. I find her students' singing to be artistic, clean, well prepared, and technically sound. I also admired the relationships that she had with her singers. She was friendly and personal without being overbearing or manipulative. Her students clearly adored and respected her. I have continued to be consistently impressed by her singers over the years. We have also shared students, who have been a joy because of their intelligence and excellent vocal training.

I admired Penelope's willingness to speak candidly about her past as a singer and how that has informed her teaching. She has obviously not travelled a straight path as a singer. As a person who walked through similar fires, that experience, though frustrating at the time, gave me a deeper understanding of vocal technique. I also developed a greater ability to work with students with similar technical issues.

Penelope is an astute, detail-oriented teacher. She is able to zero in on many different aspects of singing, but the primary issue I saw her address was breath management. She used several exercises, mainly the Farinelli breath exercise. This is an excellent tool for working with the student's breath capacity and regulation of breath flow instead of a quick "smash and grab" of an inhalation that does nothing to prepare the body. It also reinforces the three main principles of the singer's breath: the intake, the stopping of the intake, and the onset. You can read more about the Farinelli exercise in Richard

Miller's book, *Securing Baritone, Bass baritone, and Bass Voices*.[7] I had been aware of the Farinelli exercise for years, however (as I said at the beginning of this book), teachers sometimes forget very important tools because of the constant influx of students and shifting teaching priorities. It is easy for us to become trapped in our metaphorical caves and forget other techniques that we know or have used in the past. This is one of the main reasons why I started this project: to remind all of us of the tools that we have.

Another effective breathing exercise was demonstrated when she asked a student to stand against the wall with a flat back and slightly-bent knees and work on her posture for inhalation. I have used this exercise and find that the breath moves lower into the torso, which gives the singer more stable tone production.

Ms. Bitzas has a consistently positive attitude when she works with students. She said nothing negative during the lessons I observed and her instructions to the singers always were clear. She manages to keep her teaching simple and avoids what I like to call "paralysis by analysis." They never think so much about their technique that they cannot relax, breathe, and sing. It is my firm belief that we can only think about a few things at a time and exceeding that number causes a traffic jam in our mental and physical systems. In the practice room, we must work on the details. But then we must integrate those details into the whole so we can give clear and specific instructions to ourselves. I tell my singers that they can only think about two or three ideas in a section of music. They must clearly control their mental instruction to their bodies so they can respond appropriately.

Lesson Highlights

Breath Support/Control

Correcting a Clavicular Inhalation

(Instructing a female student) Go over to the wall and lean back against it with a flat back. Bring your neck down so you can really feel like you can breathe into the wall. Find your breath center lower in the body. Take a half breath. Release downward. You don't need to push the breath out.

Phonation

Caution with /v/ vocalization

(Speaking to a soprano student) Vocalizing on a /v/ can get your larynx high sometimes. Sometimes when you go up in pitch, you still want to go back into that neutral buzzy spot. Since the/v/ isn't a vowel, it's harder to think about forming a more rounded, closed vowel as you ascend. When that happens, it gets too loud, too neutral, and doesn't phonate well.

---

[7] (Miller, 2008, page 25)

Resonance

Forming an /a/ vowel

Feel the /a/ above the /iŋ/. Sing /iŋ-a/ so you can feel that /ŋ/ space until you hit your palate with the /a/ and let it go upward.

Modifying Vowels to Assist Resonance and Phonation

(Speaking to a soprano student) A wide vowel is not focused enough for your vocal folds to come together when singing piano. Can you think about closing and gathering the vowel instead?

Remember to modify upward into a tall position, not down and fat. Release the jaw and really imagine the vowel way above it and taller. As you ascend, you must find the space upward instead of downward. Thinking downward will probably also bring your palate down with it.

Registration

soprano secondo passaggio

Think tall, not wide. If you get wide in the upper middle, that will kill your top voice. The upper-middle has to be taller, thinner, and headier, otherwise you're in deep trouble.

Exercises

Exercise 1: (used with a soprano)

Tongue Trills

Exercise 2: (used with a soprano)

Lip Trills

Instructions: Feel the release before you even take the breath so you can get into a lower position. Take in your breath, suspend for two seconds, and start lip trilling.

Exercise 3: (used with a soprano)

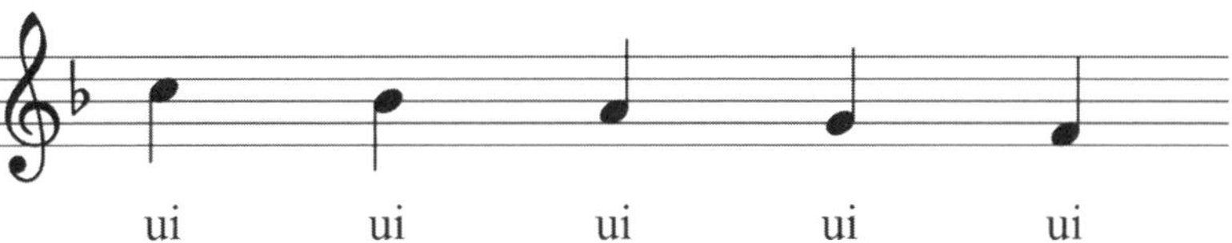

Instructions: Imagine that you're breathing into a straw. Breathe in, but don't work too hard to do it. Feel as if you are constantly inhaling as you sing and relax your jaw.

Exercise 4: (used with a soprano)

Instructions: Keep the tempo steady. Feel the cool air in your inhale and keep that feeling of buoyancy all of the way through the exercise. Bring the tongue forward.

Exercise 5: (used with a soprano)

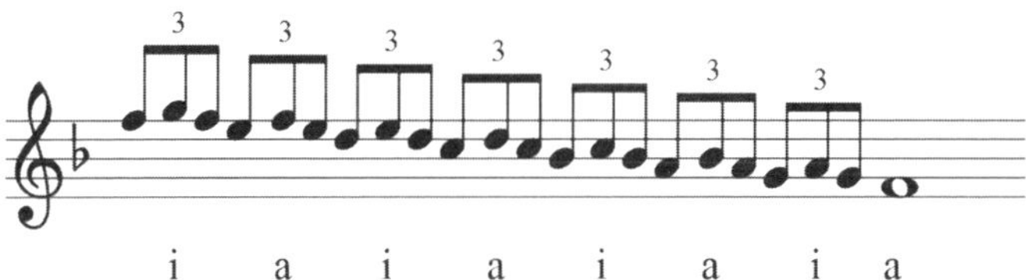

Instructions: Keep the tip of your tongue forward no matter what. Start with a tall /i/ so you don't need to move your jaw much between vowels. Find one big tall calm. Keep your palate up all of the way to the end.

Exercise 6: (used with a soprano)

Instructions: Keep your head really centered and feel the floor under you. Bend your knees and feel your torso on your hips. Zen out on how your hips center your body. Make sure your back teeth have space in between them. Low breath. Bring that dome feeling back. Go really slowly so you can feel what you are doing. Make your /a/ tall and skinny.

Exercise 7: (used with a soprano)
Sirens and glides from the top voice downward.

Exercise 8: (used with a soprano)

Instructions: Keep the sound going right through your hard palate as you descend. Relax your tongue forward. Let it touch your lip a little bit all of the time, no matter what.

Exercise 9: (used with a soprano)

Instructions: Stretch your tongue before singing this. Keep the space between your back teeth open. Put a straw under your tongue and hold it there while singing the exercise.

Exercise 10: (used with a soprano)
Speak /gagagaga/

Instructions: Put the sound above where the point of the /ga/ is. Imagine that the /g/ goes right up through your palate.

Exercise 11: (used with a soprano)
Lift your head up and back and feel the space. Now bring your head back down but keep sensing that space. Relax the jaw.

Exercise 12: (used with a soprano)

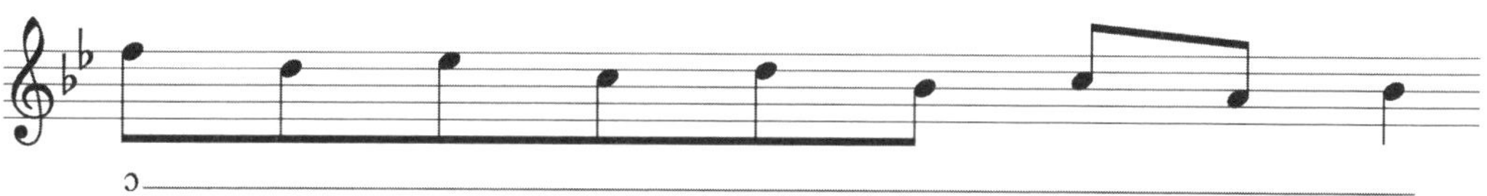

Instructions: I want to feel the head voice come downward. Really sing /ɔ/, don't just make the space for it. Find the *appoggio* in the front of your body and keep the vowel round. Find space between your upper and lower teeth.

Exercise 13: (used with a soprano)

Instructions: Keep the staccato buoyant.

JOYCE FARWELL

Dr. Joyce Farwell is a mezzo soprano who received her undergraduate and master's degrees from the University of Oklahoma, studying with the operatic tenor Joseph Benton. She received her Doctorate of Musical Arts from the Conservatory of Music at the University of Cincinnati, where she studied and coached with the famous bass baritone, Italo Tajo. Dr. Farwell is professor of voice at the Shepherd School at Rice University, and also teaches Vocal Pedagogy and Vocal Coaching for Collaborative Artists.

Earlier in her career Dr. Farwell performed in recital, opera, and with orchestras throughout the country. She is renowned now as an accomplished vocal pedagogue and travels extensively doing Master Classes and Workshops. She is on the faculty of American Institute of Musical Studies (AIMS) in Austria and is presently associated with the Voice Institute in the Houston Medical Center, presenting seminars and workshops with Dr. Richard Stasney and his staff. Dr. Farwell has several workshops established during the summer, including the *Blue Feather* on Lake Texoma in north Texas and at her home in Santa Fe, New Mexico.

The Interview

RR: *What do you think you offer a student who comes to work with you?*

JF: I think I have really good ears, and I think teaching is really about listening—not telling them everything you know, which I did when I was a young teacher. I thought I had to hurry to tell them everything I knew about it—which didn't take long—but I really think just listening and seeing are important. And what I also bring, I think in my old age, is a real understanding of who they are, and if I don't know, I've tried really hard to find out. That's really important to me—to find out who they are when they're trying to be singers. Because, I find when I can couple that with just really solid, easy work, nothing spectacular, and try and find their sound, I do them the best service. I think when you get those vibrational frequencies lined up correctly for them, they're healthier, happier, and I've done a little healing.

RR: *What do you mean about understanding them?*

JF: Well, for instance you have students come in who are so hidden, so afraid to even speak what they really think, or even to sing in a way that shows you anything about them personally.

RR: *So, they're suppressed, emotionally?*

JF: Emotionally, or just nervous or shy. It's a variety of things; it doesn't have to be a negative necessarily, but if they just come in and start vocalizing, I don't know what's going on with them. I'm just busy doing my exercises. If I have one student coming in after the other, which most of us do, I take a minute to let the other energy get out of my system and take on the new one. They're all different.

RR: *I've noticed with most of the people I've interviewed that there is a five- to seven-minute-long conversation with a student at the start of every lesson. And I know that it was true when I was a singer. Students need those first minutes to just unload—to get rid of whatever it is they're dealing with so they can relax and breathe.*

JF: And if you're sensitive to it, you sometimes sense that something is not right. There's something going on that they might even need to tell you about. But at least you have a minute to let them just forget the class they just had and try to get in the moment. They need that too, and, it gives me a clue about where they are.

RR: *And then as far as the healing part that you said?*

JF: Well, I think that what we do is healing, and if I didn't, I wouldn't still be doing it. The longer I teach, the more I work with energy. If you look at singers with whom you've worked and shown a way to sing more freely, or with the breath really in motion, there's a freedom about what they do and how they do it. That's healing. It doesn't have to be some miraculous spiritual experience. It's a physical energy thing. And I think it's important to remember that we also can shut it down. But I think it's so important that teachers stay alert and tuned in. And I know what it's like when you're teaching five or six hours a day straight. It's hard to stay if you don't just give yourself a walk down the hall or a minute to chat with them.

You can tell a lot in a few minutes by what they tell you—or what they don't tell you. And that really determines whether I start with an energetic kind of exercise or something a little slower and more legato. I have to make that decision.

RR; *You don't have a cookie cutter approach?*

JF: I don't have a certain system I use. I have several exercises that I think work for specific things; if I need to work on that issue, then that's the exercise I start with. But no, I don't have a specific *thing* that I do.

RR: *Barbara Doscher told me that teaching is based on what you listen for. She said you can have all the exercises, but if you don't know what to listen for, and you don't tell your students how they're supposed to use it...*

JF: See, that's the key, even in the exercises. The exercise in itself does nothing if you don't help your students work with it correctly. If you have a coloratura, you send her to those coloratura exercises.

There are books and books of them, and we don't need to work with them every time, but they need to know about some of them too.

RR: *So, you don't start at the same place with every singer for every lesson?*

JF: Well, I wouldn't say never—but so many problems are similar. When a singer comes to you, you don't always have a certain sense of what you would add to their voice. It all depends on how you hear it. But that wasn't always so. There was a sound I wanted to hear as a young teacher; a sound I liked best.

RR: *What was that?*

JF: It was a fairly bright vowel and free. It didn't change a lot, but I didn't start with that and try to build it in to every singer. I think that's the mistake. I don't know that my attitude toward what I want to hear in a sound has changed too much, but I don't feel like I have to impose that on a singer right away. Maybe that's not what this voice is going to be. I think we limit our students a bit when we do that.

RR: *I think that there are three ages of a voice teacher—I'm in the third one.*

JF: I'm in my last one.

RR: *The first stage is telling them everything we know. The second stage is not telling them anything and just vocalizing them. Finally, the third stage is finding your comfort level somewhere within those two paths: giving them just enough of what they need to know, but also leaving it open, enabling them to use their own intuition and intellect to find it themselves. In the end, we should be teaching them to be their own best teachers, which is what you gave me.*

JF: And that is what I tell my students. I say the real learning you do takes place in the practice room. It doesn't happen here. I can give you some directions. I can give you some ideas, but if you don't practice, nothing happens of any real or lasting value.

RR: *I remember when I was at Baylor with you that there was a student who wanted a couple of makeup lessons at the end of the semester...*

JF: Right, a quick fix. Some students take to that and some don't, but you can't help that. I had to teach students how to practice, and I think that's an important element if they don't already know how, which most of them do not.

RR: *How do you teach them to do that?*

JF: I give them a plan about learning their music. That is something I'm very organized about. I give them a way to learn music quickly. I first have them take the rhythm—no notes just rhythm—and tell them to look at the key signature and the time signature, which many of them do not. I ask them, "What key are you in?" *Not a clue.* "What's your time signature, measure signature?" *Not a clue.* Those were the kind of students I usually worked with; some bothered to look, but they were rare. They wanted to get to the music and sing the song. So, they have to do the rhythm in a tempo and take it in stages, not all of it at once. Do that rhythm on a nonsense syllable. They have to sing only three or four measures until they can do it correctly without hesitating. I also make them beat on their bodies so they have a little bit of a kinesthetic response to the rhythm. And they do that until it's right for the whole song. And then they go back and look at the text, after they have noted signature, key, and time. And I even have them mark unusual intervals. Next, they go back and do the text, speaking it aloud until they can speak it without hesitation. This is especially important if you're working on a language they don't speak, which mostly they are.

But if it's in English, I ask them to read it aloud until they can read it somewhat dramatically and without mistakes. Next, they look at the intervals and sing the melodic line with no help from the piano. I make sure they're singing the correct intervals and connecting those until they can do the melody. And that's usually not their problem—it's usually rhythm. So, only then—when all those elements are really secure—when you can go through them without mistakes or without hesitation, only then do you go on to the next one and by then you actually almost have that song memorized.

RR: *No shortcuts, right?*

JF: Not really. But that's so much easier than rote learning and so much more complete and correct when you get ready to sing that song.

RR: *That's that part of practice. Not the practice of just working on the voice. How do you teach your students to practice?*

JF: Well it depends on what's going on with them. I don't have a method that I think every singer ought to use. There are some exercises I use to work the low middle, so if they're sopranos and even baritones sometimes, they need to use that. I have them work with that every day.

RR: *Exercises for the low middle?*

JF: The middle, the low middle, which is your foundation. If they're having troubles with the *passaggio*, I tell them very specifically which exercises to work on—and they're not always the same for different singers. So, I change those up depending on the personality and the voice type. And, I think they need to have some specific exercises that they should decide on. Sometimes they'll come in with some kind of interesting comment, perhaps, "Well I tried this and it seems to help." And I say, "Great, anything that works." I do a lot of vowel work with them. Singing is about four things: breath, space, vowel, and the resulting resonance. But the resulting resonance only happens if you get your space and vowel in the right spot and the breath is working. It's not brain surgery, I tell them. In all of those elements, I work very carefully to see what is and isn't working correctly. The breath: you know, if I had a magic wand to make that all happen, I would love it.

RR: *How do you explain it to them?*

JF: They release the abdominals.

RR: *What do you mean, release?*

JF: You let them release down and that's hard, because ladies—and men too—are taught to tuck this area in. Tuck this in and then try to breathe in that situation!

RR: *So, you're talking about the inhalation?*

JF: Exactly. You release on the intake of breath. This is all Alexander work. You release the abdominals and the breath actually goes in. As I've become older, I realize I can touch people and let them touch me and it's okay. But, I always ask—just to be sure. Yes, you release the abdominals. I mean, this is how the body works. I didn't make this up. And I've talked to speech people. I've talked to doctors. It releases and the breath goes in, right? It goes only as low as the lungs go. But that pulls everything else down and I explain that. I let them feel how it's happening on my body and once the diaphragm pulls down, the breath is in; we don't regulate it. We can't. Everything makes room in the lungs for the air. Now, if we let this all collapse and move back into its position, which it wants to do, then we push all that air out. So, muscular antagonism—the low muscles—is what keeps that from happening. And it's strong down there. Does that make sense with what you think?

RR: *That makes total sense.*

JF: And that's exactly—well maybe a little different sometimes for different people—the way I explain it. Sometimes I have them get on all fours to really feel that drop and some of them can't even do it then. It's hard to let it go.

RR: *It's like yoga—cat lift and cat crunch. You talk about the generalities of all of that?*

JF: Well that's pretty specific though.

RR: *But as far as you want these intercostals to stay up...*

JF: That's more information that most of the students I work with need or are ready for. But they do need to get the sensations. I start there. But that air is going to move back out. Your job is to keep that lower abdomen supported, so everything stays in position and the breath isn't pushed out, making you lose all the air at the beginning of the phrase, which always happens. You're actually gauging [regulating] the amount of air, although I don't even talk about it that way.

RR: *What about the solar plexus/epigastrium?*

JF: I don't talk about that much because most of them get too involved, and think that's where their support is. When you tell them to feel the support system, men—most of them—will put their hand right here [indicating the epigastrium]. And what they do is tie up their breath when they do that—at least most of them—unless they know what they're doing. If you know what you're doing, it doesn't matter what you've done.

RR: *What would you say about feeling the pulse in the epigastrium area?*

JF: I think if you need to do that and it works, fine. I don't have a clue about what that even feels like. I don't feel or have any sense of anything going on in that area.

RR: *So that's basically what you tell them to do and you observe that they do it, and as time goes on...*

JF: I can tell when they sing whether or not they're doing it. Or they can tell because you'll have a student who says, "Well that's easier." Well, yes. The breath is doing the work for you, and you cannot successfully or healthfully sing without it. I know there are really good teachers who do work with that whole epigastrium area. I just don't. I haven't found I needed to.

The reason I work at this the way that I do is because I have found that it's the simplest way to discover a healthy, free sound. And I don't want to mess that up with other information. And they'll learn all that in their pedagogy class and use it if they can, or need to. I think my job is to simplify what they do in their lesson. And then they can go and experiment and come back and say, "You know, I feel that in my lower back." That's fine—some singers do; some singers don't. Once in a while when you're singing something larger you might feel a little back tension that you think you probably shouldn't be having. But a lot of singers talk about it from the back. I taught a baritone once at Baylor. He was a young man from Germany. He came in and said, "I understand. I feel like a barrel."

I try to let students find a way to talk about it that works for them. I try to give them the facts, and I happen to know they're facts because I've worked with many specialists that talk about them. I've learned a lot from speech therapists too. The vowel you place is in the back, which is the hardest thing to convince them of. If you're singing dark you're not singing back; you're singing a dark vowel. I work really diligently on the vowel color with them.

RR: *What do you mean by vowel color?*

JF" Well, it depends on where you're teaching, does it not? I had a bilingual Latina who was singing something, and I asked, "How do you say C-A-S-A?" She replied, "Casa." I said, "Will you just sing that vowel for me," and she said, "I'll try." Then it ended up being somewhere in between /o/ and /a/. And I said, "I would think *that* would be your /a/." She said, "That feels good and easy. The other /a/ doesn't feel easy." They don't always hear or respond to the same thing. And to say to them, "I'd like to hear a good Italian /a/." Really? What does that mean?

RR: *In your exercises when you do vowel work, what do you base it on?*

JF: I vary it. I will do whatever strikes my fancy that day. But, it needs to be something that's in a comfortable part of the range. For instance, working from the /a/, I found that doing the /hʌŋa/ really helps, especially when they understand that they're lifting out of the /ŋ/, not dropping. Everybody drops for /a/, and it's really all about lifting the /a/ out and up from the /ŋ/. I also work from /hʌŋai/. Sometimes I go from /i/ to /e/. I teach a really closed /e/, a French /e/, because we don't use that sound in American English. We don't sing that vowel very well. American singers don't have /e/ in our ears at all. It's not in our language center. I don't use humming a lot, unless I make sure they put their tongue really here [she demonstrated with her tongue fronted]. And then—as much as they can—put the tongue on their hard palate [she hummed] or they'll hum with the tongue down and it doesn't work.

RR: *Is there a difference to you between teaching a male and female?*

JF: I've thought about that a lot actually. I think the people I'm least successful with are the mezzos.

RR: *And you're a mezzo. What's up with that?*

JF: Most of them, I think, aren't mezzos, and I'm always working with that edging against me. I think it's what you hear best. You'd think I'd hear a mezzo—it's not that I can't teach mezzos.

RR: *I know that you can. I've heard several that you've taught very well.*

JF: Well, I'm probably more cautious with mezzos than with any other voice. I think I'm really good with tenors, oddly enough. And I'm okay with baritones. I've had good luck with sopranos. I think I do okay with most any voice. I just think you have to be careful that you know where the *passaggi* are, what they need to do, and what vowels they can use to help.

RR: *Do you find that there's a difference in vowels for a male passaggio than a female passaggio?*

JF: I do. I never let any of the females sing /ʌ/. They have to learn to sing a vowel above G[5], and they can if they let it be /e/ and sing it that way. I tell tenors, "Go watch Pavarotti sing the *Bohème* aria—his mouth is wide open and he's singing closed /e/." And I say, "You *can* do that." They don't want to, because it sounds wrong to them to sing a closed vowel in an open space. That's a hard issue to make them believe in. I have a baritone who I've always felt had options in the *passaggio*. He can do /a/, he can do /ʌ/, or he can sing /e/, but he must do something. And it will vary. I did a session once for NATS that focused on mezzos and the *passaggio*, and I said, "Okay guys, guess what I'm going to talk about? *Passaggio*!" And everyone in the house went, "Oooohh." It's there you know—face it. I had a guy came up to me once whose student I had worked with, and he said, "You know I want to talk to you about that chink in her voice. I think the cords aren't coming together."

RR: *The general consensus is to make sure the sound is clear through the passaggio and to let them darken. Since you don't want a soprano to sing an /ʌ/, are you saying that you don't want a more neutral vowel to come in too soon?*

JF: Yes, not too soon. And the thing I find I need to keep working at is either allowing the vowel to migrate to something that will work, or change the space. They both do the same thing, but sometimes it's easier with a beginner to change the vowel, and later they feel that as a different space. But ultimately, they can take the vowel they start with, go on to change their space, and it will work. That is the desired effect.

RR: *Is the breath different during the passaggio?*

JF: I think it stays consistent. Some people talk about it getting quicker. Sometimes I even talk that way. I'm not sure it happens. I talk about the vibrato sometimes. Let your vibrato be shorter. See it. Visualize it shorter. This is the crazy part: you can visualize it becoming shorter and closer together as you're sing higher. It's probably not even something that is scientifically or pedagogically accurate, but it seems to help with some folks if they're visual, and I always find that out. If they're visual I can teach them. I had a student at Rice who was very bright—I mean, scary smart. I'd say, "Tell me what that feels like to you," and she'd say, "Don't talk to me like that Dr. Farwell, I don't feel a thing." I didn't know what to do. So, I just gave her ideas and let her see what she could do with them. It was a learning lesson for me.

RR: *And you think she was being honest with you?*

JF: Yes. There was nothing artificial about that child at all. She was a straight arrow. But she was so intellectual about it all that I think she just didn't allow herself to have sensations that were a little scary for her. But it was her way. I had to learn to work around that.

RR: *How do you respond if someone sings for you and asks, "Do you think I have what it takes to have a career?" What facts would you say you would build your case on?*

JF: That's a hard question. I tell them they must have musical skills. They cannot learn by rote or listening to recordings. They must be able to be an independent musician. You cannot be an artist without being able to read music, count, and to do the arithmetic of it all. And then I say, "It's up to you whether or not you want to work hard enough to do it." I don't think I've ever felt like I could decide if somebody's talent was not good enough. If their ears are bad and their musicianship skills are bad, I tell them it's going to be a long haul.

RR: *I know you would probably never tell them, "No, you don't have it."*

JF: Well, I don't think that's our job. I have told people, "I think you're behind where you should be for what you want to do at this point, and I don't get the feeling that you want it more than you want some other things."

RR: *So, nothing about the voice? You don't really make any strong consideration just based on the instrument?*

JF: I've never had anybody ask me who just was god-awful. I don't have too many kids ask me that question, but I've had some. Do I think the Met is going call you? No. Do I think you could sing in public? Yes. I have said that. Do you want to enjoy your music and give some of that joy to other people? Yes, I think you could and that's a worthwhile thing, but to be a star—probably not. How many successful singers are making their living—fifty, or maybe a hundred? Who knows?

RR: *I think more than that.*

JF: Well, but there's a limit to how many upper-level houses there can be. There are regional opera houses all over the country that you could be singing in. But I don't think it's my job to spoil a dream. I think they come to that, most of them, on their own. But I will try to help them get as far as they can. Listen, I was fresh off the farm when I had my first voice lesson. But I could always make good sound—I knew that.

RR: *That was in Oklahoma?*

JF: Yes, and Joe Benton, who'd just been in Europe, said, "Now Miss George, I've been accused of chasing girls around the piano—I don't. Shall we begin?" I was so scared. Not of him, but just of the whole process. I asked myself, "What am I doing here?"

RR: *Over your time as a teacher, what do you think you've learned to do the best?*

JF: How to listen and rely on my ear—it's the same thing we were talking about earlier. You want so desperately to help your students. I used to lie awake at night and worry about what I hadn't done for them that day. And it was true. I had told them things, but only things I knew. I didn't really listen to understand what they needed to be told, and I didn't learn how to do that until later. I recently did a master class, and afterward someone said that there were twenty-two things I could have talked about, but that I had only homed in on one small thing—and from that one thing, everything else fell into place.

RR: *I always tell the students who want to be teachers that if you just pick the lowest hanging fruit and stay on the paved road, the other issues usually fall into place.*

JF: Usually, not always. But usually they *will* if they're quick and pay attention to what they're doing.

RR: *Do you deal with tongue positions at all?*

JF: Yes, if it's an issue, absolutely.

RR: *What do you mean if it's an issue?*

JF: Well if it's back and you see it raised up in the back, you know it's shutting off a whole bunch of stuff.

RR: *How do you get rid of that?*

JF: I try to get them to relax it, and that's hard. Sometimes I have them stick the tip of the tongue farther down and just behind the front teeth down to that ridge and sing an /i/. And it's amazing what that sounds like—if they'll do it. But sometimes they don't do it.

RR: *Even the men?*

JF: Yes.

RR: *We've covered a lot of information. Is there anything I haven't covered that you want to say?*

JF: Do you ever work with that kind of high kind of squeal thing for the tenors, like on E-flat^5?

RR: *You mean above tenor high-C [C^5]?*

JF: Yes. I have worked with that, and it helps them find their upper resonance when they're having trouble really getting above A-flat^4. I start up there and make them produce a really ugly singing sound, and then work down to about a third lower. All of a sudden their eyes kind of light up. It still sounds ugly, but they really feel a more solid tone and it helps with that upper mix.

RR: *There are singers I've had who get to G-flat^4 and it's over. Do you teach falsetto?*

JF: I don't call it falsetto.

RR: *What do you call it?*

JF: I call it "mixed high" or "strengthened high resonance." In falsetto, the vocal folds aren't really coming together. What I have them do on E-flat^5 is not that.

RR: *How would you distinguish between someone who is a young mezzo and who is a young soprano?*

JF: It's hard sometimes. It's partly the color or timbre. They're going to sound a little different in the top, and they approach a *passaggio* a little differently, even when they're beginners. For young mezzos, sometimes C^6 or even B^5 is an issue. And sopranos can go on up to D^6, and even D-sharp^6 and E^6, but then they hit it. So, they have to change a little sooner. That's part of it. And part of it is color. Sometimes young mezzos will have a color in their mid-voice. They may have as much high as the young sopranos, so I just teach them all the same for a while. But they have to do different repertoire because they can't hang up there. I had a grown lady call me one time and say, "I'm doing a Verdi *Requiem*: I heard you sing it in Michigan, and I'd really like to have you come sing it." I said, "Well, okay. And you're talking about the mezzo, right?" And she said, "Oh, no. I want you to do the soprano." And I said, "I don't do that." And she replied, "I heard you sing. I know you could." And I said, "No, I don't sing a quiet high-C [C^6]. I can sing a really big high-C, but that's not what is called for in the music. No, I won't do that." She was a little upset with me.

RR: *Do you teach people how to warm up, or is there a system you use?*

JF: I give them things I think they ought to do. I try to get them to warm the body up first. It doesn't matter too much how they do it, but they have to get blood flowing in the body. I do a lot of chewing and tongue out exercises to get the blood flowing in the vocal area. I start with the closed vowels first. For most of them, it's easier to do an /i/. Not everybody, but generally, it's easier to sing an /i/ early on than /a/. And I use /e/ too. I try to get them to warm up the low middle first, and then move from there.

RR: *You don't think that you need to start sopranos really high first, before they do this low middle work?*

JF: I know people who do that, but no I don't. I think they can do that, but I think it's a stretch, and I think it's asking the folds and the mechanism to do something it's not ready to do.

RR: *Do you use sirens for females?*

JF: Sometimes, if I think it's something that would help them. I use more of the "whoo."

RR: *You go from the low up?*

JF: Both directions. I do almost all the exercises in both directions. And I work a lot with the speaking voice. If they're having trouble with a musical passage, for instance, I make them speak it until they get a sense of what that feels like, as close to the written pitches as possible. That makes their speaking voice work in that pitch area and experience what it feels like.

RR: *You're talking about just finding the muscular coordination within the mouth?*

JF: Right. Well, and the back of the throat. After doing it twice, they almost always sing it in a better-balanced resonance than they did the first time. I'm constantly working sopranos in the lower middle range.

RR: *Do you use a spoken onset?*

JF: I had a friend from my doctoral years who said he spent three weeks just speaking with his students. They didn't sing. And I said, "Oh, my God! I don't think I could do that. I'd have them running screaming from my room." But he said, "Mine are used to it. They know that if they study with me they do a lot of speaking." And I worked with a Polish lady up in Northern Wisconsin who had me speak my vowels a lot. I learned a lot about vowels from her. The speech sound, I find, really works.

RR: *You would sometimes refer to Cornelius Reid when I worked with you. Is there anyone else that you recall about him or other historical figures?*

JF: [Richard] Miller did a compilation of what everybody's found out. I did his workshop, and it was too hard [vocally] for me; I thought it was too hard in the chest voice. My teacher studied with Jean de Reszke in France, from whom he picked up a lot about how to do the top, and he would talk to me about letting the space open as you go up. He'd sing a high-C for me when he was probably eighty years old. And he said, "Do you feel that?" I said, "Yes." And he said, "Okay. Do it that good [sic]." I said, "Okay."

RR: *So, we were going to do some exercises for the low middle?*

JF: I use the /dʒa/ with a hollering sound.

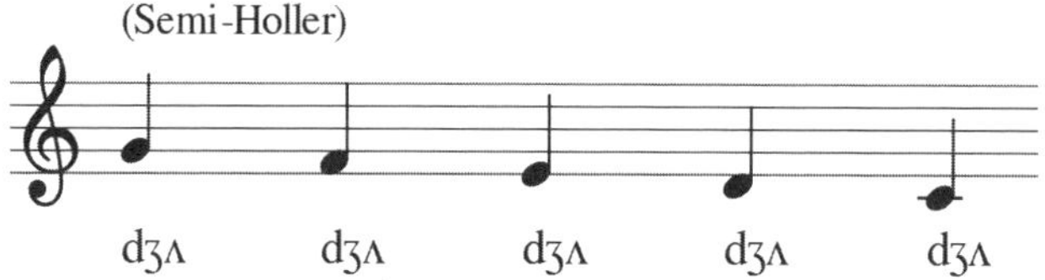

They don't really sing; they just speak it. And then I have them do the seventh and octave, so they slowly see where they have to make some adjustments. But it's just about changing the space from the beginning of that "speaky" /a/. When they have trouble I will ask them, "Okay, what happened?" They'll say, "It just shifted." So I tell them, "Right, so you must change gears as you're going up [singing], and then you can go back down.

RR: *And then go back down to that lower middle register?*

JF: Exactly! And that's just as hard for them.

RR: *So then when they say, "That feels like it's separate; it feels like the break is really large."*

JF: I have them put their hands behind their ears and listen to it, because they feel all those changes. Mine feels the same because I've been doing it for a long time. But they feel that it's in a different place. I tell them, "Absolutely, because you've gone from this lower mix of low. If this is your low, this is your high. You don't lose this [pointing to her chest], but you add this into it [pointing to her head], and it feels different." With time, they begin to understand that they're just changing the mix. I do this exercise when I feel like they're ready to go that far.

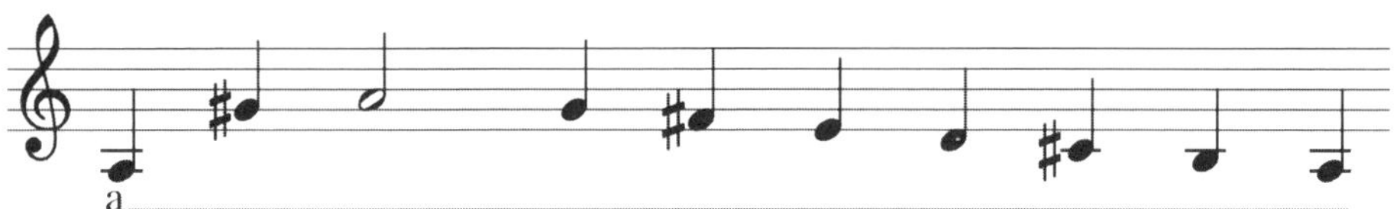

RR: *That's the one with the seventh?*

JF: Yes. I like that one because it gives them a chance to settle on the seventh a bit. The other one I do, if you have somebody who's willing to do it, usually down here [singing]. And she will ask, "Isn't that in chest?" I refuse to let them use that term, however.

RR: *You don't like the term chest?*

JF: What does chest have to do with anything? Low resonance? I talk about low, middle, and high resonance. It's okay if they want to talk about that mix in the middle, or middle resonance, but "chest" is a negative term to most people. They think it's ugly and what do pop singers do, or the rockers. So, I just make them use low resonance, which is what it is. One day I said, "Your sound doesn't really go below here." "I didn't know that. Why is that?" And I said, "That's where the resonance starts."

RR: *And you start that around A^4? This is for sopranos and mezzos, right?*

JF: The mezzos will have a different sensation with it.

RR: *And you keep them in the low resonance the whole time?*

JF: You don't lose the low; you add high. You can use any kind of vowel combination, which gives them three different resonances. And that's what I have to work a lot on. I spend a lot of time trying to get them to understand going in and out of the mixes. The students I've had—certainly the ones I had last year—had no mix. It's hard. What I work with, actually, even more than the vowel, is the legato sound. They have to run this /i/ right up against the /a/. And I talk about the fact that the first note you sing is out there. The sound wave is moving out there. You don't actually make a new sound. You change the shape of the sound that you have in motion already.

RR: *For the second note?*

JF: Yes, that makes sense. I don't think it does for most of the singers I talk to, but ultimately, they begin to understand. And then they'll say, "Oh, I see what that feels like, and I don't know where I got that, or why that's even so." It's the way I believe they need to think about it so they don't insert a glottal onset between the vowels.

RR: *What things do you do for fioratura?*

JF: I don't do *staccatti* a lot, but I do some with the sopranos and even the mezzos. I don't do it with the men much, but sometimes I do staccato with baritones so they feel the difference in the legato breath stream.

The other thing I've started doing that I think we neglect, generally, is scale passages. Most of our exercises, I noticed a while back, are all intervals. Have you ever asked one of your students to sing a scale?

RR: *Oh, yes, all the time. Every lesson.*

JF: You do scales? I had not done them much. I have really started including them, because they weren't good at it.

RR: *This goes back to our discussion about younger teachers. I realized that when I was a younger teacher, I didn't do a lot of fast exercises; they mostly were pretty slow, so that I could shoot at everything that was coming past me. And now, most of the time, things are a little more upbeat. I also do some exercises that are very slow legato exercises followed by a fast scale so they begin to understand the physical differences between the two of them.*

JF: Right, some combination. The other one I use is very slow, going from vowel to vowel without letting the sound stop. Again, I talk a lot about legato. In going from the /i/ to an /a/ or /e/ [singing], what happened? The tongue just dropped—it barely moved, and I try to have them to think this lift for /a/ and not drop. If they get a sensation of where the /i/ and /e/ are back here, and if they can think that /a/ above it, they'll usually get to it. That's the lift, and I think that can get too squirrelly looking. You're after the back lift, but if you lift the back, and that lifts too, that's okay, but sometimes you see people lifting here and nothing's happening in the back.

RR: *I constantly talk to my singers about looking at their faces. If they just look at the musculature here on the sides, they can tell whether or not they're active, if they're open in the back or not—because the tone is too somber at that point.*

JF: I've had students who would come to me nasal, and I've said, "May I look in your mouth?" "Sure." And there I see that uvula just hanging down there. Nobody's talked to them about raising the soft palate. How do you avoid that? I had a student come who had a pretty voice quality. I said, "Has anybody ever suggested that your sound was a bit nasal?" "No." And I said, "It is. Can we talk about that?" So, I looked, and again the uvula and palate were low, and she didn't know how to lift it. And I said, "What if I surprised you?" But then she couldn't sustain that. She couldn't repeat that. It was the weirdest thing I've ever had to teach.

I was thinking about another thing I wanted to tell you. Oh, the other odd thing I do, and you probably may have done this...

RR: *There's more than one odd thing?*

JF: And sometimes I use this with tenors, but I use it with sopranos, not often with baritones or mezzos. On D^5, have them do a really high, even maybe [singing], a kind of a humming nasal, very nasal, and a crescendo, and slowly let that sound open and see where it goes. And mostly, it works. Again, it's giving them some strength and a way to understand what it feels like in the *passaggio* to stay on the voice, while not letting it become breathy.

RR: *You don't think that by starting with that closed vowel, the singer is activating the larynx too much?*

JF: Not if the tongue is loose up there. I don't think so, but I don't know that for sure. But I do know it helps build some strength in that middle *passaggio*. Some people can't do it, so I stop. And some can. The other thing I've seen—and I don't do this very often—was done at a clinic, and I thought, "Oh, my God!" You open your mouth to sing and cover it with the hand, like for a soprano learning how to sing A-flat^5, and for some people it'll work. And some people never get it.

RR: *I use that. I do use that a lot in the middle of the voice. Doscher called that finding the standing vocal wave. I believe that it helps the singer understand the space for that note.*

FJ: And sometimes during a lesson I'll just think of some crazy thing that I've never used before, because I want to hear something in particular. I do more scale things than I used to do though. So, they really learn. I remember reading an interview with Birgit Nilsson about how she warmed up. She said, "I do one long scale. If I can do that and the voice feels good, I know I'm okay."

RR: *You were going to talk about passaggio exercises for males.*

JF: Tenors. I do what we just talked about with tenors, by the way. I use this for their *passaggio* too, starting on an E-flat^4.

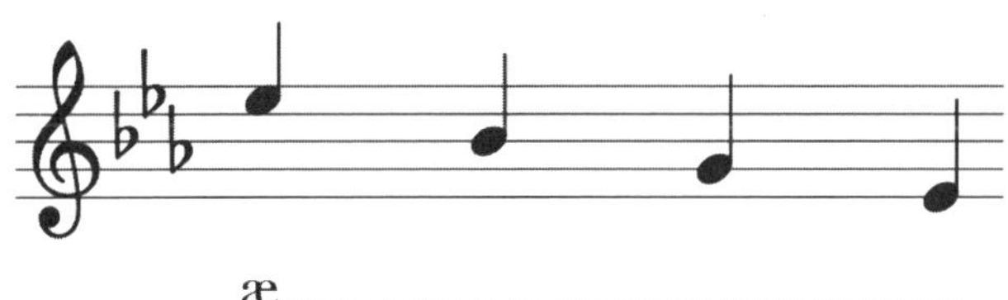

RR: *You make them sing the E-flat^4 followed by what kind of scale?*

JF: Just an arpeggio, and what they'll find is they really want to do something around the third note. I say, "Go ahead. Let it break. Let it break over. Let it go into that middle resonance if you want to." They don't always know what that means. But they know it feels like it wants to do something.

I started doing that one for the males, because I've found it took them longer when they had no idea, sensation, or experience with what it feels like, to sing a mixed B-flat^4. A lot of the tenors I taught didn't even know what that ought to feel like. That gives them the sense that what they think is falsetto isn't falsetto at all. It's a strong, high mix. And then when they get to the G^4, all of a sudden that feels like a really strong sound for them. And these are guys who haven't been singing G^4. Or if they were, it was pushed-up middle resonance, which some of them can do. I've even used it once in a while with baritones who are courageous. I also use octaves for the *passaggio*. I have them sing an /i/ and let them feel the change as they are going to the top note from the bottom of the *passaggio*. So, say, for a tenor, I would start around G^3 and do a four-note pattern, not five, because it's less distance to travel. That's very little change, but I stop and make sure they make this joint [temporomandibular joint] move a bit. I talk about this joint when we're talking about *passaggio*.

It's not about moving the jaw, it's about opening and releasing this joint. I have them put their fingers back there and feel it. The idea is that the maxilla, this upper bone, moves too. It moves a bit. Not as much as the bottom, obviously, because this upper part doesn't move. I've found this makes sense to my students, because they often have a stiff jaw. I do that on /i/ and /a/. If they can do those, I'll go on to /ɔ/.

RR: *What's the hardest kind of voice for you to deal with?*

JF: Straight-tone voices [without vibrato]. I had a young fellow who had never sung a solo; he only had sung in choirs. His voice was straight and huge, but he was using a straight tone, and so I worked with him the first day on vibrato, just having him move the voice. He said, "So the little squiggle in the sound's supposed to be there?" And I replied, "Yes, it gives it some character, some timbre." And he said, "Oh, I think I can do that." So, he went away and practiced and came back and had a little vibrato now and again. I was shocked at how quickly he developed. He was so smart–he would take anything I told him and figure it out. One day he said, "Wait, let me draw that." He drew the most wonderful diagram of the face and all of that mechanism. He said, "That'll help me remember." I said, "Could I have one of those to help me remember?" I gave him *Les Papillons* because I was curious. He sang it. I just wept. He was so right. He had tried to figure what the poem really meant and what he could do with it. That's what I mean about helping them find who they are. And I said, "What on Earth happened?" He said, "I just went where the music took me." Oh, my God! You wait all your life to hear somebody say that. And I think that's our big job. When you asked me what I expect to get done, *that's* what I expect to get done. They can somehow—even though the voice is not star-quality—somehow, they can find a way to access the music and make it a really beautiful moment. Otherwise, we're kind of beating a dead horse.

RR: *Ashes and dust, we're all ashes and dust! Okay.*

JF: Okay.

Parting Thoughts

I first met Joyce way back in my undergraduate years when I had lost my way and vocal identity. I went to see her at Baylor University because I had heard good things about her. And when I see her now, I always am reminded of our first meeting. Her presence is still so calming. It gives you the sense as a singer that everything will be alright. She helped me a lot during my time of study with her. I will always be grateful to her for that and for agreeing to be in this book. I almost had to insist she do it! As you can see, she is quite open to ideas and always has the good of the student in mind. Joyce is the first person to say that she doesn't have all the answers, while those who work with her feel that she pretty much does.

Her vocal approach is straightforward and clear. She has evolved over the years, but still concentrates on several elements that are bedrock principles to every singer: intent, immediacy of sound, and mental clarity of thought. She is patient and works at a relaxed but effective pace. She constantly deals with global ideas and approaches. Her excellent work with vowels and how they affect the resonance is the basis of a good, strong vocal technique.

I firmly believe that Joyce's approach of teaching global principles is particularly effective. As I tell my singers; if you were to plan a trip from New York City to Los Angeles, the best method is to go to Google maps and begin with a view of the complete United States. Once you understand your directions, then you can go to the street view. If they were to go to the street view first, they would never get their bearings and understand the general direction of the trip. I also believe that staying with global ideas improves the balance of the whole system, and this balance radiates to the ancillary issues, which then take care of themselves without the need to address them specifically. As a result, the singer doesn't need to be worrying about the small screws at the bottom of the submarine. Work smart, not hard.

I have always considered myself very lucky to have worked with Joyce, but even luckier that she continues to be a very positive influence in my life.

Lesson Highlights

n.b. The lessons that were observed primarily dealt with interpretive issues specific to the music and characterization, and therefore did not include many comments that have universal pedagogic/technical application. A wealth of information about singing technique is included in the interview.

Breathing and Support

Inhalation

Breathe in and let it come right back out the side. Be really definite about the inhalation and be sure you feel the air hitting your soft palate. It just comes out they way it went in—feel it on your hard palate. Just the inhalation will set you up—it really will.

Breath pressure

Now don't add more air! You don't need more air pressure. We always say, "Ooh, we're going high, so it must be harder."

Articulation

Dealing with tongue tension

You look at the tongue first. See what the back of the tongue is doing while you're trying to get yourself someplace on the page. Often it is the tongue pulling things, either pressing down or pulling up.

Singing legato

Forget the consonant. Get it out of the way—it's stopping you. Let the energy in the sound and the breath take you. Keep the sound moving. Keep your vowel moving right up to the next vowel.

Sing like you just spoke it. We speak in legato sentences, and then we sing notes. Get right off the consonant. Get to the vowel—you must sing on the vowels.

Lifting the soft palate while keeping the tongue free

When you take in air, the tongue is just lying there. Put your tongue farther down in front, behind the teeth, at that ridge, and then leave it there.

JULIA FAULKNER

Julia Faulkner is an internationally renowned master teacher who has firmly established herself as one of the top voice teachers in the world. Her students are performing globally at the Metropolitan Opera, La Scala, Vienna State Opera, Bavarian State Opera, and Lyric Opera of Chicago, among others. Faulkner is Director of Vocal Studies for The Patrick G. and Shirley W. Ryan Opera Center, Lyric Opera of Chicago's renowned professional artist-development program. She is also a Master Teacher for the apprentices at the Santa Fe Opera and has been on the faculty of the Curtis Institute since the fall of 2015. Previously, she spent a decade as professor of voice at the University of Wisconsin-Madison.

Ms. Faulkner's distinguished international singing career has brought her to many of the world's great opera and concert stages. She made her Metropolitan Opera debut in the title role of Strauss' *Arabella* in 1994 and sang major roles for many years at the Bavarian and Vienna State Operas. She received critical acclaim for her performances as the Marschallin, Arabella, Countess, Fiordiligi, Ariadne, and Capriccio Gräfin, to name a few. Other prestigious engagements have included performances with La Scala, Hamburg, Amsterdam, The Berlin Philharmonic, Cleveland Orchestra, Concertgebouw,

Dresdener Staatskapelle, Gewandhaus Leipzig, and the L.A. Philharmonic. A distinguished recording artist, Faulkner has recorded for the Naxos, EMI and Deutsche Grammophon labels, including a Naxos release (2009) of Lee Hoiby songs with the composer at the piano.

The Interview

RR: *You started to talk earlier about sitting on the other side of the table and watching auditions. Many of these singers are the best of the best. How do you make these difficult decisions? What do you think singers should remember when they audition?*

JF: When auditioning potential members of the Ryan Center ensemble, I look for a spark of creativity, great communication, impeccable preparation and above all a beautiful and interesting voice. When I sit in on auditions that our ensemble members do for agents and other houses, much of what I'm doing is just gathering information about what is important to current theaters, directors, and conductors. Tastes have changed and things are a little different from when I was a singer. The thing that has stayed the same in America over the years is that the houses are usually of a fairly generous size; therefore, the ability to be heard in these houses is an important consideration. That creates a climate, as it always has, that benefits bigger voices. I have always believed, and still believe, that beauty of sound is most important. A beautiful sound carries best anyway. I think the biggest change I've seen probably is due to the proliferation of opera and concert videos, which creates the desire for people to look a certain way. That, perhaps, in earlier generations was not as high on the list of priorities.

I think it is extremely important now that singers look the part and are able to sing it well. When all things are equal, I believe that the more beautiful voice is the better choice. I never want to see a lesser singer put out on stage simply because she weighs a few pounds less. I fight the good fight for that one. I try to impart the rather old school idea that opera is based primarily on the ability of the voice to portray the drama. Singers need to develop their acting skills and be as healthy as possible because it's a strenuous business, but I sometimes worry about the almost addictive quality that some singers display as they try to lose weight or fit into a supermodel-type image. It's just unrealistic and unhealthy. There has to be some kind of balance there.

RR: *I agree with you one hundred percent. I've often said I would rather cast an opera based on listening to audio recordings rather than by watching videos.*

JF: Me too, but it is not like that anymore. I also would say that the singers who make the impression in an audition situation are not the ones who are careful, perfect, and totally polished. They are the ones who take risks, have an individual and unique voice, and have something to say. I'm not really interested in someone who has clearly been polished to a hard sheen. I want to see his heart and soul. I want to see who he is and what he has to say, which has musical, vocal, and dramatic implications.

RR: *I noticed in the two lessons that I watched that both singers understood everything about the texts they were singing and communicated effectively.*

JF: It is very different teaching professionals who have been singing for more than a year or two, because their careers are based on their vocal identities and musical souls. In no way do I want to teach that out of them. Translating what I'm saying into their own words, into their own technique, is important.

RR: *But you also work insightfully with young singers who are still figuring out their voices and repertoire.*

JF: I think teaching that kind of student has always been the most gratifying and interesting to me. It offers me the greatest learning experience because I have to figure out how this person is going to absorb information. We have to find that common language. I have to figure out how her brain works; do I pile it all on and let her sort it out independently, or do I need to take each concept and very slowly integrate it into her singing? Working with a new brain and new circumstances inspire me to look for new ways of thinking about the voice. Right now, I have four undergraduates at Curtis. One of them is someone I have taught since she was fourteen. She and her colleague, who is also my student, were the only two people to get into Curtis a couple of years ago. I think I'm good at preparing people for their college experience when they are as highly motivated as my young Curtis students are, and willing to do the kind of work that's necessary to reach a high level of singing and artistry. I try to take one or two students of this age group when somebody special comes to me, but my current students are mostly professionals, emerging professionals, and a few excellent college students.

RR: *During your lessons, you prioritized a few main issues and outlined a clear process for the students to improve those skills.*

JF: I am always aware that students are paying me and have certain needs. I tell people right away that I cannot fix everything in an hour. There are some things you can correct that can immediately produce a noticeably better sound; other issues take longer to resolve. But I know the professional student is going to work more independently between lessons than the less experienced student. There are all kinds of elements that I have to be aware of when I teach—skill level, emotional fragility, experience—but the bottom line to me is giving them the information they need to sing their best. I help them find their way, which sometimes may include moving away from singing in their lives and careers. Not everybody is built for singing, either psychologically or physically. I don't view that as a failure. I think learning to sing is one of the great self-revelatory paths that one can take in life. Whether it results in becoming a great artist, a good doctor, or just a good person, I support all of them in their journeys.

I think it is essential for me to see the singers I work with in performance. I recently saw one of my students sing an ensemble in *Figaro* with a big company and noticed how she struggled with it. I knew the problem needed to be addressed, but not magnified, because it was already magnified in her brain. It takes time to collect that much knowledge about singers and their histories. It is really valuable for me to see my Ryan Center singers in auditions, which are completely separate, hybrid, extraordinary situations. Auditions are one of the least best ways of figuring out how someone sings, but they are a necessary evil.

RR: *When you see singers struggle in auditions, how do you help them?*

JF: I find singers usually struggle with some kind of psychological or emotional blockage. Most singers are very good at putting on a costume and getting into a character, but when there's that hybrid situation of presenting the drama while wearing your own clothes and performing for people who are there to judge you worthy or not, it can lead to every possible emotional, psychological, and, therefore, physical block.

Auditioning frequently and debriefing after each audition can help. I try to do this with students whenever possible to let them know what worked well in the performance. We try to keep close to the same repertoire each year unless something proves to be pretty disastrous. We are always doing little experiments to find the best starting aria: what sets them up best vocally, what the panel is most likely to select as the second aria, and how those two selections work together. Does the singer have the stamina for this aria combination? Is it a good fit? Of course, once you figure that out, the panel will ask for something else, but I'm usually pretty good at predicting what's going to be the second choice.

I had one case where a singer was coming off as cold and distant to audition panels. That was simply a protective mechanism. It's sad but true that you really can't be protective in an audition. You have to be open and put yourself out there. You have to take risks and perform your best in that moment. I urge singers to sing arias, if appropriate, from roles they have previously performed, because they are usually able to go back to the time, place, and setting of those productions more easily in their minds and present a more complete performance. Often, I hear terrible recitatives, even from seasoned professionals, who then proceed to sing the aria gloriously. There is nothing unimportant in an audition. The recitative comes first, so you might as well make a good impression.

RR: *The recitative is where you earn the aria.*

JF: Exactly. That's a wonderful way to put it.

RR: *You said to one of your students that she had to "do the work in the performance." Can you talk a little more about that?*

JF: You have to observe yourself to a certain extent as you perform, or be able to go back to the moment in your mind later and recall details. This is not easy because there is a heightened energy during performance; it is an altered state. It can be extremely hard to achieve that mindset in practice. It is so important to have every possible technical aspect under your control so that even that added energy—perhaps agitation and fear—will not send your body into a tailspin. Achieving that mastery takes an extraordinary amount of work and a long time. You must also observe what happens when you go into that altered state of consciousness in performance. All great performers, I think, have the potential of upping the ante when they get into that state.

The preparation and the post-performance self-analysis are necessary. I certainly don't mean to imply that you have to analyze yourself as you perform. I think most singers are adept enough to have an outside observer position while being fully engaged in the performance. In American regional houses, you might only have two to three performances of any given opera in a run, which makes that kind of analysis a little more difficult. Most European contracts have six, eight, or ten performances, which allows a singer to thoroughly learn a role and get it under the belt, make changes, and experiment. That is where a lot of growth happens. I learned more in the first year of real performing than I did in all of my years studying in school.

RR: *I tell my singers that they must control the things that they can control and be ready for anything to happen. Let's move on to some of the technical aspects I observed in your teaching, I noticed that you tended to use exercises that focused on breath movement in the middle voice.*

JF: That is accurate. I really do believe that every voice, regardless of size, needs to have agility, buoyancy, ring, and freedom. I realize that flexibility comes easier to some voices, but the ability to sing coloratura and achieve flexible movement is very important. I particularly focus on the middle voice during the warm up. When sopranos begin college voice study, there often is a gigantic hole in the middle range because they have been using their high range and a lot of chest/belt voice. Developing the middle register is what I think those years from eighteen to twenty-two or twenty-three is all about. If that part of the voice has not been built to the extent that it needs to be during that time, we have to work pretty hard on it in later years.

I think that how the singer deals with the lower register change is important to the middle voice, which happens for sopranos around B-flat^3, B^3, and C^4 in the first *passaggio* and F-sharp^5 and G^5 in the second *passaggio*. I am very clear with almost every singer, including fuller mezzos, that there must be a hook into head voice even as they transition down into chest resonance. I really do concentrate on this, because that is where the real work is. The first singer you heard today has particular issues right around F-sharp^4 and G^4 where she pulls back from her breath, disengages a bit, and raises her larynx. I work a lot on the middle voice with her. The second singer has a very different voice and is a bit of a contrast. She pushes her voice down a bit into a darker and what she considers to be a more colorful position. She needs to release and lighten. Both singers really need the middle voice work. I certainly work differently with tenors, baritones, basses, and mezzos, although I would want the same flexibility from all of those voices as well. The ability to move the voice is a sign of vocal health. If you cannot move your voice, something is wrong. That is my view.

I'm cognizant that a beautiful, rich sounding voice that comes to me is often a little manufactured or manipulated in its color. The depth and richness needs to be the result of healthy singing rather than manipulation or the product of mechanical means.

RR: *During the first lesson, you talked about three places: the top of the head, the lower abdominals, and the front of the face.*

JF: I find it useful to simplify concepts. There are many, many moving parts to singing, but it is impossible to hold all those parts in our mind. This three-part sensation, or concept, is something I use often. The first part is the placement of the sound, or the spatial presence of the sound. I like to think of this as being in front of the face or outside of the body. If singers think of the sound as originating outside of the body, they will have less of a chance to follow the pattern of manipulating and holding the sound before producing and releasing the sound. I find that works very well.

The second point is the crown of the head, where the singer might conceive of a space for singing. I feel that space is a dangerous concept for singers and fraught with consequences of manipulation and tension. For instance, just saying the phrase "Lift your palate" is an invitation to shove your tongue down, harden all the muscles in your throat, and sound like Kermit the Frog.

In truth, space in singing is much more about release of the breath and thinking through to that point where feels like it is out in front of you. It's much subtler than most singers realize. There's a lot of tension that arises from that concept of space. All three points should remain in an equal state of activation and tension between them, but not excessive tension toward any one point.

The third point is the foundation of the sound, which I identify as breath. I like that point to feel very low. I use extended speech as a model for breath in singing. It's much more complicated than that, but we do use a very unique and remarkably consistent phonation in our speech. We never think about breathing, never run out of breath, and have a good and consistent tone. We do it naturally without even knowing what we are doing.

We have that ability, and it can be related to singing. Of course, it's extended and uses an enhanced resonance, but I think it is a good stepping-off point to help singers understand the very fine control that breathing for singing requires. Thinking of that three-pronged, almost geometric spatial construct is helpful to me, both for its simplicity, and for all of the aspects underneath its umbrella that it covers.

RR: *You regularly talk about leaning on the breath. I realize that this is a known pedagogical concept, but can you go into more detail? This idea seems to vary from teacher to teacher and from singer to singer.*

JF: Yes. I think the concept of breath is most susceptible to misinterpretation or interpretations that do not work for individuals. I use the example of speech to identify both the location and intensity of breath initiation in singing because the initiation is, to me, all-important. If you get the onset right and just stay there, generally speaking, you will be fine.

To me, the problem lies in the fact that the singing breath is pressurized. The amount of pressure, where that pressure is experienced, and where/how it is controlled is the issue. Some people feel as though the pressure should be controlled in the upper chest cavity. I really believe that the gas pedal is very low in the body.

We use these muscles all the time for speech, but more subtly. It feels to me almost like an object that is football-shaped. There is pressure from below and a small bit of pressure from above as well. This concept gets misinterpreted a lot. Someone will talk about pushing out because that is the counter pressure. Another teacher will talk about pushing up because that is the pressure from underneath. To me, it is a much subtler combination of both actions.

There are also teachers who want assistance from the intercostal or abdominal muscles in the six-pack area that leads to excessive involvement with the total musculature. There are some singers who do not support, but someone who has studied for a long time very rarely uses too little muscle; they use too much muscle, the wrong muscles, or do not direct their support in the right way. Invariably, when they get it right, I hear them say, "But that feels like nothing!"

When everything is coordinated correctly, which takes years of fine muscle control, figuring it out, and laying the groundwork, it does feel like nothing, but that "nothing" took six years of work to find. It is important that we stress that it is not actually nothing. It is just coordinated and put into its place so that it functions easily and with very little perceived effort. Effort cannot be present in breathing. You have to be strong enough to support your voice with these muscles, but it cannot appear that you are trying to push a rock up a hill. You have to rest on your breath. That takes a long time to learn, but it is possible.

You do not have to have abs of steel to sing. If you did, there would be a lot of us who would be out of a job! I really do believe that when we inhale, the primary movement should be down and out and the initial activation of the sound comes from a slight tuck with a little bit of counter pressure—a gathering. I use that term [gathering] a lot to explain the internal activation of those muscles. There are so many ways to put it. Not every way will work for every singer. Some people may need to have a sense of more overt muscular activation and others may need to think about almost no muscle involvement at all. That is where you would make the judgment call as a teacher about what works for a particular singer.

RR: *Do you have specific breathing exercises that you use regularly with students?*

JF: I have them observe what is happening with the breath as they make siren sounds. "Observe" is the important word here, because if you immediately make the leap to breath work, they will activate muscles that do not need to be involved. I also use a long, slow hiss to really work on breath control. I am always clear with students about the function of each exercise and how I think it will help enhance their singing.

After that initial work has been done, we work on forming a regular repertoire of exercises that will allow them to sing with some consistency after thirty or forty minutes. We must control what we are able to control. One of those things we can control is how your voice gets set up before you sing. I think that is a very important aspect of successful singing and forming a singer's mindset. We think differently when we sing. It requires us to bridge that gap between our intellectual processing, linear thought, and our awareness of experiential sensations. Consistently singing well is more about revisiting a state of being. I think the warmup and practice rituals are crucial parts of that process. We practice so we can return to what has worked in the past.

RR: *During your lessons, I observed that you are always simplifying the process and the sound for each singer.*

JF: Yes. Singing is incredibly complex. I do not need to add to that complexity. We need to find the essence of what we do because the most beautiful singing always seems to be a direct expression of a person's soul or emotional intention. Getting there can be extremely complicated. There are so many aspects to great singing, but ultimately it is a simple act. The ground has to be prepared, and then you have to let go, which is the single most difficult thing to accomplish. We are taught to hang on to all of these concepts simultaneously. We carry our experiences with us, accumulated through years of work, and the investment of thousands of dollars in training, so how can the answer be so simple? In fact, it really is. The song is always there, even as we are trying to perfect the instrument. It is just waiting to be sung. If we can find that with our imperfect human bodies, then we really do have a chance to connect to something very meaningful and deep. It is an incredible joy to explore that with another human being, within myself, and share it with people.

RR: *What are the two or three most important things that singers need to have if they want to have a career in singing?*

JF: They must be willing to risk and to persevere in the face of rejection. They always must be true to themselves. But please, please, please learn how to sing before you pursue a career, because a career is not going to help you learn how to sing. You have to know how to sing first. If you do not have the skills, find someone who can help you, because it does not get easier when you add costumes, a conductor, and an orchestra.

RR: *Who are your influences as an artist and a teacher?*

JF: My strongest influence was my teacher, Margaret Harshaw. I was also greatly influenced by the environment at Indiana University. There were a lot of wonderful singers and colleagues who have now gone on to have careers: Vinson Cole, Nadine Secunde, Michael Sylvester. The list goes on and on. I was lucky enough to have a *fest* [secure] contract in Munich as my first real job. I entered the ensemble right at the end of a lot of great careers, so I stood on stage with Astrid Varnay, Christa Ludwig, and Brigitte Fassbaender. I even sang a performance with Hans Hotter on his eightieth birthday. I was incredibly fortunate to sing with Dietrich Fischer-Dieskau and to have come in contact with that great generation of old school singers. They are still the singers I listen to. At the Met, I covered Kiri Te Kanawa. That was a great experience. I did a master class with Elisabeth Schwarzkopf—I feel like I am passing that torch to a certain extent.

I think I am influenced by European old school singing first, second, and always. They had beautiful techniques and very individual voices—not always perfect, but text and sound-driven above all.

RR: *What was it like to sing with Dieskau? Was it a large voice?*

JF: No, not large at all. I remember singing a Blumen Mädchen when he sang Amfortas in *Parsifal*, which is a huge role that requires incredible stamina. I have never ever heard anyone who had such a command of the language. I became friends with him and his wife, Julia Varady. He let me sit in the wings on a little catwalk looking directly at him during a recital that he gave in Munich. The man could hold an evening like no one I have ever seen. Even in his late sixties, he was still a magnificent artist.

He gave me my single most important and, to this day, most moving musical experience. When I was a sophomore in college he came to Chicago and did *Winterreise*. I remember being with a friend of mine who was so overcome by the experience that we literally had to support her on her way out. I felt the same way. We just could not speak. It was a formative experience. I am so glad I have that because I think it did much to inspire the direction that I wanted take in my life and my musical world.

Parting Thoughts

Julia is the director of vocal studies for The Patrick G. and Shirley W. Ryan Opera Center, Lyric Opera of Chicago's renowned professional artist-development program. The lessons I observed were in the opera's beautiful facilities. Both singers I heard that day were accomplished and already well on their way in their careers. Despite their advanced stage of study, Julia concentrated mostly on the connection of the breath to the body. The breath initiated everything in her exercises. She worked on the breath gesture in a different way with each singer, with excellent results. She used few specific anatomical terms, concentrating instead on the process of the breath flow and how each singer responded to her ideas. Periodically during the lesson, Julia would ask each singer to begin a note or a phrase using a high sigh as an onset to set up a feeling of higher resonance and breath initiation for every movement.

Another aspect of the lessons that I specifically remember is how she had the pianist play all of the interludes and introductions while working with the singers on major roles, which allowed them to properly prepare for each entrance and to think about how their character should evolve during the singing breaks. With such challenging repertoire, this is as important for self-preservation as much as it is for performance preparation. I felt fortunate to witness Julia passing the torch to the next generation of professional singers.

Lesson Highlights

Breath Support/Control

The primary importance of breath

Breath has to carry the sound. When that gets compromised, you have to use something else to support. Then you have several choices at your disposal, but none of them are good.

Resonance

Singing with forward resonance

When you are aiming for a forward feeling or position, make sure you are not shoving the sound toward us. The sensation of forwardness is a byproduct of palate and jaw release assisted by deeply grounded breath. You really have to think into that palatal pocket while continuing to direct the flow of sound through and out. Create the space without holding or jamming the breath. Use the breath to activate your connected system.

Finding throat release

I can tell you what throat release is not: it is not a feeling of opening the throat by pushing and flexing the tongue. Throat release is the release of those muscles, as they do right before the start of a yawn. Look for that sensation that happens the moment right before the stretch starts. There is an unlocking that leaves everything flexible. If you go into the stretch, it becomes inflexible. Use the breath to keep things open and buoyantly stretched.

As soon as you think of lifting your soft palate, you are back with your tongue. Get the sound way out in front of you. That will free the space. If I say, "release the back of your tongue," you'll start pushing the tongue down. In all of these directives, we are trying to get people to release something back there. You have to think through and out so that the energy moves to the focus point in front of you. These are all psychological tricks to get you not to think back where your tongue is. We can talk about it but I don't like to focus on it. I want to give you something else to think about that will be more helpful.

Articulation

Singing an /a/ vowel

Try this image: when you think of /a/, feel as though you have the dome of an opened umbrella floating against your hard palate. The point of the umbrella extends up through the hard palate and between the eyes on the inside of the face. This is where the primary vibration is experienced.

It is the place where nasality would happen if you put the back of your tongue up. But instead of putting your tongue up and going nasal, make sure the breath is finding that spot with an open throat.

Registration

Singing through register transitions

I think it is important to speak of registration issues as transitions and not breaks or shifts. I often use the analogy of the ideal being automatic transmission instead of manual. Many singers sense the approach of a transition and either preemptively shift, or hold back the shift until one is forced to "jump" into the new register. Both create the sensation and sound of a "break" at the transition point. This is why I am adamant about *passaggi* not really being anything more than an automatic transmission. The mechanism can move seamlessly between those positions. When one avoids manipulation of the larynx at transition points and supplies adequate breath, movement through the transition takes place. I like sliding exercises for registration work because they require you to be on your breath so you really can feel those shifts. Stay with the vowel and let the shifts happen by slightly backing off and then moving forward and leaning through.

Singing through the second passaggio (soprano)

As we get to F-sharp^5 and G^5, make sure you have a little more space. Redirect the breath into the extra space that you need, instead of continuing to roll it out. Compensate for that extra space by feeling the resonance tilted a bit more forward. To me, it is just like maintaining the pressure/counter-pressure that you should sense in the tautness between the triangle's three points. Those three points should move away from each other rather than closer together. To counteract that slight raising, really ground the sound.

When the larynx tends to go up slightly here in the *passaggio*, the breath gets higher and a little more compressed. To counteract this, stay deep with the breath. The breath holds things in place and allows the mechanism to be supported without using external muscles like the tongue and the jaw. As you learn to do this, you will strengthen that skill by going to the place where the sound feels a little unstable. This is usually a sign that the sound is being freed from manipulation. This can be very hard to do while you are performing until you make it a habit.

Instead of backing off on your breath pressure, which makes the larynx climb, keep things in line so that the breath has to be under you and flowing. Lean on it even more. It's going to feel coarse to you, and not as refined.

Performing/Preparation

Learning music

(RR) Julia worked very carefully on the rhythm and diction in each phrase with students and combining it all into a precise flow. She often directed her student to keep the buoyancy of the breath connected with a precise and clear delivery of the text while keeping her jaw and tongue as relaxed as possible. They repeatedly spoke the text correctly in rhythm with as much legato as possible.

Surmounting technical challenges

If there is any trick, as you asked me earlier, to getting over a technical challenge, it is deciding to be more brave than protective when we go out and perform. It comes with having more and more success and not caring about any one performance except as a laboratory in which to grow. Then your success in that moment will grow into long-term success.

Exercises

Exercise 1: (used with two singers, both of whom were female)

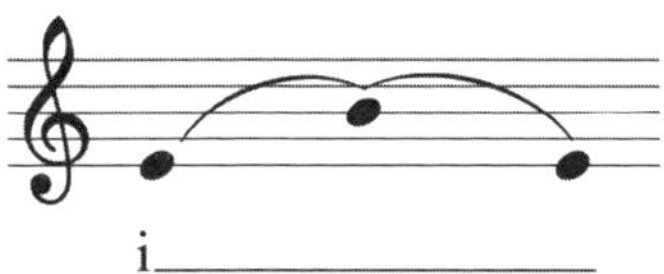

Instruction: Just speak sing. Remember to vibrate and not bear down on the sound. Make sure your jaw releases at the end.

Exercise 2: (used with first singer)

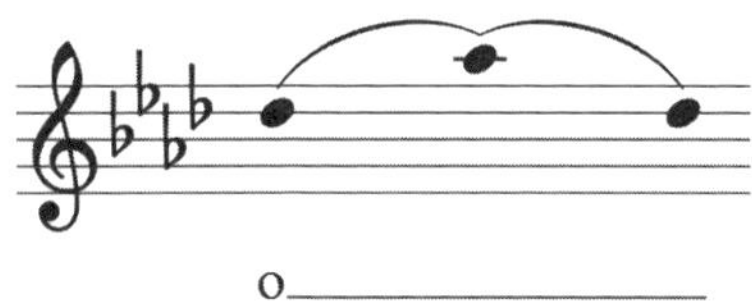

Instructions: Think about leaning down as you go up.

Exercise 3: (used with first singer)

Instructions: Keep thinking in a forward direction. Allow a little tilt into chest resonance as you descend and maintain that hook from the top.

Exercise 4: (used with first singer)

Instructions: Move only the tip of the tongue, not the jaw. Remember that the focus point is created with that long tube. Now, connect it to the lean. This is an exercise using different vowels/consonant combinations so you can work on maintaining the flow behind them. They are easy to do on one vowel, but become more difficult when you start adding consonants and vowel changes. The articulation and accuracy of the vowel happens with that tongue movement. It is almost though you feel a separate space behind that feels kind of like an "uuuuhhh." Everything gets filtered through that very open feeling.

Exercise 5: (used with second singer)

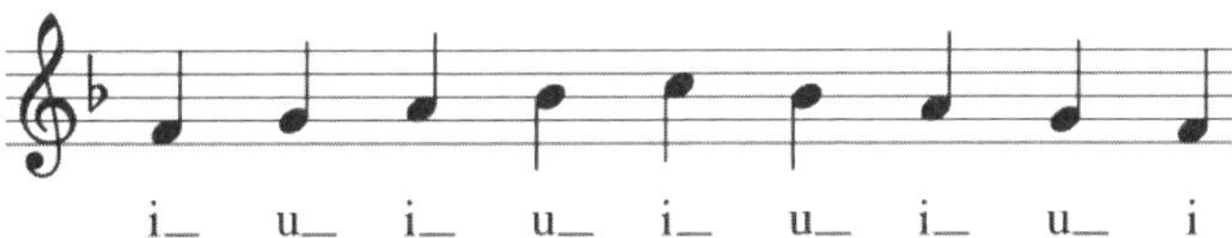

Instructions: Use your tongue clearly for the /iuiuiu/. Make sure that there is sound flowing back up, above, and over.

Exercise 6: (used with second singer)

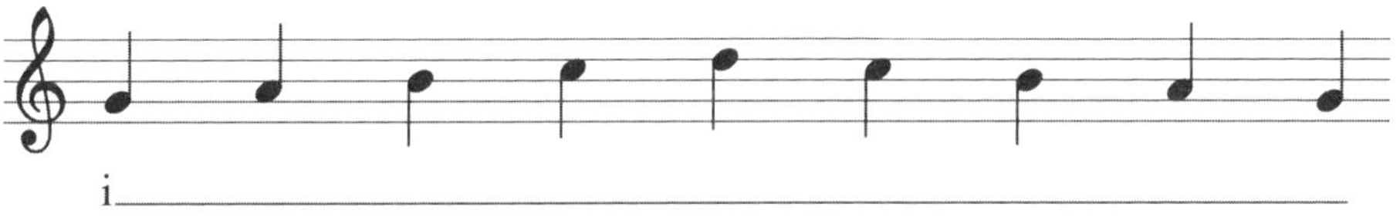

Exercise 7: (used with second singer)

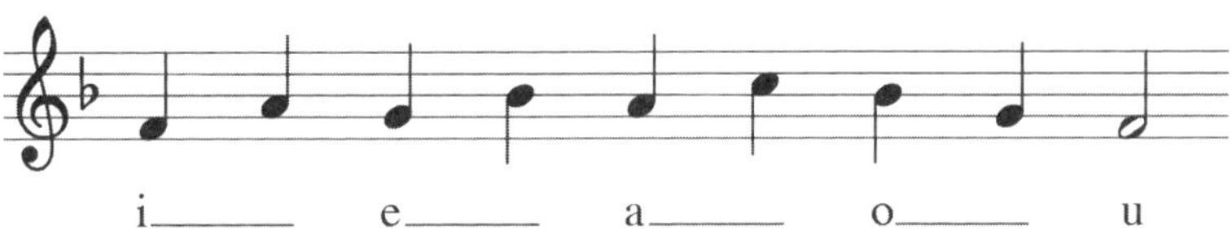

Instructions: Just speak-sing /ieaou/ first on one note. Let everything feels as though it flows over that shelf up here, never below.

Exercise 8: (used with second singer)

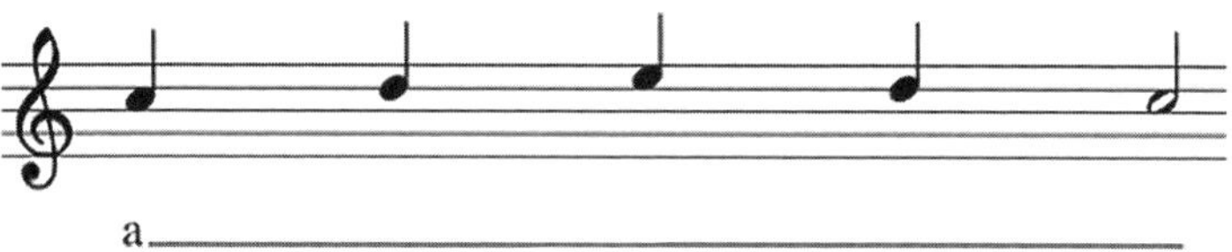

Exercise 9: (used with second singer)

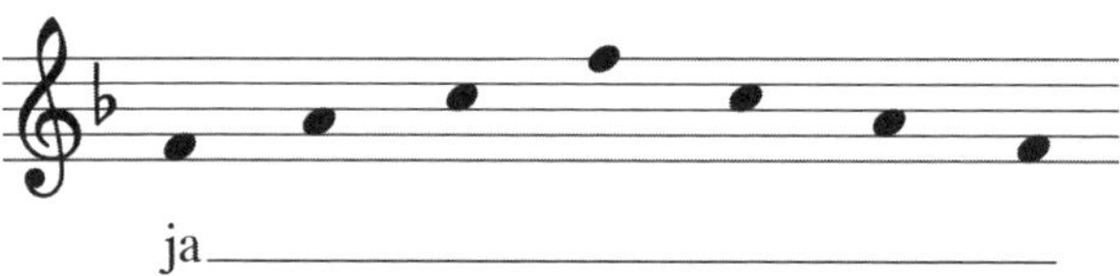

Instructions: Don't shy away from /a/. Sweep through with your breath.

GEORGE GIBSON

A native Texan, Dr. George Gibson's formal education began at Texas Lutheran University, followed by degrees from the University of Miami, The University of Texas at Austin, and The University of Southern California. He studied voice and opera at the Munich *Hochschule für Musik* as a Fulbright scholar. His teachers included Hedwig Fichtmüller, Rupert Gundlach, and Hans Altman.

Dr. Gibson has spent the majority of his professional life in the teaching field, having held positions at Northwestern State University of Louisiana, The College-Conservatory of Music of the University of Cincinnati, the Eastman School of Music of the University of Rochester, the University of Arizona, and Wichita State University, where he was Professor of Voice and Director of the Opera Theatre for twenty-nine years. He also taught voice in opera houses of Germany, Austria and Switzerland. During his tenure at Wichita State, the Opera Theatre grew to be one of the finest of its kind. He served in all capacities: producer, director, coach, and conductor. Some eighty-five different productions were given under his leadership. His former voice and opera theatre students include Samuel Ramey, Joyce DiDonato, Alan Held, Barbara Honn, Catherine Cook, Karla Burns, Stephen Tharp, Thomas Baresel, Jonathan Retzlaff, Beverly Hoch, and many others. His students have sung or are singing in all the major opera houses and concert halls of the world.

As a singer, Gibson's repertoire consists of some sixty-five leading roles in opera, oratorio, and musical theatre. He has appeared with opera companies of Miami, Tampa, Shreveport, Wichita, Santa Fe, and Los Angeles. While residing in Los Angeles, he sang American premieres of operas by Richard Strauss, Paul Hindemith, and Gottfried von Einem, and the west coast premieres of operas by Christoph W. von Gluck, Luigi Dallapiccola, Benjamin Britten, and Carl Orff.

Dr. Gibson is a long-time member of the National Association of Teachers of Singing, and has served as a master teacher in their Intern Program. He maintains a voice studio in the Washington, D.C. area where he travels once a month from his home in Tucson, Arizona. He is in demand as a master teacher and clinician.

The Interview

RR: *You talk a lot about equalization of vowels and breath with students. Do you believe in shaping with the lips at all?*

GG: Not a lot. The reason is because I feel it has the tendency to bring the sound down too far forward [demonstrates]. When I do this, it gives me a totally different resonance feeling inside my head. It's what I call "fish lips," or "pucker." I do a little bit of it, but I don't talk a lot about it.

RR: *I also notice that you did not talk specifically about what to do with the lower body while singing. Instead you used images like "spinning the breath" and similar ideas.*

GG: I talk about it if I see a drastic deficiency in that area, but nine times out of ten, the problem resolves itself when they get the connection of the breath that I'm looking for. I may talk differently to men and women about where the basic expansion occurs. I have noticed that men breathe a little higher. I basically feel my breath move when I sing from here [indicating the lower abdominal area]. I feel it moving through my body. This part of the body [the lower rib area] stays open once I breathe and never collapses. The activity occurs in the abdominals.

Many teachers want you to stay expanded in the abdomen after you inhale. This I don't understand at all. The ribs can stay expanded, but how can the abdominals? I have run across teachers who have put their fists on the abdominals, and say, "Push against me. Now sing." This seems to be diametrically opposed to the natural support of the sound.

I spend more time with my male students on activating the lower abdominal area than I do with female students. I'm a very physical teacher. I always ask my students, "Do you mind if I touch you?" Never have I ever had any student say, "No, I don't want you to touch me." I think it's very important for the student to physically know what's going on in the support system.

RR: *Would you explain what you called "vowel flow?" I like your idea of mapping out this concept of the vowel line.*

GG: That was so drilled into me by my early singing teachers. The teacher that saved my life, as far as my career was concerned, was the teacher I studied with on my Fulbright, *Frau Professor Kammersängerin* Hedwig Fichtmüller, a Wagnerian dramatic mezzo who taught at the *Hochschule* in Munich. She was a *Kammersängerin,* but never sang in this country [United States].

I received the Fulbright right out of undergraduate school and was singing way too heavily—I was going to set the world on fire, you know? She just tore me up one side and down the other. I vocalized for six months. I thought, "I came over here on a Fulbright to vocalize for six months?" And, in retrospect, that is what saved me. I would never have had any kind of a career had I gone on singing the way I was. I would have lasted maybe five, ten years at the most. She insisted on exactly the same connection from vowel to vowel. She would yell at me, "I want the same, same, same. I know you have the vowel change, but I don't want anything else to change." I sang that until the cows came home. And she said, "I don't want any outside movement. I want everything inside." I try to teach that, and I think it makes a heck of a lot of difference. In other words: more tongue activity, less of everything else. Otherwise the line gets so choppy, with inconsistent, uneven resonance.

The other main idea that was ingrained in me early on was from a teacher at the University of Miami. She said, "I want to make your singing as natural as possible; look at singing as being nothing more than vocalized speech." I'll never forget the first time I did a musical, which was *South Pacific*. It scared me to death, because I had never done dialogue before on the stage, other than *Magic Flute*. She asked me, "Have you ever thought of using your singing technique when you speak the dialogue?" And once I got that into my mind, as far as using the same breath concept for my singing as speaking, I began to get the idea of going from one to the other and using the same technique. This too has saved me. I can teach here from ten in the morning until eight at night, and I'm just as fresh at the end of the day as I am at the beginning. I'm very proud to say that. My throat is totally relaxed, simply because there is always air moving. There is absolutely no feeling of strain or any pressure. That's my general philosophy, to use a totally natural approach. I don't care whether my muscles down here are at a thirty-seven-and-a-half-degree angle when I sing an E-flat^4. Who the heck cares?

I always impress upon my students that the answer to every problem comes back to two things: vowel and breath—maybe not immediately, but eventually. That's where we start. It's this business of trying to make your approach to singing as natural and forthright as you possibly can, and build on the idea of vowel purity, which will result in purity of sound, rather than a tone that may be breathy or shrill. I speak of resonance a lot. I speak of where the *passaggi* lie. I try to instill in them where the breaks in the voice occur, but allow the breaks to happen on their own without placing them.

RR: *I noticed that you worked with your tenor student using falsetto.*

GG: From the top down.

RR: *Do you do that kind of falsetto work with all of your male students?*

GG: Some baritones. Not much with basses. We don't do it a lot, but it at least gives them that feeling of up and over that is so important. I don't like the idea of always approaching everything from underneath. I also work with students on putting consonants in the same place as the vowel.

RR: *I noticed that you have a very old school Italianate sound when you show students how to sing without excess mouth movement.*

GG: But singing without a lot of mouth movement does not mean the jaw is tight.

RR: *Or that your text is muddy.*

GG: No. In fact, it's just the opposite. When I was at Wichita State and Eastman, I gave freshmen Gilbert and Sullivan patter songs, just to get that idea of working the tongue versus extra outer movement. They always looked at me kind of funny, but I would say, "No, go home and learn the first verse. Come back next lesson with it learned." Then we would work on it from the standpoint of working the tongue versus bouncing the jaw.

Barbara [Honn] speaks much more about vowel modification than I do, which is fine.

RR: *She really helped me. I remember she would always tell me, "Modify the space, but not the vowel." She would constantly tell me that, which helped a lot. She told me that she didn't believe in modification.*

GG: Exactly. I consider Barbara one of the finest teachers in the country. I'm extremely proud of her. After she graduated, I saw her sing in four or five productions in Germany. She was unbelievable. That was very fine singing. When she came back to this country after nine years of singing over there, she taught for us at Wichita State for a year and then moved to a position at the University of Texas. She called me when she received that job offer. I told her, "Barbara, you are going to be one of the finest teachers in this country. Believe in yourself, let the students be your sounding board, and you will go places."

RR: *She has been an icon for so many singers and teachers. So, if an undergraduate student came to you and asked what he would need to be successful as a singer, how would you answer?*

GG: It's so individualistic. I don't think you can say anything definitive. I've always been told that the keys to success are the three "Ds:" desire, determination, and discipline, but I don't think that tells the whole story. I do not encourage my students to go into the singing field because I know how difficult it is, but that doesn't mean I don't encourage them if they show me certain strengths. The one thing I look for, even if they don't even want to go into singing, is a certain "germ" that gets my ear. I can't tell you what it is. It is a spark—something that makes me feel that I must listen to them. I have no choice. I have to listen to it. That needs to be combined with an extraordinary work ethic, a certain innate musicianship—which cannot be taught—and a little bit of luck. When I worked with Sam Ramey during his undergraduate years at Wichita State, for example, he sang Figaro in my first production of *The Marriage of Figaro* and then the title role in *Falstaff*. He was superb—I always knew Sam would make it. Sam was not the strongest student or musician at that time, especially when it came to passing the piano proficiency exam. But he had an innate musical flexibility. That's why he was so successful in the Handel repertoire.

In Barbara's case, I put this germ of a career into her head. I asked her, "Have you ever thought of trying to make this a career?" And she answered, "Well, I have children and responsibilities." Soon after, she won the Southwestern Division of the NATSAA [National Association of Teachers of Singing Artist Award] competition and a scholarship to AIMS [American Institute of Musical Studies]. During her time at AIMS she auditioned for agents and they picked her up immediately. Have you ever seen Barbara on stage? She's dynamite. She can really move with grace and command.

RR: *If you had someone like Sam Ramey now, what advice would you give him for approaching a career?*

GG: I would take him as far as I could, and then send him to somebody else who has good connections. I don't have any connections with agents in New York. Therefore, I would try to connect the person with someone who does, like Bill Schuman, for example. He would need someone there who would be interested in his development and have him sing for the right people. I'm pretty good with repertoire, but don't necessarily know which arias to assign students when they go to New York. I can put them in the right *Fach*, but I'm not aware of current casting trends.

RR: *How much do you teach during your typical trip to Washington?*

GG: I arrive on a Tuesday, teach Wednesday through Saturday, take Sunday off, and teach Monday through Thursday. I start at 10:00 a.m. each day and finish at 8:00 p.m. I used to go from 9:00 a.m. to 9:00 p.m., but I quit doing that. I usually average about sixty-five to sixty-eight lessons per visit.

Luckily, my wife and I don't mind traveling, and I don't get tired. I find this studio interesting from the standpoint of diversity. About fifty percent of the students are professional singers, many of whom are older. Washington is a real choral town with a huge number of choral organizations. I have a few students who are members of these organizations and they come in with horrible ideas about technique. I've been successful with some of them, not so much with others. And then I have vocational singers who are lawyers, a federal judge, and even people who are affiliated with the Central Intelligence Agency (CIA) and the Environmental Protection Agency (EPA). Brilliant minds! They all simply want to keep up their singing.

Parting Thoughts

George is, in large part, the catalyst for this book. I heard about him for years as a young singer and really wanted to know about his approach. Every singer I met who had studied with him loved working with him and sang very well. George is a true gentleman, with a youthful demeanor and energy that belie his chronological age. He is eternally young.

George works vigorously with every singer to line up singing vowels with minimal movement of the throat and mouth, which is another cornerstone of the Italian *bel canto* approach. He is consistent about keeping each vowel connected to the next and not allowing intervals or consonants to disturb that connection. Consequently, his students sing with excellent diction and tone clarity.

I was also delighted by how much time he spent assisting students with score study. They discussed many small, but extremely important, details. My very first voice teacher during my high school years, Mr. Herbert Coursey, used to tell me to, "Sing to the smartest person in the room." He knew that singing at that level creates the best performance for the entire audience. Even people with no musical knowledge can sense that there is something special going on when a singer performs with that level of detail, intent, and commitment.

What the composer wrote is important, and we owe it to the composer to study the score carefully. I will never forget a time in my opera classes with Alberta Masiello when a singer brought in Verdi's "Stride la vampa." As the singer began, she sang a musical turn rather than the written trill. Of course, Miss Masiello insisted on a trill. After trying it a few times, the singer stopped and said, "That is much harder!" Miss Masiello, in her signature dry manner said simply, "No. It is correct."

Lesson Highlights

Breath Control/Support

Breath management when singing fast music

If you breathe too many times during a fast song or aria, you're going to get too much breath inside of you. It will be breath on breath on breath, to the point where you will feel something akin to hyperventilation.

The importance of pure vowels when singing long phrases

Sing open /ɔ/, exactly, not an /a/. I guarantee you that if you hold onto that /ɔ/ vowel in your mind with the right concept, you will have no trouble making it to the end of that phrase. When you widen the /ɔ/ too much you lose too much breath to finish long phrases.

Inhalation with vowel shapes/prephonatory tuning

When working with one vowel in a vocalise or song, especially if it is a narrow vowel like /e/, /i/, or /u/, there is no need to change your vowel concept or structure at the end of a phrase before starting the next one. Just breathe. Don't disrupt what you already have gained by breathing. Leave it alone.

A teacher used to tell me a long, long time ago, to inhale through an /i/ vowel regardless of what vowel you start with in the forthcoming phrase. The /i/ vowel has an arched tongue position, with the tip right behind the teeth. It took me a little while to get used to inhaling in the /i/ position, but the whole point of that little rule was to negate the temptation to drop the tongue when breathing in. You must move in both directions simultaneously when you breathe—up with the soft palate and down with the breath. This gives you the idea of what I call the "lift of the breath."

Phonation

Managing swollen vocal folds

Visualize in your own mind that you're only using the top half of your tonal core and approach each note from above. If you let it fall and start using too much of the folds, especially when they are swollen, then you're up a creek without a paddle and the voice will start cracking.

Resonance

Oral Resonance

Sing in your mouth, not out there somewhere. That's what gives you your unique quality. All that extracurricular jaw and tongue movement does is dislodge the resonance you have within your body.

Vowel purity and modification

To my way of thinking, a vowel is pure from the top to bottom, or bottom to top. You absolutely can open up your jaw when you get up in the upper pitch range. But, do I purposely modify a vowel above the break? No. Now there are some teachers who I greatly respect who say, "Modify toward /a/ above a G^5, period, especially sopranos." I don't personally understand that way of thinking. That's just me. Why do I have to modify a vowel above a G^5? Instead, I'll drop the jaw, give the vowel shape as much verticality as the pitch demands, and keep the pure vowel concept. Can I sing a high B-flat^4, or can you sing a high B-flat^5, on an /i/ vowel? Absolutely. You will modify it as if you're going to sing /a/, but your concept is still that /i/.

Registration

Accessing the Female Upper Range

As you ascend to pitches above B^5, maintain the high soft palate and widen the space between your ears. Try pulling up and out on your ears as you sing pitches from B^5 to C-sharp^6. This helps you stay inside your resonance in this range.

Articulation

Tongue movement

Leave your tongue alone. Let your tongue respond to your mind.

Articulation, Text, and Expression

When approaching text, find a basic vowel structure for each word or syllable. For example: the word *nun* in German would be closest to /u/. Speak the text with that vowel clarity, and then sing the text again, focusing on less activity outside and more activity inside. The extra outward movement that expressing a dramatic text can inspire doesn't make a singer more successful. Don't let the drama get in the way. I made this mistake often as a young singer. Finally, my teacher said to me, "George, just sing the song. Don't do anything. Interpret from the inside, not the outside." Love these vowels and words from the inside. Make your inside as involved and alive as it can be.

Italian Diction

In Italian, the consonants that you are singing must be in the same place as the vowel. If the consonants are outside the vowel flow, your cords are not going to phonate. You're slapping your consonants outside the vowel flow rather than softening them and pronouncing them inside the openness of your vowel channel on pitch. You don't need to lessen the consonant. It just needs to be in the right place.

Expression

Singing Recitative and Arias in Mozart Operas

All of the drama takes place during the recitative in Mozart operas. Once you get to the aria, you stand there and you just sing it. It's purely vocal beauty. You've had your dramatic moment already. Just sing.

Exercises

Exercise 1: Lip Trills (used with women)

Instructions: Lay the tongue right behind the bottom teeth. Keep the soft palate raised as you traverse through the lower middle resonance into the chest register. Don't give yourself a lot of vertical space in this part of the voice. Make the opening of the lip trills small so the breath channel can be appropriately narrow. Make sure you are using enough air, but not more than that.

Exercise 2: Lip Trills (used with women)

Instructions: Do this exercise quickly and lightly. Feel everything sighing from the top down.

Exercise 3: (used with a tenor)

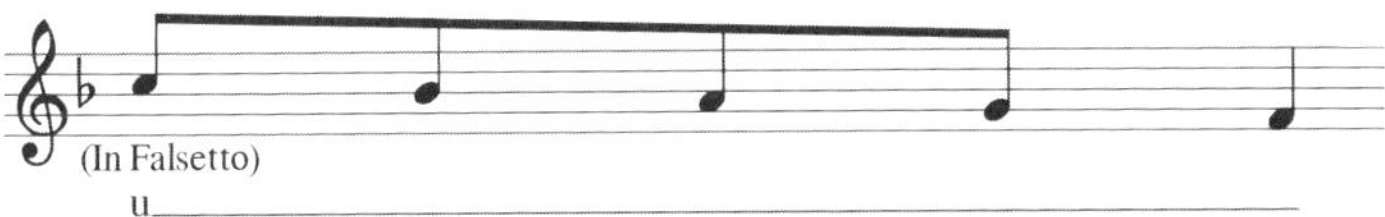

Instructions: Take everything from the top (in falsetto) and carry it down as far as you can. Shift to your connected voice when you need to and apply a little more strength to that sound.

Exercise 4: (used with a mezzo soprano)

Instructions: Approach the phrase from above.

Exercise 5: (used with a soprano)

Instructions: /i/ is a tongue vowel and /u/ is a lip vowel. There should be no lip tension in either vowel. This is something I fight about with choral singers all of the time. The tongue is the major mover, going upward with the /i/ and sliding down into a grooved position for the /u/.

Exercise 6: (used with a soprano and a mezzo)

Exercise 7: (used with a soprano)

Instructions: Put your hands on either cheek and hold your jaw open in a comfortable position. Move your tongue into each vowel position without involving your jaw.

Exercise 8: (used with a tenor and with women)

Instructions: Make sure to get the base of the tongue to the right height for /i/. Only use the amount of breath you can control. Don't overflow.

Exercise 9: (used with a soprano)

Instructions: I want this vowel change to happen as fast as I snap my finger. Don't accent the vowel changes; just make them quick and exact.

Exercise 10: (used with a soprano)

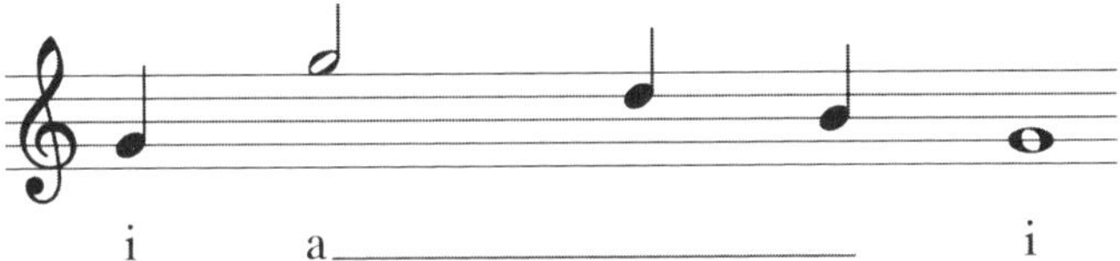

Instructions: Take two fingers and put them on either side of your nostrils. Push up gently on that area as you go to the top pitch. Never lose the feeling of the hard palate in any vocal range you are singing. Don't pull the sound back behind the hard palate as you approach your head register. As you descend, let the changes in resonance occur on their own.

Exercise 11: (used with a soprano)

Instructions: Keep the relaxation in the base of the tongue as you ascend. Make sure you avoid tucking your head downward as you go over the top.

Exercise 12: (used with a soprano)

Instructions: Don't drop the jaw much when you sing /a/ in the middle range.

Exercise 13: (used with a soprano)

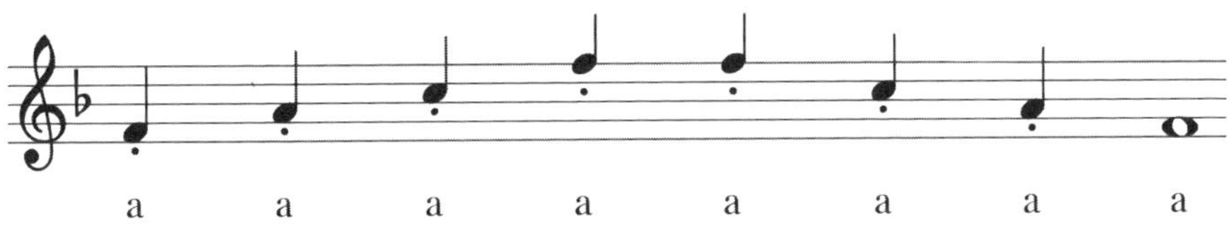

Instructions: Think vertically. Look at it as nothing more than detached legato so you find a real connection to each note.

Exercise 14: (used with a mezzo and a tenor)

Instructions: Release the jaw at the top. Try to put every vowel in exactly the same place.

Exercise 15: (used with women)

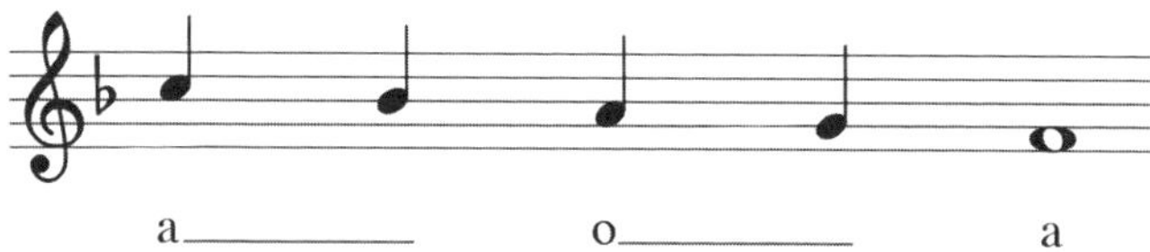

Instructions: As you approach the lower register, don't make that register switch quite so obvious. Stay in middle voice. All right, now fill your chest for the scale between D^4-G^3. Easy! Don't push it. Just let the air pass over the cords and drop your jaw.

Exercise 16: (used with a mezzo)

Instructions: You do not need many jaw adjustments in this part of the range. Only do what is necessary. Be very, very careful that the vowel and the vowel concept stay very pure.

Exercise 17: (used with a mezzo)

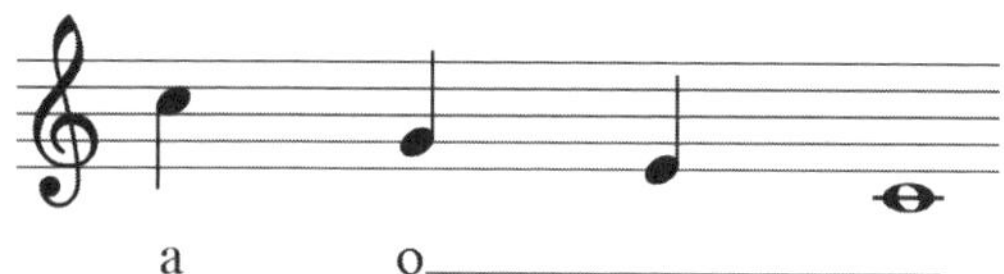

Instructions: Up with the palate, down with the jaw. Don't hesitate at the climax of the breath or at the attack. Once you start the process of breathing you must not hesitate. The palate should really stretch up when you drop your jaw. Achieve both directions in one operation. Do not let anything drop when going into chest voice, just change your resonance.

Exercise 18: (used with a tenor)

Instructions: Keep the tongue tip at the lower teeth. Inhale through an /i/ vowel without puckering your lips. When you finish the /u/, breathe through that position for the next phrase and start the next scale with another /u/. At the end of that scale, you will finish on an /i/ and breathe through that vowel for the next repetition that begins on the /i/, etc.

Exercise 19: (used with a tenor)

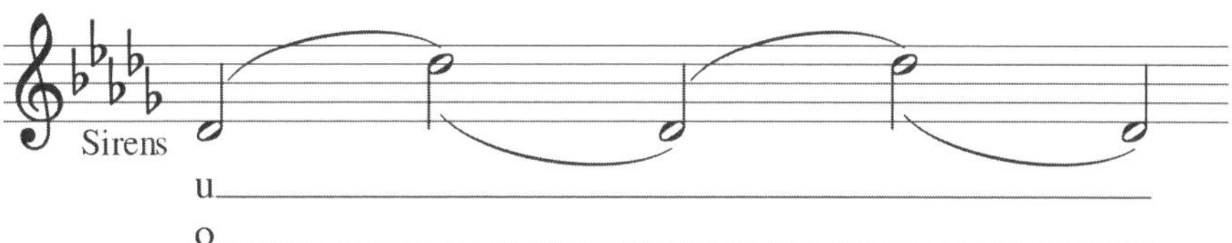

Instructions: Really slide between the pitches with lots of height. Don't worry if it goes into falsetto, but try to keep it in your connected voice whenever possible. Use only as much breath as you are comfortable with. Don't over-blow.

Exercise 20: (used with a soprano)

Instructions: Just sing /i/. No other vowel. Keep your head up and hold onto that vowel concept. Make a decrescendo on the top note, let it float for a moment, and then crescendo before beginning the descending scale. Don't lose the back-head resonance when you crescendo.

Exercise 21: (used with a soprano)

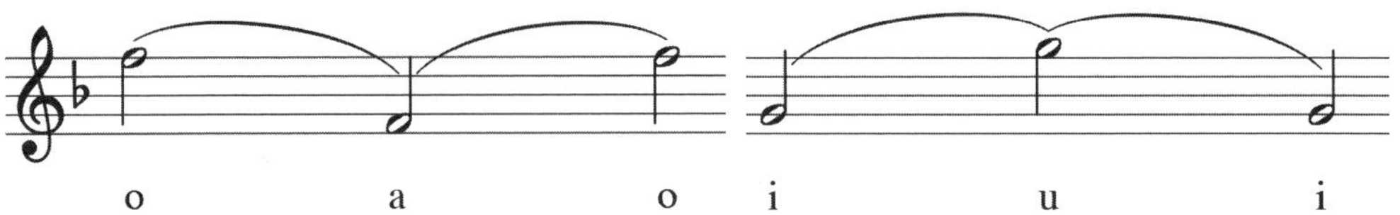

Instructions: Find a little more verticality on the top and open up the back a bit more through the ears. Find the width in the back-resonance space.

Exercise 22: (used with a mezzo)

Exercise 23: (used with a mezzo)

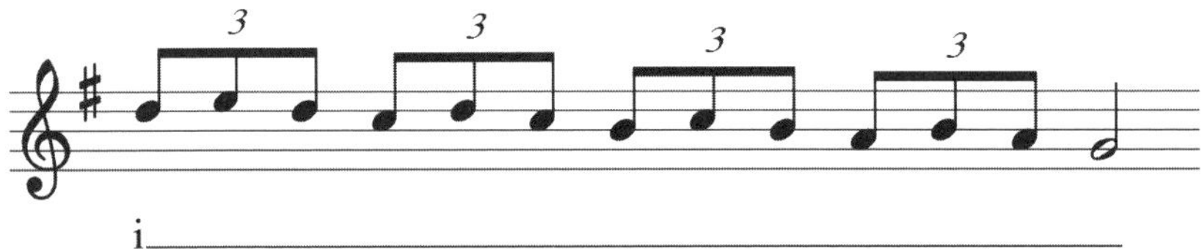

Exercise 24: (used with a tenor)

Exercise 25: (used with a mezzo)

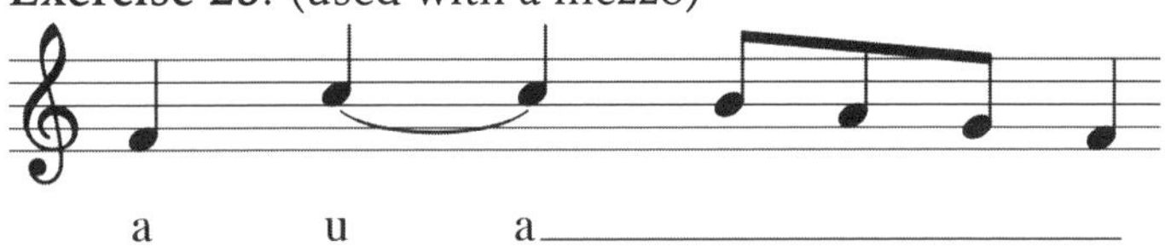

Instructions: Keep your tongue up nice and high for the upper note. Keep a feeling of elevation in the back when you switch to /a/. Keep your /u/ and /a/ in the same place.

RUTH GOLDEN

Internationally recognized voice teacher Ruth Golden serves on the faculty of Manhattan School of Music with over twenty years of teaching on the faculties of the Academy of Vocal Arts (AVA), Long Island University Post, and Bard College Conservatory Graduate program. As a guest master teacher, Miss Golden has worked with young singers at the Glimmerglass Festival, the Juilliard School, Songfest, North Carolina School for the Arts, the Chautauqua Institution, the University of Southern California, and Eeh Wah University in Seoul.

Her students have gone on to perform with the Metropolitan Opera, Royal Opera House Covent Garden, San Francisco Opera, *Bayerische Staatsoper* Munich, *Deutsche Oper* Berlin, New York City Opera, Spoleto Opera, Opera Theatre of St. Louis, Santa Fe Opera, Royal Swedish Opera, Minnesota Opera, and Wolf Trap Opera, among others.

Under the direction of Beverly Sills, Miss Golden appeared at the New York City Opera as Mimi in *La Bohème*, Marguerite in *Faust*, both Pamina and First Lady in *Die Zauberflöte*, Zerlina in *Don Giovanni*, and numerous operetta heroines in *The Student Prince*, *The Mikado*, and *The Merry Widow*. In addition to appearances on *Live from Lincoln Center*, she appeared at Carnegie Hall, Alice Tully Hall, Weill Recital Hall, Symphony Space, and

Merkin Concert Hall. Concert engagements included appearances at the Kennedy Center, Los Angeles Music Center, the Ravinia Festival, the Aspen Music Festival, and the Music Academy of the West.

In addition to touring thirty-five of fifty U.S. states, Miss Golden appeared with the Canadian Opera Company, *Orchestre Pasdeloup* in Paris, Prague Philharmonic, and the Orchestra Royale in both Madrid and Lisbon. An alumna of the Thornton School of Music at the University of Southern California, she appeared with Marilyn Horne and Martin Katz for the Koldofsky Memorial Scholarship Fund.

Miss Golden's discography, originally recorded for Koch International Classics, includes works by Delius, Warlock, Vaughan-Williams, Rodrigo, and Samuel Barber. The Warlock and Barber recordings have been re-released on EMI.

Miss Golden received the Van Lawrence Fellowship from the Voice Foundation, and serves as a member of the panel of judges for the Metropolitan Opera National Council Auditions.

The Interview

RR: *How would you describe your approach to teaching?*

RG: I had an incredible music education at USC, where I studied with one of Vennard's students and worked with Martin Katz. But there still were questions that weren't answered for me as a singer, which is what started me on my journey. Part of my journey, both as performer and certainly as a teacher, was to find ways that people could apply things quickly and practically. I've read every pedagogy book and read every article. I've been to every master class. I feel I can hold my own with anyone's scientific knowledge. I go to the Voice Foundation and talk to all the doctors. I'm not sure what all the medical terms mean, but I know what they're talking about. But, ultimately, if I'm in the room with someone who is seventeen or twenty-seven, I know that he or she doesn't really need to know all of that at this point. What I can say is, "There are structures that are doing xyz, and what you probably need to feel is this." I'm oriented more kinesthetically than scientifically as a teacher. But if I'm with people who are really cerebral, and I know that's where they want to go, I'll give them reading assignments and we'll talk about pedagogy and science. I try to address each student as an individual.

What really brought me a lot of information physically and practically was the Alexander Technique. I started doing it twenty years ago. When I was performing at Lincoln Center and dealing with the physical and mental rigors of doing repertory opera, I found that the Alexander Technique really helped me return to neutral in my own body. In my teaching, I work with the practicality of posture, the sensations and mechanics of breathing, and how they might feel the stretch of the phrase. How I might do that depends on whether the person is seventeen or twenty-seven.

RR: *So, it's not a cookie cutter approach?*

RG: No. There are some exercises that I use with many students, such as lip trills. I don't even call them "lip trills" anymore. I call them "breath trills," because I want to see if they're connected to their breath. The first thing I do is to evaluate their posture, whether their neck/jaw relationship is free, and whether the tongue is independent of the jaw. Those things will always be staples, but it all depends on who's in the room with me. So, I would say that what I really bring to people is how technique can be practical and applicable. And, if you want to know all the science behind it, I will definitely point you in the right direction, but I'm not going take your voice lesson time to teach you that. There are classes for that and many books. But mostly it's learning to manage their bodies. They come out of high school with the joy of singing, and I hope they leave college with more information and more joy.

RR: *I hope that I can listen to some of your exercises today. But also, I'd also like to understand your reasoning for using them. Some people believe that if they just buy a Concone book, it will teach them everything about what to do!*

RG: Boy, I had some teachers like that!

RR: *Did you know Barbara Doscher?*

RG: I did not know her, but I read everything she wrote.

RR: *I had the fortune of working with her, just for two weeks, in the first NATS intern program. She said, "Robin, you need to know all of the science, but as soon as you sit down with a student you must forget all about science and use your ears."*

RG: That's right.

RR: *What do you think are the top attributes of a successful singer?*

RG: A beginning singer? A mid-career singer?

RR: *Let's say a successful young professional who is out of school and going to auditions.*

RG: Okay. That's good, because that's much of the population I work with. Successful singers must have unquenchable intellectual curiosity about everything—about opera and about the business. They have to want to know everything. They have to be over-prepared. They need to do their research and go to the opera a lot, if they can. They need to take full advantage of what's available on the Internet. If only we'd had YouTube videos to look at in our younger years! I didn't get to see my first real professional opera until I was seventeen. With YouTube, you can see full productions any time you want. It's incredible!

RR: *Do you remember which opera it was?*

RG: Oh, of course! It was *La Bohème*, with Luciano Pavarotti, and Teresa Stratas.

RR: *Oh, wow. Mine was* Manon, *with Alfredo Kraus at Dallas Opera.*

RG: And there you have it. I saw *Bohème* at San Francisco Opera, so when I went to Merola, I thought, "Thank you. You're the opera house that changed my life." Young singers must be incredibly open and flexible to hearing what a trusted few are saying to them, because singers never really hear themselves the way they are heard in the world. You can get too much input from lots of people and be completely confused, or you can take the other end of the spectrum and take no information from anyone. Both approaches are potentially limiting.

The students I love working with are the ones who make the commitment and do the work week after week. They know that it's not just about preparing five arias for an audition. Really successful students and professional singers look at their ongoing development as a big discussion about how best they can serve the music. So, it's the curiosity, open-mindedness, commitment to being really physically and vocally healthy, and the wisdom to be patient. The body and the voice change. What might work at twenty will not work at twenty-five. Teachers have to find ways to communicate gently, compassionately, and realistically so we can say, "Sure you can go sing *Tosca* now, but that may eventually take a toll on your voice and your whole infrastructure of breathing, vocal folds, and physical stamina."

RR: *What do you look for in a voice? Or is that less of an issue for you?*

RG: Well, my own particular thing is it's not *the* voice, it's *your* voice. It's *his* voice or *her* voice, because a lot of people will say, "The voice is beautiful." But you *are* your voice. That's a whole other psychological discussion, but there needs to be a sense of ownership and responsibility. So, if someone comes to me and says, "I'd like more warmth in my voice. What am I doing technically that is limiting me?" that is a good place to start. I rarely attract students who are already fantastic and finished. They come here because they were missing something in their previous training. I look for a beautiful voice or an aspiration to developing an even, aligned, beautiful voice that is functional, useful, and can respond to the needs of the music. Secondly, are they emotionally open and can they put their heart and soul into repertoire that is right for them now? When I was twenty-two, I wanted to sing *Tosca* more than anything, but I was a lyric soprano. It was never going happen. So, I say to them, "Are you willing to make the commitment, to love what your voice can do now—while acknowledging the possibility that with work it may evolve and change?"

RR: *Would you say that there are specific technical skills that you teach very successfully?*

RG: Yes. I think that the best thing I do is teach people to move the tongue, jaw, and head independently so their articulation becomes very fluid in the upper torso and connected to a real understanding of and reliance on their breath.

RR: *How would you describe the intake of the breath? What do you tell them to do on the intake and while they sing a phrase?*

RG: When I was researching the literature a few years ago for a paper on breathing, almost all the authors agreed on what happens during the inhalation, but there was no consensus on what should happen during the exhalation. What I tell people is, "Let the exhalation happen as freely as you can, not relaxed, but with energy and buoyancy." I try to use adjectives that people can feel and ask them to describe sensations in their words and experience. I can say something fifteen ways, but using their words helps us develop better communication. For me, language is important. It doesn't need to be accurate scientifically as long as it means something to the person who's requesting it from me.

So, I tell them to release the knees and the hips, feel elasticity in the rib cage, release the shoulders, keep the head/neck/jaw nice and loose, and feel the expansion in a 360-degree way. A complete inhalation is 360-degrees. I'm really opposed to glottal onsets in the exhalation, even in English-language opera.

I always think, "You just took all the dome and height off your voice by smashing your cords together. What if you let the air go over the roof of the mouth so we can hear the vowel?" I try to avoid the hard, glottal onset. I do believe in the idea of leading with breath so the *Bernoulli Effect* can happen. Now, how to achieve that with each person, of course, is the big mystery. I don't use the phrase "press down and out," because I locked up when I was taught that way. So, I say instead, "Feel the buoyancy. You're going feel some sort of pulse, which you can manage, somewhere between the pubic bone and above the belly button." Where you feel it exactly depends on the length of the torso of the person. You can help guide the breath in a feeling of pulsing. So, if people ask, "Are you an up and in, or a down and out" I would say I'm an up and in, but not drastically. I feel like there has to be this buoyant cushion of air and a little more help for certain places in the repertoire.

For example, I think repeated notes must be rearticulated; otherwise they decay or get tight, especially in the *passaggio* or higher register. Another example would be certain initial consonants or consonant clusters, especially in German. If you have three consonants that have to be timed before the beat so the vowel is with the orchestra, you have to give them some extra help. I think that the exhalation is not even throughout the line, and this is where I diverge with some people who just advocate for an even, efficient flow. I find that people don't use enough air. I'm not talking about blowing air through your folds and splaying them apart. I'm talking about giving gentle encouragement or energy to maintain breath flow if there's a particular phrase that needs highlighting. When there's a run with *staccati* underneath it, I might say to a student who is learning the piece, "Pulse each of those a little bit" [singing]. Once it is really in your body, you may not consciously do it anymore. Your body might just need to do it initially as a way to encourage a strong, flexible approach.

I often have beginners come up and feel my breath support mechanism, because I'm very strong but always flexible. That's the opposite of locking. I worked with a baritone voice teacher for a while who was all about pressing down and out. All it did was lock me up, tighten my throat and tighten my neck. I lost my high notes. So as much as I believe in expansion, I don't believe in rigidity. I read an article by a respiratory physiologist in Arizona, Thomas Hixon, who studied vocal physiology and breathing in singers. All of the subjects described what they did during exhalation, and, of course, none of them were doing what they said they were. I just laughed out loud, because I thought, "They're not using any language that he would relate to as a physiologist, but it made sense to them." The exhalation is the most crucial and misunderstood part of singing. I certainly have not measured what I tell people to do scientifically, but I have pretty close to a hundred percent success rate. So, I'm going to go with that. It's a combination of strength, buoyancy, and the ability to always feel that you have a little more.

When people use the full breath, their recoil reflex can then help them breathe more easily for the next phrase. People are so afraid they're going run out of breath that they resort to locking, which keeps them from using all of the breath that they have. Sometimes I say to students, "Look, you're not going pass out! Keep going! I promise you that you won't fall down!" If you've developed your musculature correctly, you can find this easy, energetic inhalation in time for the next phrase, regardless of whether you have an eighth note or a whole note to rest and refuel.

RR: *Do you feel that any of this is different with male versus female students?*

RG: I think that's a really good question. For me, it's not so much male and female *per se* as it is torso, body length, and the gender difference in pelvic structure in relationship to the rib cage. So, when I start with a student, I let each person show me on him or herself where the expansion is felt. I'll have people bend over to feel the expansion in the upper rib cage. I'll have them release the lower back and hip joints to feel if they can get a lower, wider breath in the back. I try to relax the really high sternum that some of the men I work with have been taught to maintain. They shouldn't be concave, but I think this overarched military posture is detrimental. The issue with more of the women is that they've been told their whole lives to hold their tummies in for vanity, so getting them to really let it open can be a challenge. Alexander Technique has informed a lot of what I do in terms of what I feel and what I can help other people feel.

RR: *If you had a student who wanted to read more about Alexander Technique, is there any specific author or book that you would recommend?"*

RG: Well, there are many books, but I think it's most important to work with a person one-on-one. Bill Connington, with whom I've worked with for twenty years in New York, has published a book titled *Physical Expression on Stage and Screen*, with online video instruction on Alexander Technique and performance, published by Bloomsbury Methuen Drama [London]. I think you can read everything, but Alexander Technique is an experiential rather than an academic subject. You have to feel it in your own body.

RR: *How do you find the right repertoire for singers?*

RG: How long do you have? I'm judging five Metropolitan Opera regional competitions this year, which I'm thrilled about. I highly recommend Kim Witman's lists of arias that she compiles from the Wolf Trap auditions. Those lists and her blog are so useful to young singers because she talks about the process from the other side of the table. I think singers need to think about that.

RR: *Looking at the question a different way, are there signs that someone is singing the wrong repertoire when you are judging a competition?*

RG: Yes.

RR: *How would you describe that?*

RG: What I try to do is look at the age and stage of the singer. How old is he/she? How much training has he/she had? What is this voice, really? I know they're in the wrong repertoire if they're struggling to make the sounds or to meet the demands of the music. People usually don't sing something that's too light. They usually sing something that's too heavy. In comes Mimi and she wants to sing Tosca, or in comes Despina and she wants to sing Mimi, so it usually tends to skew that way. I'm also very wary—probably from the twenty years I've been judging the Met Competition—of singers who do not demonstrate a well-rounded technique in their repertoire. If I see a list of five arias that have no high notes and no coloratura—basically the same aria in five different languages—then I know they are struggling. In those cases, I would say in the feedback session, "It's not just about having a variety of repertoire. You must show that you've mastered the basic skills of singing." So there has to be something where you have movement, even if you are a voice the size of Deborah Voigt or Stephanie Blythe. You have to move your voice. One of the great joys of my life was hearing Stephanie Blythe and Marilyn Horne sing *L'Italiana in Algeri*. Here are big voices that can really sing runs. So, don't tell me, as people have tried to many times, that your voice is too big to move at the age of twenty-five.

The last suggestion I give competitors is to consider presenting contemporary and Baroque repertoire. In the twenty-first century, there's more of a demand for contemporary music than when you and I were studying. Handel is now standard repertoire as well. So, if their voices would be right in that repertoire and it's not on the list, I need to ask why. Is that an omission because you can't handle the technical demands, or were you just unaware that this is an option?

One of the great gifts to me in all these judging experiences is sitting with conductors and artistic administrators of top tier opera companies. One of them said to me quite pointedly after three days of auditions that he was really tired of people shouting at him all day. There is this true misconception on a national scale that opera needs to be loud all the time. It still has to have dynamic contrast. So, if singers can't do that, if they're singing big all the time, if they can't move their voice, if they're struggling with high notes or low notes, if they can't easily field and smooth the natural register changes, all those things would indicate to me that they aren't ready.

I also appreciate my own ongoing education from professionals in the business. I'll ask them, "When I was young, I heard everybody from this type to this type sing Gilda. Who do you like singing Gilda now?" That's today's performance practice. If a full lyric says to me, "I want to sing Gilda," I'll respond, "I love that, and you sing it beautifully, but you should know that the casting trends is toward a lighter sound in this role right now." That's neither good nor bad. It's just acknowledging what is.

RR: *How do you know when singers really need to change their Fach or if they need to move up to a higher voice classification?*

RG: You mean if a baritone comes in and he's avoiding his high notes?

RR: *Or needs to move up to fuller or higher repertoire?*

RG: First, I try to judge if I am really hearing free, supported singing. Then I determine where the voice is the freest and the fullest in terms of *tessitura*. Where's the sweet spot, if you will, or the four or five notes where I think, "Bingo!" And if someone comes in over-darkening or trying too hard to make low sounds because she thinks she's a mezzo, but sings freely and beautifully a fourth higher, I think, "Hmm." More often I find singers avoiding the top range rather than people singing too high. But before I would make that suggestion, unless it was someone I work with weekly, I would just say, "I think you need to consider or discuss with the people you rely on whether or not this repertoire is right for you now or in the long run."

I frequently find very talented lyric mezzos with great, easy high notes. You'll hear one of them today. She's not a soprano, in my opinion, but people tell her all of the time that she's a soprano because she has an easy C^6. No, she's not. You have to really, really listen to where she excels and the color, comfort, and tessitura when she's completely connected. Maybe she'll sing soprano repertoire when she's forty, but not at twenty-six. I think a lot has to do with age and stage of development.

RR: *When you're working with your singers, do you prescribe some sort of vocalization regimen for them?*

RG: I believe singers should start in the middle, not at the extremes of the voice. They should start in the middle and work from the top-down, instead of bottom-up.

RR: *All singers?*

RG: All singers. Most of us were taught to start at middle-C and sing five-note scales. All of these sopranos would have issues turning over and going to the top of the voice, and I thought, "Well, what if you turned it around, and vocalized in the other direction?" Boom! No problems. I only teach a couple baritones. I have mostly tenors, sopranos, and lyric mezzos. Even my dramatic sopranos vocalize that way.

I'm an advocate of lip trills and long arpeggios. I'm an advocate of fast onsets that ring cleanly and freely without time to create problems. If the women are having issues with finding the thin edges of the vocal folds when their voices start to grow and get bigger, we find them on an /n/ or an /ŋ/ and really do a lot of top-down work.

I have one full lyric coloratura singer who came to me with intonation problems, mostly because of medical issues. I said, "Let's just start with descending chromatic scales, so we can really calibrate your sense of where your voice is." She couldn't find a half step. And this was a really good musician,"

RR: *And that worked out?*

RG: Yes. Her pitch is precise now.

RR: *How long did you have to work on that with her?*

RG: Maybe a month. She really worked hard. I know she practiced consistently because the scales became better every week. I can give the suggestion, but it's the dedication of the student that's the key piece of the equation.

And as a woman who's survived all of those hormonal changes, I'm keenly aware that the medical field doesn't always understand how hormones can affect a woman's voice when she's young. Opera houses in Europe for years would have it in women's contracts that they wouldn't have to rehearse or perform on certain days of the month. That kind of acceptance and awareness that a person's voice may not be in the best condition during that time helped to minimize the problems it can cause. I always tell all my female singers to eliminate salt and exercise frequently during that part of their cycle, because it reduces the edema.

RR: *You tell them to physically work out?*

RG: Yes! Go to the gym. Sweat it out. Get on the elliptical trainer. You'll feel great, and you can mitigate some of the symptoms. Not all of it, but some of it. Practical tips from the road.

RR: *How much singing a day do you advise students to do? Do you want them to practice every day?*

RG: If can get the young singers to practice five days a week, that's great. They are all so busy with classes and jobs. For the majority of those you will observe today, I would say five to six days a week. I don't think someone should sing three or four hours a day—that's excessive. There's so much other work you can do mentally, visually, and aurally. I used to do my memorizing while I was on my elliptical trainer. I was always someone who could multitask.

I've started to do two-hour lessons to build stamina with students who are going off to do competitions, but I wouldn't do that with a beginner. I only do that with people who are around twenty-six to thirty-two years old and have already sung a little professionally. An occasional two-hour lesson to prepare a lot of music can help them. With a competition, you need to start singing a little more each day to prepare for the inevitable fatigue that comes with adrenaline. Like in an athlete, stamina is important.

I also hope these longer sessions improve students' concentration levels, because that's what you need in competitions and auditions. If I have someone in the studio for two hours, I can really explore phrases, discuss the student's perceptions, and review specific technical and artistic concepts. By modeling that process in the lesson, I'm helping them to learn *how* to learn. I think that's something people assumed students understood when we went to school, but I don't assume it anymore. With most people, I feel like I'm teaching them not only to learn their music, build their stamina, and build their technique, but also how to learn.

They also must learn how to rehearse for seven hours with a company without sacrificing vocal quality and mental clarity. You are never "safe" now, you know. The Internet has destroyed that. Before you've taken your makeup off, someone has posted your performance online. People used to say to me, "Go off to somewhere and try out this role." And I could! Nobody knew if I did well or not, except for me. That doesn't exist anymore. You can't really try something out, because everyone talks to everyone, and everything ends up online. So, I feel like I really need to empower people with these strategies of how to use their voices healthfully in a rehearsal period.

RR: *Do you recommend marking?*

RG: Marking is helpful if it's done well. The problem is that a lot of people don't teach singers how to do it. I talk about it as singing softly with lots of intense concentration and breath. And if the conductor goes back three, four, five, or six times, you just start marking after the second time. What's really difficult are these concept pieces where the director wants everybody sitting in the room for all seven hours of rehearsal whether they are in the scene being rehearsed or not, which is really fatiguing. We developed a good strategy for a student of mine in that situation. She would just go in the corner of the room, put on her headphones, read a book, or just try to divorce herself from what was going on in the room. It was very tiring for her.

Parting Thoughts

The cornerstone of Ruth's technique is breath management. In observing her lessons, it is hard to keep track of the number of times that she talked about breath flow or a using the breath to give you "room to bloom." How to achieve the breath flow is where many teachers go in different directions. I loved Ruth's statement that there is no consensus on expiration technique. When I recently spoke about this with one of my graduate students, his conclusion was, "Basically, the method through which you find the consistent stream of air is irrelevant so long as you create a consistent stream of air."

Ruth is completely engaged with her students during every minute of the lesson. She constantly is interacting with her students and giving them instructions as they sing, which helps to keep the singer's concentration on the task at hand and allows the lesson to progress quickly.

Often, we have students who come in for a lesson and just don't feel right about how their voice is responding that day. I was impressed with how Ruth helped one of her students as he really struggled with congestion. I also admired the student for managing to accomplish so much in spite of these difficulties. We need to know how to focus and operate under less than optimal circumstances. The singer sounded excellent—except for the occasional dry response from the instrument. So, as singers, we need to remember that input and output are completely different things. What we as singers hear when we are singing is not what others are hearing. Many times, the things that bother us in our singing are not apparent to anyone in the hall.

Lesson Highlights

Breath Support/Control

Exhalation and Natural Rhythm

One of the really good things about realizing what your inner metabolism/tempo is in singing is being able to recognize whether you are a rusher or a dragger. If you are a rusher, I don't want you to rush your exhale in warmups because I want you to feel the buoyant, energetic release without feeling like you are in a hurry. The onset in a piece may be different, but this is what you need to do when you warm up. Just feel low and slow.

Singing descending phrases

One of my mantras is to "breathe up." The phrase may descend, but we must keep the air coming up so that the notes don't drop too far. Maintain the opening and expansion at all times. As you descend, allow yourself to embrace the architecture of the line with breath. Just thinking up isn't enough. I want you to feel you've built yourself a really good infrastructure so that all your phrasing is possible. If you start without thinking about that in advance, you can't find it mid-stream.

Finding the Breath Anchor in a Performance

When we get nervous, our breath loosens and we lose that grounded feeling that we need. What helps me is to back into the piano to give me something to breathe against. I would create blocking for myself in each song, like singing against the piano or leaning fully against it, so I could find the anchor in that physicality. Once I felt really in my body and was no longer levitating with adrenaline and nerve energy, I could step away and feel safe.

Returning to Neutral

You need to sing vocalises that bring you back to neutral. Every role you do is going pull you in some direction. The physical roles that have you hopping and skipping can really unground you if you aren't careful. You need to be more in the feet, ribs, and have this feeling of body underneath your sound. This is returning to neutral.

Phonation

Vocal Onset

Remember that the onset is the most important task for a singer. Once you have sung into the phrase, it's really too late to make changes. That's why you must take your time, think about what you want the first note to sound like, and feel where you want that note to be before you begin.

Pedagogy

Learning How to Practice

(From a student, explaining what she has gained by working with RG) I definitely needed some structure. I told this to Ruth when I first started working with her. I just didn't know how to practice, so when I would go and practice it was just a free-for-all. She helped me come up with a system and figure out what to work on. After that, I was able to easily measure the progress. Once I had a solid set of exercises for practicing, everything was so much easier. I started feeling so much better vocally and mentally within a few months. I felt more confident too, because I had a plan.

Being in Perfect Voice

The great soprano, Elizabeth Schwartzkopf, told me that ninety-five days out of a hundred you will be in less than perfect voice. Those five days of perfect voice will likely be on days that you don't have an audition or a performance. To be a successful singer, you have to learn to deal with your voice on the other ninety-five days.

Exercises

Exercise 1: (used with a soprano)
Stretching/Body Preparation

"Plant your feet, roll those shoulders, and just twist. Feel that long, low engagement as you breathe in, and notice the knees. Release the hips. Breathe in. Exhale. See if you can feel the release of the hip joint as you inhale. Release the ribs out. The shoulders should be uninvolved.

Exercise 2: (used with a soprano)

Instructions: Really use the air. Breathe in wide. Do a slight plié as you exhale. Take your time.

Exercise 3: (used with a soprano)

Instructions: Tuck the tip of the tongue behind the teeth. When we sing /i/, the tongue has to move more upward, which means that the breath has to move sooner. Otherwise, we get a mushy vowel. Allow the tongue to create the /i/ space and let the breath take over. Give it "room to bloom." Grow with the air. Let the bloom be in the back of the head.

Exercise 4: (used with a mezzo soprano)
Stretching/Body Preparation

Instructions: Lean against a wall. Feel your shoulder blades slide down the wall followed by your knees. As you get the balls of the feet into the floor, feel the space between the toes.

Exercise 5: (used with a mezzo soprano)

Instructions: Sing a nice /a/ vowel: feel a breath pulse, get the balls of your feet into the floor, and keep the upper torso completely uninvolved. The vowel on the /ja/ needs a faster air speed to find the height and depth of the /a/. Sing this against the wall: release the knee and hip joints. Feel like you're just falling back into the wall as you sing. Let the shoulders relax and the shoulder blades go down the wall while your head gets taller.

Exercise 6: (used with a mezzo soprano)

Instructions: I want you to feel your body under as you run from the low to the high, but don't add weight. Stay on the floor. Remember the speed of your air and leave room to bloom on each note. Sing all of these notes with the same tender-loving care.

Exercise 7: (used with a soprano)

Instructions. As you go up, feel your body lengthen. Let the breath be lower and the vowel be taller. Put your tongue on the teeth. Breathe into the back.

Exercise 8: (used with a soprano)
Breathing/Body Preparation

Lean over and press into this stand. Bend the knees and feel wider. I'm going to put my hands on your back. Now, breathe into my hands and go wide. Release the shoulders and send the air in. It's very important to open the back as you are singing each day. Get yourself into a posture where you can do it using a chair, table, piano, or whatever.

Exercise 9: (used with a soprano)

Instructions: Give yourself enough time to really feel the back expand while you inhale.

Exercise 10: (used with a tenor)

Instructions: Bend gently and release your knees and toes. Fill the space between the toes. Feel the space lengthen from the last rib all the way down to the back of the hip-bone.

Exercise 11: (used with a tenor)

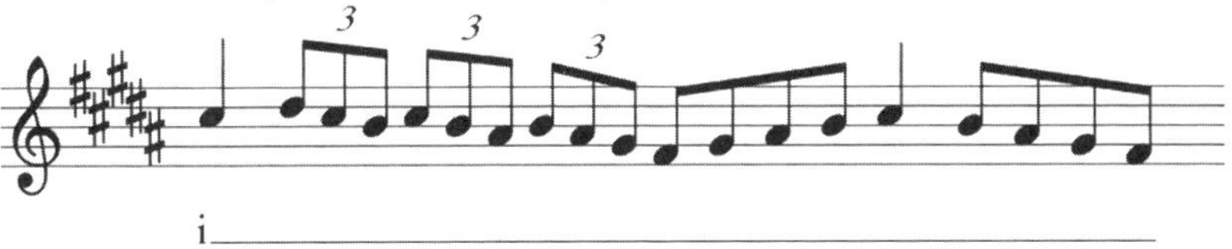

Exercise 12: (used with a tenor)

Instructions: Find the depth in the /u/ without dropping the jaw. Widen and go lower in the body as you ascend in pitch. Plié and release the neck.

Exercise 13: (used with a tenor)

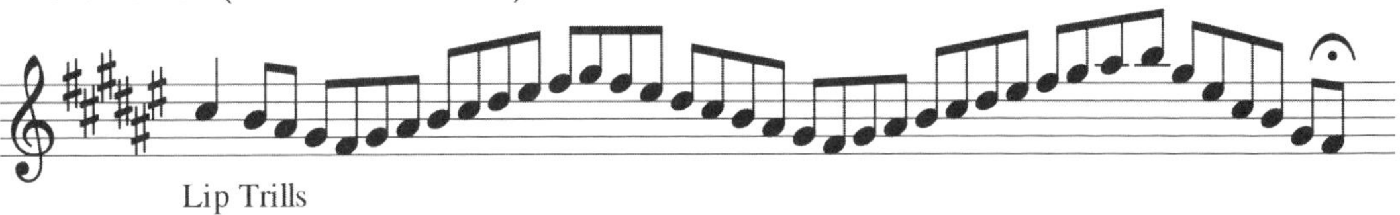

Instructions; Do a plié during the last part of the exercise. Open your back. Sing your intention. Speed up your airstream.

ROBERT HARRISON

Robert Harrison is now a retired Professor of Voice from the Indiana University Jacobs School of Music. Previously, Harrison taught at the University of Colorado-Boulder for twenty-three years and was the Chair of Voice for ten years. Robert's teaching encompasses all voice performance, including early music as well as nineteenth and twentieth century music.

Professor Harrison completed his doctoral degree in 1986 at the University of Arizona. He began his career as a freelance chorister in New York City, where he sang under Bernstein, Shaw, Stokowski, Brubeck, and Gregg Smith. He has performed at the White House and at numerous national meetings, including NATS, CMS [College Music Society], and the Sonneck Society. Robert was a Master Teacher for the NATS Intern Program and has given master classes and performances at the American Academy in Rome, Argentina, Egypt, Madrid, Barcelona and the *Hochschule für Musik Hanns Eisler* in Berlin. His students have won the Truman Award, the Metropolitan Opera National Council Auditions, Denver Lyric Opera Guild Competition, and performed with the San Francisco Opera, Central City, Opera Colorado, New York City, Santa Fe, Glimmerglass, and

Ohio Light Opera Companies; the Boston Symphony, Tanglewood, Philadelphia Orchestra, and PBS Great Performances.

The Interview

RR: *You talk a lot about the /ə/* [schwa]. *Can you define that a little bit more for me?*

RH: I regard the /ə/ vowel as a neutral vowel, located between /a/, which is the most open, and the /i/, which is the most closed. It's the essential vowel we use when we breathe in a relaxed fashion: when we are not panicked and when we are not in shock. When our nerves are "in neutral," that is when the tongue, throat, and jaw are in their most relaxed positions. That's why /ə/ should be incorporated into the mix with other vowels. When in the schwa posture, you can easily get air through the glottis, and if you can get air through the glottis, you can efficiently phonate. If you can't phonate with ease of emission, you have nothing. Who cares about resonance, after all, when you can't phonate?

RR: *So, when you refer to the /ə/, you're talking about finding a pharyngeal posture?*

RH: Right.

RR: *Would you want them to use this in all vowels and in all parts of the range?*

RH: Absolutely, but never in the same amount. For example, there will be less of it at the top of a tenor voice, but it's absolutely imperative that there be some. They may have more of it in their lower voices. In fact, they may be more open than a /ə/, but I like the /ə/ because it allows the two folds to vibrate with great efficiency.

RR: *Tell me about your concept of power singing versus non-power singing.*

RH: I define power singing as taking advantage of as many of the high, midrange, and low overtones as you can, as a result of a decent fundamental frequency and good use of the filtering/resonating system. We want this resonance so we can compete with the orchestra. For any sound that we use is that of a secondary color or that might be used to communicate something lighter mood, I might filter out some of the low and midrange overtones so I can feature the bright/high overtones, as an orchestrator might do if he/she desired a similar effect by featuring the first flutes with the first three desks of the first violins.

RR: *I was also struck by your description of the catch breath to one of your students.*

RH: What I was asking the student to do this morning was to use some air movement to get his cords vibrating in the top voice aerodynamically, rather than myoelastically. I want the cords to approximate with air, rather than being pushed together muscularly with air forced through them. Where I don't want fast air movement is in the inhalation, because you're doing the same thing to the folds; the air is going through those folds at such a high velocity that a vacuum is created in the glottis. The folds, then, have no other choice but to come together abruptly and brutally, resulting in the catch breath.

RR: *Would you explain your definition of "face" vowels versus "tongue" vowels?*

RH: I explain to the students that the larynx is there to accommodate two actions, neither of which is related directly to singing or speaking. One is to close the airway while swallowing to prevent aspiration [by adducting the vocal folds and closing the glottis]. But during inhalation, the larynx must be in an open position to allow air to enter the lungs [by abducting the vocal folds and opening the glottis]. So, singing comes out of those two particular postures. And when you take food and liquids into the mouth, you create a closed, narrow, lateral position—unlike the opposite: the open position.

RR: *That /ə/ position.*

RH: Right. The schwa creates an action of the face. The face creates this kind of posture, so the air can go in and you can take food into the mouth. To swallow, it goes laterally. All of the sounds of any language are based upon those two postures. So, you have face-related vowels and consonants, and you have tongue-related vowels and consonants. And everything in between. Voice teaching has to be structured around these principles.

The larynx responds to a position of the face, where the air and the food enter. You don't have a choice. If a teacher asks a student to move the air more and release the air with a swallowing articulation, it isn't going to work.

If you find students who are singing with high pressure, you can invariably see that they're electing swallowing positions and postures with too much action in the tongue, and excessive adduction. If the sound is airy, with too much airflow at high velocity, they are too open. And that is absolutely indisputable, because the larynx will respond. The position of the larynx, action of the depressor and elevator muscles, and tongue posture are all contingent upon an action of the face. It's just physiology.

RR: *It is like what Barbara Doscher told me: if you don't prepare, you are sunk before you even begin.*

RH: That's exactly it. Our preparatory beat is how efficiently the air gets in, which is the singer's necessary preparation. When you breathe, it communicates what you're going to say and it prepares the instrument for proper phonation.

RR: *What do you think has changed about your teaching over the years?*

RH: I think it's natural to change, because we are practicing an aural art, a listening art. We can't avoid listening; listening brings about change, or it should, in the teacher. If I've learned anything from teaching, it wasn't so much so from a pedagogy course. I learned on the job. I wish pedagogy courses would teach listening and the relationship of actions that create certain sounds, but they don't.

I taught a pedagogy seminar course for doctoral voice students at IU that was structured on the model of the NATS intern program. The doctoral students would teach in front of the group teachers and receive critiques. Almost every student asked me the same question when they began, "Dr. Harrison, how do I start?" I nearly hit the ceiling the first time someone asked me that, but then I thought, no, I can't react that way. That's where the student is. But I finally asked, "Have you ever thought of listening as a start?" That was a revelation to a good share of those students. Then I asked them, "Have you thought of what you're listening for? Do you have any concept of what a finished sound is in the human voice and if that sound is communicating to you?" They have to know what a competitive sound is and how to figure out every student's vocal thumbprint. What is *his or her* sound? The way I figure out their sound is by setting up the conditions of a /ə/. The tongue, jaw, and throat are in restful, neutral positions. To me, that's the thumbprint. From there, we build.

RR: *When I recall watching you teach previously, I remember you doing a lot more onset exercises with the students.*

RH: You are absolutely right. That was the progression. I still work onset more now if a student has a tremendous amount of fuzz in the voice and is really, really underphonating. Now I use more and more vowel structures that will let the folds come together as a result of facial position. If that doesn't work, then I will try onsets.

RR: *I know Doscher and Coffin were a big influence on you, but would you tell me how you got into teaching?*

RH Well, the economy really went south after I did about eight years of freelance choral work in New York City. Major orchestras like the New York Philharmonic started hiring Westminster Choir College and other collegiate groups for a lot less money. There was suddenly less work for professional choristers. My wife and I talked about coming back to the Midwest, and I wanted to do a Master's degree at the University of Wisconsin Madison with Bettina Bjorksten—she taught me the intellectual side of music—so we gave up New York and came back to the Midwest. My wife was teaching public school. We had no children, and a comfortable income. I didn't need the money, but Bettina asked me if I was interested in a teaching assistantship for my second year. I had no idea what I was going to do after the master's degree, so I decided to try it. They gave me a class full of voice majors who couldn't get into a faculty studio and a small number of applied students who were in their sophomore year.

I had done all the preparation for this initial voice class, which was my first teaching activity on the first day of school. And then I met these twelve students. Their faces, every one of them, had a look that said, "Okay, buddy, show us what you can teach us. We're silently angry. Show us what you can do." I was so intimidated that I literally closed my notebook and said, "You're going to have to excuse me. I hope to see you on Wednesday." I got up and left. They were, in some ways, rightly mad. They received a TA [teaching assistant] with no teaching experience.

So, I went home absolutely defeated, but somehow, some way, collected myself and taught the next class. That experience, combined with my private students, really grew on me to the point that I knew I wanted to teach. After that, I had three one-year sabbatical replacements. We had to do three long-distance moves with no tenure-track position in sight. I started thinking that I should just change careers, but then the tenure-track position came open at University of Colorado. I remember Barbara Doscher telling me, "You have such outstanding ears. You know what you want. You don't have the information about how to get it, but you're going to learn how. This is the reason why we're hiring you." I observed her teach after I started working there, which was revealing. She was so efficient about taking control of a voice and giving students exact action verbs to get the change she wanted. She wasn't vague. It was incredible to me how quickly she could create positive change in a singer's sound. It really inspired me to learn more.

As I tell my doctoral students who are interested in teaching, you will see an undergraduate student for approximately thirty hours in one academic school year for four years. If you divide that total one hundred and twenty hours by twenty-four, you come out with around five days to six days of instruction. That's all the instruction they have as undergraduates. To think that a singer is made in but a few days—are you kidding me? When I realized that, it really provoked me to be efficient through using what we know about the physiology of the larynx, its anatomy, and acoustics. There's no time for anything but the truth, to the extent that I understand it, and also passing exact actions to students so that they can get the job done sooner. I decided to figure out how to do that, mostly through self-study, because I didn't learn how to do that in any pedagogy courses. It's not so important that everyone like the sound of the students they hear. What *is* important is that I'm giving them precise actions to create what they are producing. And that is what really makes teaching this craft fun.

RR: *Do you use the same action verbs with different people, or do you tailor them to the individual?*

RH: The action is always the same; air goes in. I will sometimes use a different action or command with a particular student. If I sense that a student gets overloaded very quickly, I can't give that student as many actions to think about, and the development process might be a little longer. But the actions are just based on these two pieces of flesh in the throat that do this or that, and are designed for closing and opening the airway. I can give them language sounds and commands to alter their singing behavior. Because an /i/ does more of this [raises and forwards the tongue] more than an /a/, and there are variations and gradations of closed and open, we can get all the variations between this pole and that pole through the language sounds they know. And then I have to determine if there is too much of this or too much of that. And if there's too much of this I need to find actions that will reduce it and get it closer to that. That's all through listening.

RR: *Do you find any overall similarities in female singers as a group, or male singers?*

RH: I don't find similarities between any two people, not even any two mezzos. Rarely have I found two mezzos who sound alike. I suppose there are general patterns. A mezzo voice might work more efficiently with closed vowels in a particular area of the voice as opposed to open vowels. There are going to be those general rules. Tenors seem to enjoy, for example, more closed vowels on the top as long as they have enough space, as opposed to females, who like to have more open vowels at the top as opposed to the bottom. I've discovered through the years that there are no two sopranos who are alike. They all have their own thumbprints and DNA, which has been a joy to discover. I let every singer display his or her own special gifts.

RR: *What kind of singer do you like to work with? If you hear fifty singers and get to choose ten of them to work with, how do you make that decision?*

RH: Well, to me there are three general standards that all singers need to meet. They must sing accurately, both with respect to pitch and rhythm, use correct diction, and by all and every means, be able to communicate effectively. They must say something to me in a performance that changes me from what I was when I walked in the room; I want to be changed. They must enlighten me in some way, intellectually and artistically. They can touch my heart, my intellect, or both. Especially if I've paid them, I want to have something that I can take home in my mind after a performance, even though I may have walked into the performance annoyed that the grocery store was out of skim milk and I couldn't find a carton of eggs that wasn't broken. You might have noticed that I didn't say anything about a beautiful voice.

RR: *Right. That was going be my next question.*

RH: A beautiful voice that says something enlightens me. I'm also okay with a voice that is not so beautiful but that says something to me.

RR: *How do you work with students on expression?*

RH: I often ask them to speak the text and ask them if they have an experience that allows them to understand it personally. If not, I will ask them to set up a hypothetical situation, complete with what the character's likes and wants. For example, if it's an individual who likes hot red cars, I'll ask, "If you could afford any car in the world, what kind of car would you buy?" And maybe they'll say a BMW, or an Audi, or a Benz. And then I'll tell him, "Okay, pretend that you have been asking your parents for a BMW for three or four years, but they never bought it for you. Christmas rolls along. You wake up on Christmas morning learn that there's a BMW in the driveway for you that you've always wanted. You don't call me on Christmas morning to ask me how you should sound and what kind of expression you should use to show your parents how elated and overjoyed you are. You already know. Now put your life into that character, because a good singer is always someone who is ultimately providing an autobiography of him or herself." When we hear somebody sing, they're not talking about that character. They're actually talking about themselves.

To some degree, young students are limited as to what they can say and how they can say it, because they haven't had enough life experiences. But I will try to find songs or arias they can relate to, and identify experiences they can incorporate into their interpretations. I also like to make them aware of the particular sounds of each individual language, and how they can use those sounds to express ideas. Sometimes I ask them to say an /uwa/ sound with either a happy or sad expression behind it.

RR: *Do you often start off lessons with lip trills?*

RH: Oh, yes. Absolutely. Lip trills have been proven effective by voice science over and over again. If students can do a lip trill, raspberry, or even a rolled /r/, that creates the correct proportion of airflow to air pressure for every tone that they can lip trill. The correct ratio of air pressure to air flow changes for every pitch. When they are phonating, they are creating the proper ratio of air pressure to airflow, and that results in a fundamental frequency. So, lip trills and raspberries teach the production of fundamental frequency, and when you have the most profound of fundamental frequencies, you then have all of these overtones available that we can filter in or out as we wish as a result of changing and alternating the shape of the resonator.

RR: *If students come in without knowing how to do a lip trill, how would you help them learn to do it?*

RH: I haven't had that happen. If they did not pick up the ability to lip trill quickly, I'd probably send them over to the speech communications department and have a speech therapist work with them. I've had students who can't do them at first, but they always figure it out quickly. If they couldn't do it, I would have them do hums, but humming doesn't ensure the correct pressure ratio that is necessary for singing.

A good M-hum is nothing more than that pencil width of space, a loose, slack jaw, the tongue resting on the floor of the mouth, a released jaw that is neither hyper- or hypo-extended, and the larynx sitting in its most neutral position, and of course, with closed lips—an /m/ position. When the air speed gets high enough, it draws the cords together just enough to use the edges. When we need something stronger, we incorporate more cord as a result of creating fundamental frequencies based upon lip trills or raspberries. In a lip trill, you're using a little more cord, but still using mostly the edges. If you're creating lip trills that have no detectable air leak whatsoever, then you have a really decent fundamental frequency, which is everything in terms of sound. After establishing that, I move on to open mouth sounds.

RR: *Any specific part of the voice?*

RH: In the middle. It's the most comfortable area. Language developed there. The throat is probably in its most neutral position in middle voice. Then I work from the middle to the top and back down.

RR: *How do you generally instruct students to access their top voices?*

RH: Through increasing air velocity, which will automatically decrease air pressure. I will give them vowels sounds related to air movement. If I want to decrease air speed, which raises the pressure, I'll use tongue vowels; to increase air speed and decrease pressure, I use face vowels.

RR: *Can you explain what vocal qualities you hear when there is too much pressure in the sound?*

RH: A closed, pinched, overly bright sound, generally with high amplitude high frequency overtones. I hear an over-ring in the voice, to the point where the sound is almost static. I tell the students that it would be synonymous with listening to a symphonic recording on your home sound system with only the tweeter speakers. My ideal is, particularly in a power sound, a tone that would be coming through the subwoofer, midrange speakers, and tweeters together. I want thorough resonance with the least amount of cord use. *Chiaroscuro.* And to achieve this, you're going to have to combine a back vowel with a front vowel. We're constantly singing mixed vowels. Mixing and equalizing the vowels results in getting the highs, mediums, and lows.

RR: *Would you tell me about your use of falsetto with male students?*

RH: I use it because there is no question that, physiologically, the larynx has to ascend for high frequencies. We just can't allow it to become that necktie tenor sound. We have this thing called "stable larynx," but that should never imply that the larynx is sitting in one place and only one place for each and every pitch; the larynx does have to ascend as the pitch ascends, and to access falsetto or whistle voice. The elevator muscles should be allowed to strengthen so that they can battle and compete with those depressor muscles that add some hookup. Ideally, there are a certain number of pitches where we can combine both mechanisms and use some elevator with some depressor. With every semitone or quartertone or eighth-tone that you ascend, you're giving up a proportional amount of depressor muscle. If you go high enough in the male voice, you're going to be in total falsetto. There's a point at which you can no longer create a supported falsetto, because the depressor muscles just simply can't contract.

RR: *How do you talk to your students about using their lower bodies during singing?*

RH: I talk about it a great deal during the first few lessons with every new student. Those first session are *Breathing 101*, no matter where they've come from. I think that lower body involvement is optimized by the quality of the inhalation. If they have more time to take the air in, they're going to get a deeper breath. The breath will go, as we might call it, lower into the body.

RR: *Do you have exercises you use particularly for this purpose, or do you just explain what you want them to do?*

RH: If I have students who can't achieve that simultaneous contraction of the diaphragm against the muscles of exhalation [making a hissing noise], I will have them try to lift, or imagine lifting, something heavy. I also have them do pliés while singing. As soon as they are required to do any kind of load-bearing activity, the diaphragm is going to engage and bring the folds together. Otherwise, they can't bear the load. If they don't have an ample amount of air, there's no way they can make a decent fundamental frequency. Going back to the lip trill will also engage the diaphragm

RR: *When you do that lip trill, do you feel an outward resistance?*

RH: I feel the result of the diaphragm descending and displacing what's beneath it. I feel an expansion all the way around the ribs.

RR: *And what happens during the exhalation for singing?*

RH: Then I'll ask them to do a lip trill, and the diaphragm will engage.

RR: *Do you want them to think of the singing exhalation as a slow movement inward, an outward position, or do you not specify?*

RH: I don't talk about that. What I'm more interested in is the diaphragm remaining comfortably contracted so that the muscles of exhalation can work unimpeded.

RR: *I noticed that at times you allowed your students to use an embouchure concept. You did not specifically tell them to do it, but they do it.*

RH: Yes, I've been criticized for doing that. Some call it "trumpeting" when you round the lips. For power singing, it's absolutely essential. There's no other way it can be done.

RR: *So, if you had the chance to give advice to young teachers today based upon your career of experience, what would you tell them?*

RH: I would remind them that music is a language. The mission is, through singing, to say something to change the life of a listener who has often paid to be at a performance. We have a responsibility to say something to them that will change the way they feel and the way they think.

Parting Thoughts

Because Barbara Doscher was a formative influence on both Robert and me, I appreciate his adeptness at tweaking and mixing vowels throughout different registers and registrations. The end result, like the other teachers on this book accomplished, is to get the student to move less, while exhibiting a sustained and easy release of the instrument.

Robert's lesson with a young bass baritone was truly instructive. A young male voice is sometimes a little wild, especially when the student has a larger instrument like this one, which can be unsettling. His struggles reminded me of some of my own struggles early on as a singer. Why did some notes near the *passaggio* stay open when those same notes might close and go into the top resonance in other situations? Soon, I learned that closed vowels naturally go over sooner in the registration and open vowels naturally go over later. The keys are the breath flow and acoustics: closed vowel sounds and quieter dynamics require a narrower breath flow and will go over sooner. Consequently, the open vowels and larger dynamics require a larger breath flow. The result is the larger the dynamic, the more open the vowels must be to accommodate the breath flow and vice versa.

Robert was careful to direct each student not to hold on to the ends of the phrases. Excessively sustaining a note can add unintentional syllabic stress to text that does not enhance the syllabic flow or intelligibility. Equally importantly, it wastes the singer's energy and reduces the preparation time for the next phrase, which often can make the singer late for the next entrance. All of these results are unacceptable. The singer must make the time to prepare for each phrase. If the composer does not provide enough time, the singer must figure out a way to create it. I always ask my singers to listen to one of my favorite Callas recordings, "Egli non riede ancora" from *Il Corsaro*. Her lesson to us in breath management is extraordinary in this aria. Her last breath at the end of the cadenza after the trill is one of the most expressive sounds I have heard. Lastly, in this world of sound and sensory bombardment, the use of silence can be a very powerful and expressive tool.

The other integral part of Robert's approach is the use of the structure of the /ə/. Since many vowels tend to intersect within the /ə/, this position has many merits. My good friend, vocal coach and colleague, Ed Bak describes the ideal /ə/ as a French schwa /œ/, which is formed by creating the:

space of /a/
tongue of /ɛ/
lips position /ɔ/

If one shapes this style of /ə/, the movement to other vowels can be appropriately small and add stability to the singing system.

Lesson Highlights

Breath Control and Support

Taking the time to breathe

By the way, you are paid to breathe. Don't be afraid to earn money for not singing. I don't know of anyone yet who can sing without air. No air, no sound; no sound, no dollars. You can breathe in the middle of a word if you have to. If Aretha Franklin can get by doing that, and she did, so can you [he sang "li..., takes a long breath and finished ...berty"]. That's an expressive breath. It works. The breath you don't want to show your audience is the one that broadcasts, "I'm in trouble breathing. I'm in trouble. I'm in trouble."

Never, ever get too low on gas. Don't get the needle all the way down to empty in this last section. Stay high, wide and beautiful. Keep the chest high, wide, and get them up on the shelf, because you don't want the chest sitting down on those lungs. Create an ample amount of space for those lungs to inflate and the diaphragm to drop. My students know well my oft, repeated axiom with regard to breathing and its relationship to singing: *no air, no sound, no dollars.*

Inhalation and Laryngeal Positioning

Take more time to breathe, because the faster you breathe, the more you're going lower the larynx. It's a gasp of fear, so every time you breathe that quickly you're just pumping up the laryngeal depressor muscles more and more. That quick breath also prevents you from taking a full breath, because it lives up to its name: the catch-breath. It catches, stops, and literally draws the folds together.

Phonation

Onset

We want an aerodynamic effect to start phonation in the upper voice. We want the *Bernoulli Effect* to bring those cords together. Believe me, you can go up there and squeeze them, but it's not a good idea. You don't want any hard onsets in the top voice. It's a way of bringing the bottom up. If you want to protect the top, I think the best way to do it is through air movement, rather than onsets. You can onset in the bottom, and the middle, but not at the top.

Resonance

Mixing vowel resonances

For power singing, you're probably always going to want some back vowel with the front vowels, and some front vowel with the back vowels. A good vowel pairing to practice as an example, is /e/ and /o/. You want to find the high, medium, and lower overtones in the sound. Let the tongue do the work for the /e/, but keep some of that /o/ in it, since it is an articulation for air movement that allows you to move the air through the glottis and achieve the front vowel. Pucker a little bit if you want to add warmth to the front vowels and add a bit more closure and brightness in the back vowels to balance the sound and line.

Managing the tongue and creating "face vowels"

Leave the tongue in more of an /ə/ position for the /o/, and allow the face, rather than the tongue, to create the /o/. It is no more effective to call on the tongue to create a face vowel than to call on the face to create a tongue vowel. So, if you want more /u/, get it from the face. Leave the tongue completely in that restful position. Don't use it or move it whatsoever to create a face vowel. Let the face do it.

The tongue is just a blob in the mouth. It will find its place as a result of the face moving. The tongue is rather dumb. It follows the command of the face by following its movement. It will also follow a face command to accommodate chewing and swallowing. When food and air enter, that sends the action command to the throat and larynx to open. They adjust oppositely the glottis for swallowing.

The /a/ vowel and /ə/

Margaret Harshaw always instructed her students that /a/ was the most difficult vowel, according to the people who worked with her. She maintained that it was made up of all of the other vowels. I say that in another way, but it kind of means the same thing. I think every vowel should have some /ə/ in it. Another great Harshawism is this one: You cannot have nuance without sound.

Closed vs. open vowels in "power singing"

(Speaking to a mezzo soprano) If you want to close that /e/ on B^5, and I'm all for doing that, you cannot then try to power sing it. Don't ramp up the air pressure quite so much. Send the air a little faster. Open is to power as closed is to lean. Don't try to power sing it. You cannot get all that sound through such a small bore.

Registration

Arias that spend a lot of time in the passaggio region

I would rather you develop a good sense of singing above or below the *passaggio* comfortably than spending all of your time negotiating the *passaggio*. It's such a narrow place to sing, like the waistline of an hourglass. It can be incredibly draining. If you never sing above it, then you will always be barreling up toward it. The higher you go, the more you have to give up on the bottom. If you never find out what it feels like to get out of the bottom and into the top, you will always bring everything up. I suppose a few mutant singers can survive that, but not many. So, go ahead and jump over that range. I don't even care if it yodels! Don't worry about feeling the rise and the drop in the larynx. You need to find that upper sound, even if it isn't ideal. It may be unhooked, too closed, or a bit airy. I'd rather that than make you go up there with an immense amount of pressure.

The reason I have you do all of that lip rounding is to stay away from any kind of wrong articulation, which causes over-adduction. I want the air to release. If there's no release, there's no way you can get above the *passaggio*. You can't physiologically do it. So, if there's more air in the sound, I am all for it right now. I want the air to move when you go through the *passaggio* and get out the other side. It can easily be taken away once you feel comfortable in that part of your voice.

Female Chest Voice

Show that you have some power. Put on your power suit of sound, and if it takes on that red color down there, that's just fine with me. I have no problem with chest voice, any more than I have with a high voice with a lot of /æ/ in it. You don't have to create the same postures that you're creating on the top for the bottom.

Pacing High Notes

(Speaking to a mezzo soprano) If you slow the tempo, you're adding time, which is going to use up your breath, giving you less breath for the top note. It's a no-win. Don't slow down so much, unless a composer actually requires you to do so. The grand dames do not slow down very often before a high note. They'll approach a high note quickly, arrive, and then add time and slow down. The more you slow down on the way to the high note, the more of your vocal fold you are going to use. If you use more vocal fold, you won't get to the top because you're taking up so much weight. You can power sing once you get there.

Articulation

Modifying Italian Diction to Assist Phonation

I would change that /t/ to almost a /d/ to help you approach that G^4 a little more easily. Though the /t/ is muted, you are still introducing a vowel in the top voice with no air movement. That makes no sense to me. If you start with a /d/, a slight little tip of the /d/, almost like a flipped /r/, then you are really starting that vowel sound with sound. Introducing a vowel with sound rather than silence is a good idea, so don't be afraid to replace that /t/ with a flipped /d/ or /r/ in those situations.

Get rid of the /f/ consonant. I like to get rid of consonants that have no sound/voicing so that your default is going to be a legato line. Instead, add a short /v/. Put a /b/

on that "piangi," rather than the unvoiced /p/. If it's quick, it won't be a problem and will link everything together.

You're going into a swallowing articulation because of the /l/, so we need to find a similar consonant that is voiced and in an air movement posture. In this place, we can use /r/.

Jaw Opening

We're not really going to close the jaw past a /ə/, which is one pencil width of space between your molars. Stay there in that posture for all of this Italian text. If you want to articulate consonants, just let the tongue and lips move, but don't lose the one pencil width of space between the molars. That will let you move your air. If you close more than that, you are in the swallowing posture, and that's when you are going to create excessive air pressure. You don't have a choice; it's just the way the throat behaves.

In fact, there are no mandibular consonants. You will never hear a speech pathologist, scientist, clinician, or linguist, declare that there is a mandibular consonant or vowel. They don't occur. You either use your lips or your tongue. That's it! The jaw moves, but it's a secondary articulator. It's not the primary articulator for any consonant.

When we have to power sing, we will use more than one pencil width, which means that the consonants become less of a concern. We don't want consonant articulation in those places; the articulators can't reach that far. If you went to two and half or three pencil widths between the molars, the lips can't stretch and meet, so consonants are out. The tongue can't stretch that far to articulate. So, at most, those articulators are doing partial articulations. If you can articulate fully with the tongue and the lips while power singing, you're doing it wrong and it will tire you out.

Exercises

Exercise 1: (used with a tenor)

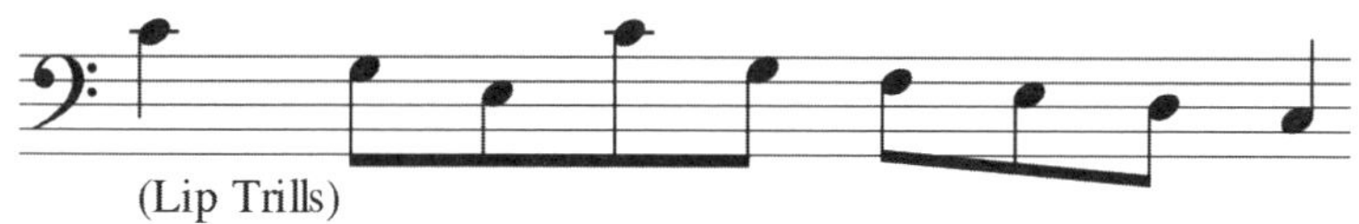

Instructions: Phonate in your lip trill right through that interval and don't allow it to yield whatsoever as you change pitches. If anything, slur, but don't stop the sound. As you approach the area around E-flat[4], you might want to release the air a bit more and speed it up a little. The speedier the air, the more immediately those cords are going to come together. Speed the air up as you return to the upper pitch in the octave. Break a little wind.

Exercise 2: (used with a tenor)

Instructions: Add a smidge more /o/ to your /e/ just to give the sound a few more lower overtones.

Exercise 3: (used with a tenor

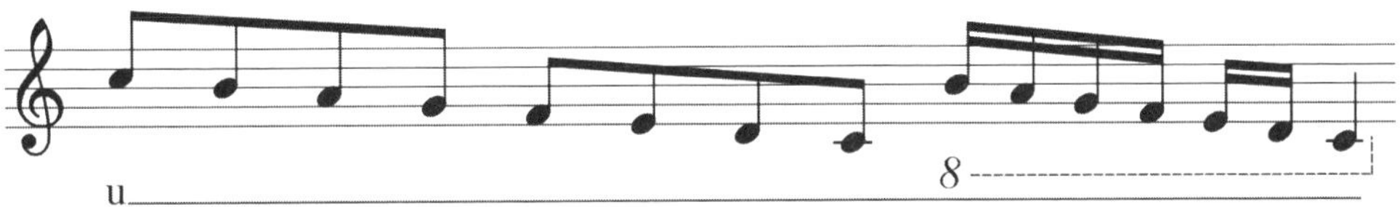

Instructions: Start in falsetto and mix on the fourth scale degree, by adding some /U/. Use a pure /u/ with no excessive air pressure and a bit more mix on the top.

Exercise 4: (used with a bass baritone)

Instructions: Don't compromise phonation one iota. Link sound with sound. Don't carry the top down low any more than you would carry the bottom to the top. Feel the rumble in the lower pitches.

Exercise 5: (used with a bass baritone)

Instructions: Give me a little /ə/ in that /e/. We want both vowels to have a similar color. Protect the quality and integrity of the timbre through every vowel change.

Exercise 6: (used with a bass baritone)

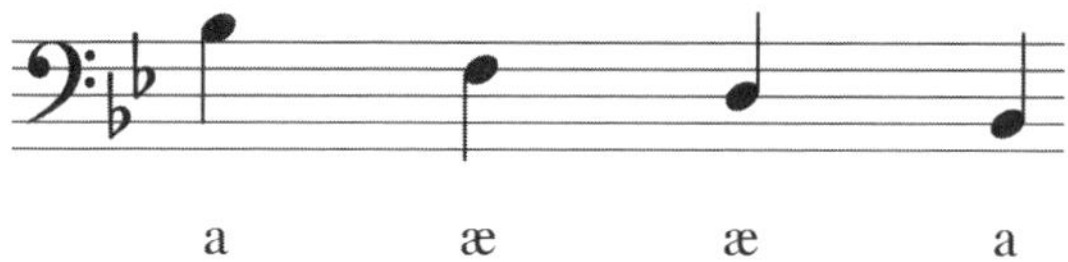

Instruction: Add a little bit more /a/ to the /æ/, and keep the tongue tip at the lower teeth. Make sure you narrow a bit toward /u/ as you go through the *passaggio*. When you get to the other side, you can open back up again if you want to.

STEPHEN KING

Stephen King is the Lynette S. Autrey Professor of Voice and Chair of Vocal Studies in the Shepherd School of Music at Rice University. Additionally, he is Director of Vocal Instruction for the famed Houston Grand Opera Studio and Head of Vocal Instruction for the Domingo-Colburn-Stein Young Artist Program of the Los Angeles Opera. King is also a longtime artist-faculty member of the Aspen Music Festival and Ravinia Festival's Steans Institute for Singers.

Internationally recognized as a teacher, King's students sing on the major operatic and concert stages of the world. He is sought for his expertise in training singers and teachers alike, having twice been a Master Teacher for the NATS Intern Program and appearing in a featured master class at the NATS National Conference. Mr. King also has taught for the Santa Fe Opera, the International *Meistersinger Akademie* (Germany), The Samling Master Classes (UK), and at various venues in Russia, China, and Italy. Mr. King's teaching was profiled in the University of Minnesota Ph.D. dissertation, *Three Exemplary Voice Teachers: Their Philosophies and Studio Techniques* (2008), by Jenny Elizabeth Dufault.

Mr. King maintains a large professional studio of international-level singers who have been winners of The BBC Cardiff Singer of the World, Operalia, George London, Richard Tucker, Metropolitan Opera National Council, Vinas, ARD and Belvedere competitions. These singers appear at the Metropolitan Opera, *Wiener Staatsoper*, La Scala, Chicago Lyric, San Francisco, Houston Grand, Los Angeles, Canadian Opera, Royal Opera Covent Garden, Paris, Berlin, and numerous others.

The Interview

RR: *You directed a student during a lesson to "put more cork in it" a couple of times. Would you please talk more about that idea?*

SK: Was I talking to a man?

RR: *Yes.*

SK: I was probably trying to get a firmer setup: more closure, more "ring," not blowing so much air through the tone. It seems like there are lots of students who think, "The more air we blow, the better it's going to get." That's probably what I meant when I said to "cork it" in the attack or onset. None of this is original to me, but I think they can forget about everything else if they don't get that right. If there's no closure, then there's no real hookup to the body. Where's the resonance going to come from?

RR: *You didn't talk very much about exactly how to manage the lower body. Do you generally leave that part of the body alone and see if it naturally falls into place?*

SK: I do talk about it, but how much detail depends on the student. If somebody's empty from the ribcage down, and doesn't seem to feel anything in that part of the body, I have the student sit on an exercise ball, on the floor, or in a chair. Sometimes I have people lean over the piano or act like they're going to pick up a sack of potatoes to feel some sort of lower body release. It's just a question of whether or not they feel it when they stand up. Not everybody does that very well. Of course, when you start talking about it too much, they overdo it. "Push this out, pull this in"—they lose the balance. This is the hardest thing to learn and takes the most patience to teach. In the way we train singers today, there is not enough time allowed for this most important aspect of developing and maintaining a professional level voice.

RR: *So, you stay away from telling them exactly what you want the abdominal wall to do?*

SK: I tell them how it works, and then, we constantly revisit the *appoggio* through exercises and especially breathing and singing through straws. In my weekly studio class, we'll have several sessions or a whole month when we focus on the physical setup of breathing. Many students don't really release and inhale efficiently. Others don't exhale completely. Some breathe, but then collapse at the onset of a sound. We get to parse out what works, since different people do things differently. I believe some of the sensation has to do with body type. Pear or apple-shaped students feel it in one way and the tall, slim ones feel it another way almost all of the time. So many tension and fatigue issues are related to the "don't push" mentality that has been cultivated. The resulting energy deficit leads to all sorts of problems in sound production. What an operatic singer does is more akin to an elite athlete. So, it stands to reason that the coordination of the body is fundamental to the sound production. This takes time, patience and constant vigilance. Any high-level athlete has a foundation/anchor to the setup of whatever they do to create leverage, which is often found in the posture or grounding. Because the descriptions of what happens vary among singers and teachers, we have to stick to the facts, and then know what to listen and watch for as we move toward a consistent support.

RR: *You also talked about the tongue angle a lot.*

SK: The curve of the tongue, yes.

RR: *Would you explain that concept more specifically?*

SK: The tongue needs structure because it's a muscle that continually is being flexed; it is following what our brain tells it to do. I think the tip of the tongue should be at the top of the bottom teeth. It needs to be, at least initially, at the leading edge of the bottom teeth. With problematic consonants, students probably are going to pull the tongue back. The tongue should always have that convex angle—never, ever concave. Of course, people hear that, and say, "You mean the back of my tongue can't be down?" My response is, "Well, yes, the back of your tongue is connected to the hyoid bone while the blade of the tongue is singing a vowel, whether it's toward the front of the mouth or farther back in the mouth."

RR: *You don't think it is helpful to create a ridge in the tongue blade?*

SK: That curve/angle does create a ridge. If I sing an /i/ vowel and the horizontal flex of the tongue is not toward the fourth tooth or so, I'm not using a good setup for /i/ or /e/. I have to figure out what's going on if it's too low.

I was in a master class recently with a tenor, and there were a lot of young singers there, so I asked them, "What's the favorite vowel for tenors in the *passaggio* on F-sharp^4 and G^4?" They said /a/. I stopped and said, "really?" I guess the idea out there is that if you flatten the tongue enough, there will be more space in the throat, which is really the opposite of what's happening. I use /i/ and /e/ in the *passaggio* so I can get a lot of backspace and stretch upward with tenors. Of course, it's different with women.

RR: *I noticed that you work similar ways with men and women in the passaggio, but approach the acoustics differently.*

SK: Yes, there is a difference in the acoustic, but also the laryngeal function. The women are singing completely with cricothyroid function, so when sopranos go up to an F-sharp^5 or G^5 with their mouth wide in a big, spread /i/ vowel, I ask, "How are you going to do that? Has no one told you that you have to open your mouth there?" That seems like fundamental information to me.

RR: *What is the best advice you could give to an aspiring singer?*

SK: The harder you work, the luckier you get. Somebody else has said that already, but everybody I know that's doing well at this is working so hard. You can be lucky for a while and skate by on talent, but these are not the people who are making major, long-lasting careers. It's very individual, because some people have a lot of talent and don't work hard, but others who have average talent make it on really hard work.

You must cultivate a sound without being a copy. I don't think that's possible without trial and error, because there's so much scraping away that usually has to happen before finding it and believing in it. There's so much individual work to do, regardless of the teacher. Singers rely too much on teachers.

There are a lot of teachers who have the information you need, but how much are you willing to put into *yourself* to figure out your voice? That factor makes the biggest difference. Singers must find their individual sound and really own it. I keep telling students, "If you don't own this, the good and the bad, how can you really be an artist? Don't just mime what I told you, or what somebody else told you, or what you saw." I think that's really hard to do.

RR: *You introduced me to the [Paola] Novikova writings.*

SK: Yes, that's great stuff.

RR: *I've really enjoyed reading them and have shared them with my students.*

SK: She taught Nicolai Gedda, George London, Zinka Milanov, among others. I don't hear many people nowadays who sing that way, or who even try to. Maybe it's a sound that's not currently in our ear.

RR: *It's hard to find it in the culture right now, but I do think that we've been overly dominated by* chiaro [brightness] *in recent years, which takes a toll and compresses the voice into too small of a box.*

SK: You're right. There's been too much of the *chiaro* in current pedagogy. For whatever reason, too many teachers and singers "chase the ping" rather than the process that results in complete resonance. People misinterpreted Richard Miller or something. Chapter one, verse one is not *chiaro*. Chapter one, verse one is onset and breath management, which is very Italianate and traces more to Manuel Garcia. When you listen to Pavarotti the *chiaro* is there, but he didn't need to create it. People have different ears and different aesthetics, but I think if you get onset and breath management right, a lot of other issues become clear.

RR: *How did you first start teaching?*

SK: Necessity, I suppose. I thought of myself first as a singer who taught, but then I soon became a teacher who sang. In my late thirties, I made a conscious effort to stop trying to sing because I was balancing too many things in my life. I just couldn't have a family, travel to sing, and teach. My first job was at a little school called Georgetown College outside of Lexington [Kentucky]. Later, the University of Kentucky contacted me and asked me to apply for a temporary job. I took the job, which turned into a permanent position the next year. In 2003, I was asked to teach the singers at Houston Grand, which led to joining the faculty at the Shepherd School. For the past twenty years, I have been able really to focus on teaching. Fortunately, I have been able to teach many talented singers.

RR: *Someone told me once that good students make good teachers.*

SK: The teachers get a horrible rap from the professional side of the world. I always say to them, "I could go out to the middle of an Iowa cornfield and find someone who can teach voice, but since they haven't taught eight Metropolitan winners, or the best singer in the world, you think they don't know anything." Famous teachers happened to be in contact with really great talent. I think that forces you to constantly evaluate and refine the way you approach each person's training.

I don't think every teacher is for every singer, no matter how talented, but some people can deliver it better to certain types of singers. I find that I'm more attracted to working with certain kinds of singers, which sounds biased, but it's true.

RR: *What do you think you bring to your students?*

SK: I try to find out what they need as quickly as possible; if it's not broken, don't try to fix it. Some students, usually because of what they mask, are just harder to figure out. It may take more time, or you may not get to them at all. I keep telling singers, "Most of this is *you* figuring out *you*. The more you figure out yourself, not just your voice, the better you're going to do with the things that reasonable people ask you to do, and to know when it's an unreasonable request. Trust yourself more than teachers and coaches." The professionals don't need this message as much. Teaching them is like doing an alignment on a car. They come in, get realigned, and leave for the next assignment.

RR: *Did you read a lot of pedagogy books when you started teaching?*

SK: I read a lot. I sang for Bill [McGraw] periodically who gave me feedback. I was in the NATS Intern Program. My master teacher was Shirley Emmons, who taught me a lot about teaching women. She was a brilliant person and was the first to watch me teach and encourage me toward growing as a teacher.

RR: *Do you teach men and women differently?*

SK: Yes, since they are primarily singing in different mechanisms and because the acoustics are not the same. Men must lengthen the vocal tract to ascend in pitch past the modal/speech range and avoid elevating the larynx. This takes time and much experience. As women ascend above the staff, the vocal tract shortens and the larynx slightly elevates. Obviously, this fact alone influences the acoustic values [vowels] that are chosen. Due to the differences in subglottic pressure, I think we must constantly be aware of the way the breath energy is being used. Men rely heavily on a strong closure of the folds to create the necessary pressure to generate an overtone that can be enhanced with vowel acoustics. Women need to find only the first overtone to be heard over the orchestra. Teaching them with the same ears seems rather absurd to me now.

RR: *How many lessons do you teach a day?*

SK: Seven or eight on most days.

RR: *That's tough. How do you do that?*

SK: I don't know. I think part of it is because I teach such a range of students. I don't get bored. I teach undergraduates and graduate students at Rice and slightly older singers at Houston Grand Opera and Los Angeles Opera who come from all over the world: Mongolia, Korea, Wales, Russia, Western Europe, South America, Canada, and Mexico. All of these singers are gifted, so it's not fatiguing. Most days I feel that I have learned more than I have taught. For some of them who are already working, it's about maintaining the work and helping them improve. After 4:00 p.m. most days, I see professional singers who schedule online or with my personal assistant. My Rice students are in opera workshop or opera rehearsal in the late afternoon and don't have evening classes. I teach around one hundred professional singers, so we all have to plan ahead.

RR: *That's a university policy?*

SK: It's how we do things here. We put them through the ringer during the day and get them out by 7:00 p.m. It's something we came up with to try to give them more time in the evenings for study and reflection. It also fit the general school schedule better.

RR: *Do you travel frequently?*

SK: I teach at the Domingo Studio in Los Angeles about once a month for three days. In the summer, I teach in Aspen and at the Ravinia Festival's Steans Institute. I don't travel that much. My life is very busy. If I can get out and play golf on the weekend or do something like that, I'm rejuvenated. When I exercise, I have plenty of energy. I start getting tired if I don't.

RR: *Do you have a certain kind of regimen that you want your students to follow when they're warming up?*

SK: I think it changes. I have a routine that I go through with the young students that we add to periodically. All I try to get them to do at first is to phonate on the breath, since that's what ninety percent of them can't do. Maybe it's the musical aesthetic of our time, or too many misunderstandings of how the voice works. Ninety percent of my teaching is built around onset, breath management, vowels, and legato line. For me that's what it has all boiled down to over twenty years. This is my twenty-fifth year of teaching, but I don't count the first five or six, because nobody knows how to teach when they start.

That's why we have the NATS Intern program. Being a young teacher can leave you discouraged when you watch master teachers who have experience in listening, watching and knowing just what to say. When I did the program, we all had to teach in front of our master teachers. I was told I had talent for listening and describing how it might change. That was probably the first time anybody said anything like that to me. None of my teachers had ever said that, maybe because they just worked on my voice and didn't worry about all the other skills. I probably started taking it a little more seriously after that. I generally don't demonstrate for students. I sometimes demonstrate for men, but really avoid it with women. I've had students say, "I've never heard you sing in the studio. You need to sing." I tell them, "No, your job is to be a lot better than me. If you don't sing better than I sing, I have failed you."

RR: *What do you think are the top attributes of a successful singer?*

SK: You need a sound that I remember, which can't be taught. The really great singers that I've known or taught all have an identifiable sound. They don't sound like anybody else, and the more you try teaching them to sound like other people, the worse they get. Some have good technique, some not as much, but they have that signature sound and can say something with music that makes you forget about anything technical. They have the gift of going straight from the music to the emotion without getting tangled up. There are certainly some functional, serviceable singers working in the profession who are good actors, but would I pay money to hear them? There's a shrinking market for these people, and yet we keep recruiting students in schools and conservatories, acting like there are going to be jobs. It's not true. It doesn't mean they can't study and do something. They can be you or me, after all.

Ten years ago, we cut the Rice program from sixty-five singers to thirty-six singers—twenty-four graduate students and twelve undergrads. I doubt it will get bigger, because we tried to figure out the best way for us to give the greatest resources to our students rather than the fewer resources to a greater number of students.

RR: *How do you deal with the interference of other people and situations into your professional singers' psyche so you can keep them on track and focused?*

SK: There are a number of advisers in this field. Like doctors and lawyers, we are all in the "practice" of our chosen profession. Some are better practitioners than others. I am part of a small team including the artist manager, coaches, and conductors who give advice to singers. It is an endlessly fascinating, confusing, and sometimes frustrating relationship. In short, the singer gives great trust to the advisers, but must ultimately be very discerning. With professional singers, I've occasionally had to say, "If you want a teacher in Houston, then I'm happy to help you. But if you want a teacher in San Francisco, New York, or Europe, I don't have time to see you for a fly-by lesson." There's nothing proprietary or possessive about this information, but I don't want to be a part of any confusion, and I don't want to have to reinterpret what somebody else has already told you. I'm the voice specialist, just like there are German and Italian specialists that you go see. That's what I do. We're not set up to have one teacher for life, but I find that singers get lost when they've had six, seven, or eight teachers. Everything you tell them is filtered through five different lenses. I'll take professional students who are really having problems only if I think I can help them.

RR: *Do you sometimes say no?*

SK: Yes. That's part of a communication I send out to the professional singers. It says, "If you are coming to have a lesson because someone suggested that you work with me and are currently working with another teacher, please tell me." Then I give a consultation lesson. I'd really rather work with people over a period of time so we can have a conversation that goes deeper, rather than see someone occasionally. If that means working with fewer people, that's fine with me.

RR: *What are your goals now for the short term?*

SK: Other than fly fishing or playing golf? Well, I'm just really enjoying what I do and feel like a kid in a candy store. I didn't set out to do any of this, to be honest with you. We all know how singing works, but say different things and come from different paths. I think what keeps me interested is the challenge of finding new ways to explain the same concepts to different people in a way that really helps them.

Parting Thoughts

I heard singers with different voice types during my time with Stephen. His rapport with students and how much was accomplished in each lesson was remarkable. He works very similarly with both men and women, but he makes adjustments acoustically for each different singer. His ear and the resulting sounds are what guide him.

I was very pleased that my approach to working with singer's vowels is similar to Stephen's. So, his use of vowel combinations is quite easy for me to understand. For years, I have felt that this was a very tangible way to get singers to understand space and acoustics. Such as, for sopranos, in approaching the higher extension above B-flat[5], many will gravitate to /ʌ/ space with /æ/ placement. So, one vowel is used for the concept of structure or space and the other for placement or resonance.

Along with this idea, Stephen also was aware of the aperture of the singer. As I see it, the lower the jaw, the more front space that a singer will have, which will increase the body's need to fill that space with breath. So, if the aperture is too large in the middle voice or the pre-*passaggio*, then the resulting breath flow will be larger and require more work. So, you can imagine what the result will be once the singer moves into the top. The result will be a heavier than needed mechanism and the access to the upper voice will become increasingly labored. One mustn't move toward a Maria Sharipova tennis grunt when moving into the top voice! The great singers will keep the aperture in the middle voice reduced, which allows for a better balancing of the system. One of my mantras is, "The adjustment will bring the power to the voice." Don't get me wrong, I love full, complete singing, but we simply cannot power the voice into submission.

I was also impressed with his discussion about listening to other singers and being careful not to mimic their sound. They should listen to singers and their *work*, not their color or size.

During the lessons I observed, Stephen referred several times to Luciano Pavarotti as an example of great singing. At one point, he spoke about a picture he shared with his students that shows the typical way he shaped his mouth. Here is a copy of that picture, which I actually keep in my studio beside the mirror. I use this picture as a tool, and as singers make progress, they learn to understand the musculature well enough not to rely on the embouchure quite so much. This is what I call, *"Singer's Position-101."*

Lesson Highlights

Breath Control/Support

Sustained singing

If your car is going at sixty-miles-per-hour, it won't stay at sixty unless you keep your foot pressing the accelerator pedal. The air behaves the same way. So, when you sing A^4 to A^5, you've exactly doubled the speed of the pitch. The air needs to match it with intensity and acceleration. It's not more or louder—that's where most of us get confused. It just feels more intense and has a sense of openness.

Breath Flow

If I say, "Use the breath," that's different than, "Throw more breath into the sound." When the cords are together, just concentrate on accelerating the air all the way to the end to the end of the phrase, regardless of where the pitch is going. Just think about the acceleration. This does not require a lot of air. Some people are better off taking a really quick breath and singing, because their tendency is to grab more air than they actually need. That raises subglottal pressure a lot, which tempts them to sit on that pressure in an attempt to find some kind of connection sensation. Some people don't have to think about maintaining consistent airflow after they begin phonating cleanly, but there are singers who have to think about it very actively so they don't grip and hold their airflow.

Descending phrases

Make sure to stay connected to the air as you're descending and don't let go of the acceleration or the energy. If you let off that energy, you will lose stability. Clearly restate the vowel. When the pitch comes back down, you're going to keep turning forward and "tilting" in the throat while letting the sound keep coming over the arc of the tongue. If you do that, [the larynx] won't rock back and depress in the back.

Alignment/Body Positioning

Lowering the larynx

Let the tongue be wide so it feels like it's touching your molars. This is the inner smile. It's the prepared breath.

Put a finger under your chin, swallow, and inhale. As you breathe in, you will feel everything descend, but not depress. When you swallow, everything goes upward. The larynx must be suspended—not shoved down. If your tongue is sitting up toward the teeth, it can't improperly depress the larynx. If you do, it's like putting a stopper in the bottle of wine. We can't enjoy it because the wine won't come out. When you breathe into the straw, or think about the snore, the larynx should feel stable. It should feel firmly engaged, not loose, or bobbing around like a Ping-Pong ball in your throat.

Zygomatic Arch

The zygomatic arch should be engaged and elevated without outward tension. However, if it's engaged too much, the masseter muscle tightens, the risorius muscle contracts, the larynx rises, and the sound becomes tight and inflexible. Lengthen the nape of the neck and allow the mouth to be in a pronounced "hmm" posture. Singers confuse the sound they think we want to hear with how to do it. It's not that the information is wrong. I think the information is right. The problem is how the information gets used over time.

Phonation

Squeezing versus Closure

Make sure you don't feel like you're doing anything that feels like squeezing. I'm not squeezing to try to control the narrowness of the sound. I think that when we say the word "narrow," a lot of us subconsciously react by squeezing. Let everything feel open. Maintain a cushion around the closure. When you start narrowing manually, the throat gets tight.

Piano Singing

Your piano must have your forte in it. You must intend to sing it the same way. So, if you're going to scale it back, don't scale it back past the point where you can sing with the same energy. Start "fluffing" around with the attacks and you'll hate yourself later.

Messa di voce [sustained crescendo and dimuendo]

When you execute a *messa di voce*, you must constantly reenergize it; opening and closing the mouth achieves the crescendo and decrescendo. It's really hard to push if you do it that way because you have to start in that smaller space and bloom out of it. You can't start at full throttle. You're still singing the same pitch with one foot on the gas pedal, regardless of how loudly or quietly you are singing. There must be flexibility, not locking.

Resonance

False chiaro

Don't feel like you need to "place" the sound. We don't need to make a falsely bright sound, so you don't need to fix it that way. That's sort of the student shortcut. Someone says, "You're too back!" The student says, "Oh, okay!" and sings it with false brightness. Well, who wants to hear that in an opera hall? That's like country music on steroids. When Pavarotti was asked, "Maestro, Maestro, where's all the resonance? How do you achieve the *squillo?*" Pavarotti pointed to his throat. He knew where it was coming from.

Great Singers of the Past

When I listen to the great singers, to me there's a sense that they have an underlying structure for the production of tone. It's seems a dangerous word to use, but they're manufacturing the vowel and supporting that to maintain consistency. And yet, you are sometimes hard pressed to find a teacher who will admit that or say that you should be controlling the sound or controlling the vowel in a certain way.

Registration

Working with the tenor passaggio

When you move to the higher pitches, you should feel a fuller environment. That smaller space where you start allows you to open up, bloom, grow, and increase your resonance. If you just hear the pitch and stay connected, your voice will protect itself and "cover" through vowel adjustment or what is now known as formant tuning. If you don't protect it that way, it will either fall back or you will have to jam it forward. It won't be able to stay the same. It's a fine line that you walk, because you have to stay connected as you feel the voice begin to turn. You can't just drive the sound through the range between middle-C and F^4. Men must allow the sound to move into the "second mouth" as they approach the second *passaggio*. This means not allowing the jaw to travel down too much and coordinate the speech posture with rising pressure. Start the process a little earlier and let it tilt. Don't wait.

Working with the baritone passaggio

Around B-flat^3 through C-sharp^4, just narrow the focus a little bit. You decrease the opening in front and increase it in the back. It's a reverse cone effect. You could say that's modification, or that we're manipulating the resonance, but I think that's just what you need to do to keep that part of the voice stable. It's the "turn," and the voice is going have to adjust. Otherwise, we start bringing up too much of the speaking sound. There's nowhere for that to go. You're adjusting to do what? Maintain stability as the pitch rises. If you don't start feeling that adjustment happen in this range, you lose back-space and resonance. The voice doesn't turn and you don't go up as easily.

Working with the mezzo soprano primo passaggio

When working on the lower middle range, make sure that it's covered, just like a guy's voice in his top. It needs to be *copertura* [covered], or turned. It should feel really big in the back and small in the front and very dark. You don't use your tongue to do this—the tongue is up at the teeth—but with where the sound is going. This eliminates the impulse to push the sound.

Working with the mezzo soprano secondo passaggio

A general rule of thumb when you get to the *passaggio* is to think /o/ or a little /u/ when you get to the very top of the *passaggio* and move into the bigger top voice. If you do that while maintaining your position you will get more head voice behind it. Open the vowel, but not the mouth in the *passaggio*. You can't sing up there the way you've been talking an octave below.

Articulation

Diction

I get the words, but I already know the words. You can't assume everybody does, but it's not just about the diction. It's about using the language to bring more color to the music. The colors come from what you think about the words. So, if you don't think anything about the words, the audience will think, "Oh, it's vocally fine, but boring. Use the words, not in a diction way, but in a vocally dramatic way. You won't hurt yourself if you continue to concentrate on starting well.

At any moment, we can sing four different versions of an /i/ vowel to give more context to the language. If we're thinking about making diction sounds for accuracy, we tie ourselves in knots. If we make the right sound, everybody says, "Hey, you sound great, I love your diction." The baritone should get the most compliments for his diction. He's singing ninety percent of his pitches in his speaking range. The sopranos don't. The tenors spend some of their time in speaking range and some out of it. That is one of the reasons why it's so hard to train tenors.

Tongue

This business of just relaxing your tongue doesn't work. It needs a structure in it the whole time. (Talking to a tenor student) Think about balling it up and making a fist with your tongue, like flexing your biceps, and then keep the curve in it and anchor it at the front. When you move from vowel to vowel, the tongue just goes up, down, back, or forward a little tiny bit. That alters the resonance and makes us think you're singing in a different vowel, but you haven't changed the basic structure. That's the key if you're going to sing in the upper range. Once I get up there and make the turn, the changes get smaller the higher I go. If I change the vowel, the adjustment gets smaller and smaller.

Exercises

Exercise 1: Raspberries (used with a soprano and a tenor)

Sung with a Bronx cheer (raspberry)

Instructions: Bring it all the way down the head. Keep the larynx tilted forward. Don't let it rock back and open up.

Exercise 2: Raspberries to /i/ (used with a soprano and a tenor)

Instructions: Keep the tongue blade high in the /i/. Create space behind the tongue.

Exercise 3: (used with a soprano)

Instructions: Use a lighter contact at the beginning. It's more like drinking in air rather than blowing out. Think about inhaling or sipping through a straw. Sing a true /u/ vowel. Stay behind your tongue to get a better vowel and let the mouth come along for the ride. Move your tongue. Hear your vowels before you sing them.

Exercise 4: (used with a soprano)

Instructions: Let the tongue sit at the teeth and make the [vowel and consonant] changes with your tongue, not the jaw. Make sure the consonant has a smaller space when you start the /l/. If we start well, then we just have to stay level and let the pitch change without any extra help. You don't need to change the game plan as you rise in pitch. If you're connected, it is much easier to feel those subtle shifts, or turns, as you enter different parts of your range. If you splash air through consonants, you lose your connection. Keep the connection slim.

Exercise 5: (used with a soprano)

Instructions: Inhale on /i/ to prepare. Avoid lunging toward the top. Focus on connection and feeling some resistance. Sing /a/, but think /u/. Tilt down and forward in your throat, otherwise you will push. Remember that the sound should not start abruptly. Like the violin, we start moving the bow, make contact, and then increase intensity. Otherwise, that's where the air stops. We have to keep the pressure steady.

Exercise 6: (used with a soprano)

Instructions: Sing this quickly. Let the larynx tilt down so the sound can turn over more. If I ask for more mask in the sound, I am really searching for more room in the resonance space behind the tongue. Don't hold the breath.

Exercise 7: (used with a soprano)

Instructions: As you are focusing on vocal fold closure and finding full contact, also find room around it so it feels more cushy and breathy at the top of the phrase. Bring the tongue a little more up and away from the back of the throat. Think about adding the idea of an /u/ to your /a/ as you ascend.

Exercise 8: (used with a soprano)

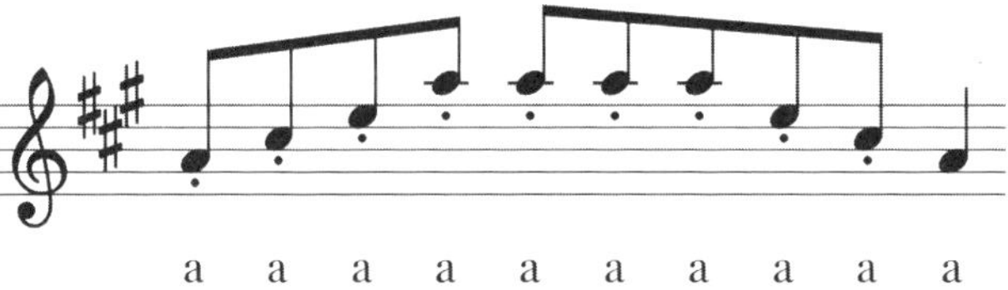

Instructions: Use a laughing /a/. You don't need to push any air into the sound.

Exercise 9: (used with a soprano)

Instructions: You don't necessarily have to get louder as you ascend. Just maintain the velocity. The mouth will do what the mouth needs to do. If you throw the mouth open, you lose some of your sense of balance. It will work better if you don't open your mouth until you get above the staff. Wait until your body tells you that it needs to open.

Exercise 10: (used with a tenor and a baritone)

Instructions: Focus on more height, release, and tilt. Instead of thinking about singing bright, think about how you begin. Make sure the voice is prepared and keep the mechanism balanced and coordinated. If you ascend and pull the speaking voice out of the sound, there's not enough tilt in the larynx. It needs to feel deep and fundamental.

Exercise 11: (used with tenors)

Instructions: Sense a more spacious, deep, released environment as you ascend. Let the voice "flip" without getting louder. Focus on tilting down in the throat. That is the stretch people talk about. When you feel that stretch, you can sense more back space and more freedom in general. You can tune the vowels the way you need to when you're connected and stable. Keep the breath pressure constant.

Exercise 12: (used with a tenor)

Instructions: Let the space stay open in the back. Keep the structure in the tongue shape. The tongue should be anchored and make small adjustments for the vowel.

Exercise 13a: (used with a tenor)

Example 13b: (used with a tenor)

Instructions: The higher the range, the smaller the tongue adjustment should be when you switch vowels.

Exercise 14: (used with a tenor)

Instructions: Modify/adjust your /a/ in the *passaggio*. Keep your lips separated and teeth apart. Avoid using "trumpet lips" because it tends to lead to laryngeal squeezing.

Exercise 15: (used with a baritone)

Instructions: Slide from head voice downward. When you come to the crack, make sure you've rocked down in the front rather than falling back. Bring it as low as you can bring it.

Exercise 16: (used with a baritone)

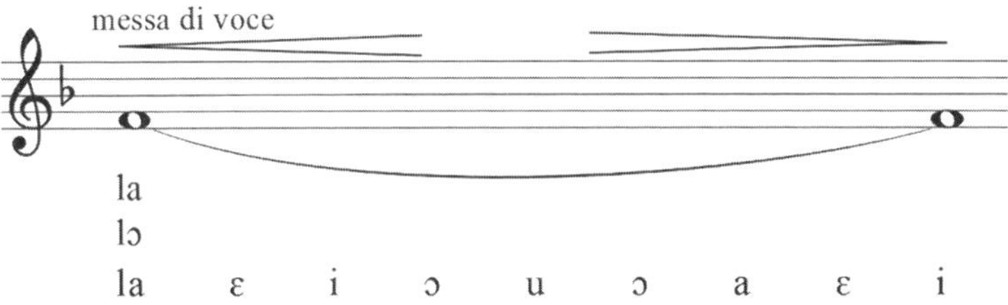

Instructions: You must stay pliable. Don't hold. Change the aperture at the mouth opening to get louder or quieter. We're singing the same pitch, so we still need one foot on the gas regardless of how loud or quiet we sing. When you sing all of the vowels, the tongue should have a high angle that aims toward the center of the hard palate.

Exercise 17: (used with a baritone)

Instructions: Bring the structured vocal folds together and focus on accelerating the air that you have all the way to the end of the phrase, regardless of where the pitches are going. Just think about acceleration. This doesn't require a lot of air.

Exercise 18: (used with a baritone)

Instructions: Shape the mouth for /ɔ/ when you sing all of these vowels. It's like you build a wall in the center of the mouth so the sound cannot go through that space. It must bypass it and go another way. Keep the integrity in the height of the middle tongue. Use more resonance, less effort.

Exercise 19: (used with a baritone)

Instructions: Think of threading a needle or going through a smaller aperture so you can control your air a little better. Keep turning down and tilting all of the way to the end of the descending line. Maintain the inhalation posture in the body and feel more resistance and depth as you ascend. Put the/ŋ/ in a smaller space and aperture. This exercise is easier to navigate if you think about an /o/ opening in the mouth. When in the B-flat^3 to D-flat^4 range, close a little in front so you keep more inner lift and space. If you close the first mouth [the mouth opening], you open the second mouth [the throat].

Exercise 20: (used with a mezzo soprano)

Instructions: Bring the top voice down farther and farther. Call on that sensation every time you breathe. Find the height in the sound. Let it feel big in the back and small in the front.

Exercise 21: (used with a mezzo soprano)

Instructions: Use a "hooty" sound.

Exercise 22: (used with a mezzo soprano)

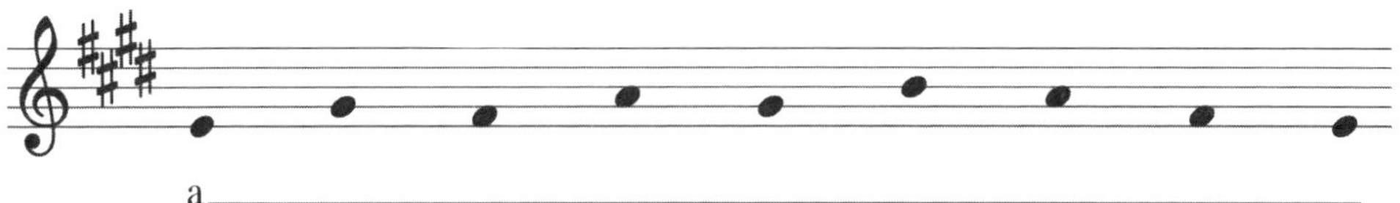

Instructions: Keep head voice in the tone and a narrow focus. You must feel the flip [register transition] around the E^4 and F^4, otherwise your F-sharp^4 and G^4 will require you to drive the sound too hard.

Exercise 23: (used with a mezzo soprano)

Exercise 24: (used with a mezzo soprano)

Instructions: When the pitch comes back down, keep turning forward and down in the throat so the sound can keep coming over the arc. Don't let it rock back and depress in the back.

Exercise 25: (used with a mezzo soprano)

Instructions: Begin this exercise in the lower middle voice and repeat at progressively higher pitch levels. Make sure your tongue is down in the front. Find your resonance space. Think about biting an apple in the front and find more lift in the back. You don't need to drop your jaw.

Exercise 26: (used with tenors)

Instructions: Find the tilt at the larynx so you can get more closure and stretch. Shape an /a/ in the mouth and an /o/ in the tongue for the top note. Make sure the /ε/ is giving you maximum *vertical* space rather than horizontal or forward. It needs to be taller in the back. Try a *messa di voce* on the top note. Use the /l/ to linger on the pitch for a while. Feel the structure on the top note and bring it all of the way down the arpeggio. Find more head voice and balance in the attack.

PATRICIA MCCAFFREY

Regarded as one of the world's most sought after vocal technicians, Patricia McCaffrey is currently on the vocal faculties of the Curtis Institute of Music, Brooklyn College Conservatory of Music, Lidal North in Oslo, Norway, Meitar Opera Studio of the Israeli Opera, Berlin *Staatsoper,* Young Artist Program, the Metropolitan Opera Lindemann program, and Ravinia-Steans Institute, as well as maintaining a private voice studio in New York City.

For more than twenty-five years, her students have sung in the major opera houses, festivals, and concert halls of the world, including The Metropolitan Opera, The Lyric Opera of Chicago, San Francisco Opera, Houston Grand Opera, Covent Garden, English National Opera, Vienna State Opera, Berlin State Opera, Bavarian State Opera, La Scala, Paris *Bastille* and *Chatelet,* The Salzburg Festival, Bayreuth Festival, Carnegie Hall and the BBC Proms. They have also distinguished themselves as winners of numerous competitions and awards, including the Metropolitan Opera National Council, Tucker Awards, George London Foundation, Marian Anderson, Operalia, Vinas, ARD, *Das Lied* Competition, Gerda Lissner, Puccini Foundation, and the Grammy Awards.

In addition to teaching a classical music technique for singing, Trish McCaffrey also teaches performers who appear on Broadway, in motion pictures, television, and commercials. She has also prepared numerous students who hold voice positions at colleges and universities in the United States and Europe.

McCaffrey has sung mezzo soprano roles at the Metropolitan Opera, New York City Opera, Miami Opera, Zürich Opera, The Wexford Festival, Starlight Musicals, and other venues throughout the world. She is most noted for her portrayals of the title role in *Carmen*, Eboli in *Don Carlo*, Brangäne in *Tristan und Isolde*, Santuzza in *Cavalleria Rusticana*, Octavian in *Der Rosenkavalier*, the Composer in *Ariadne auf Naxos*, Amneris in *Aida*, Charlotte in *Werther*, and Herodias in *Salome*.

She has served on the voice faculties of Arizona State University, University of Minnesota, University of Michigan, The Hartt School of Music, Manhattan School of Music, and has taught at the young artist programs and studios of The Santa Fe Opera, VoiceExperience Foundation in Disney and Savannah, Intermezzo Foundation in Hartford, Connecticut and Bruges, Belgium, International Institute of Vocal Arts in Chiari, Italy, and the Israeli Vocal Arts Institute in Tel-Aviv, Israel.

The Interview

I was not able to sit down to interview Trish in person because of our conflicting schedules. We did, however, have some email correspondences, the content of which are included below.

TM: Some people find my unorthodox methods of teaching a bit "crazy" because I say absurd things, like "jellyfish" and "drown the minions," and because I am a really intense, screaming teacher, but I try to be silly to try to balance it all out. I really want them to get it. I really want them to get their money's worth. And if that were not true, they wouldn't come back. Once they get it and really feel how free it can be, they won't be happy with how it was before, even if other people like it.

RR: *I noticed that you spend a few minutes during lessons with each singer working on particular vocalises. Would you please explain what you try to accomplish with those exercises?*

TM: I only do brief warmups with each student in a forty-five-minute lesson and expect them to vocalize before they come; however, I do not believe in excessively long warmups in any situation. Five minutes should do it for a person who is singing regularly. My students use a lot of exercises, but they are not really meant as warmups. They are used as technical exercises. What I do try to accomplish in this time is to establish a connection to breath/support through lip trills, matching vowels in mixed voice, and establishing a lot of contact with chest voice, falsetto with men, and whistle voice with women.

I spend more time with singers on technical exercises when I have not worked with them for a long time or with students who are new to me and less familiar with my technique. For example, I might use an exercise to explain the action of consonants, principles of legato, mixing head and chest voice, or the function of agility.

RR: *What exercises do you use to work on different aspects of technique?*

TM: For the tongue, I use descending five-tone scale exercises on 'ng', /lui lui/ or /glddi glddi/ to encourage quick tongue actions.

For legato, I do the [Rosa] Ponselle series of exercises that "cry" downward on an arpeggio with the longest possible *messa di voce* on the final note.

A middle voice exercise I use is singing the phrases "mio amore" or "amore mio" on one tone, starting quietly, with the longest possible *messa di voce*.

For breath, I have them pretend to inhale through a straw while expanding the ribs, and release the air through a hissing sound as long as possible without letting the ribs collapse. The goal in this exercise is to reach a forty to sixty second exhalation comfortably. I also ask them to sing scale exercises in one breath.

For registration, I spend a lot of time with the men identifying where the chest voice is and at around what pitches they start to notice a turn in registration to solidify their understanding of that action and sensation. I do the same thing with women. I make them sing every day to E-flat^4 in chest voice and then turn the voice. But I ask them to only use a thread of that chest voice when singing. I like having presence of chest in the head voice. I also use yodeling exercises for registration. For me, it is imperative that singers stay connected to their bodies and that they have the ability to differentiate between chest and throat.

For jaw freedom, I ask them to imagine having holes in their ears and fish lips, suck their thumb, and sing an exercise using the syllables "yah, yah, nah, hah" to release the chin [not the jaw].

RR: *You mentioned that you think working with falsetto in male singers is important. Would you share more of your thoughts about that?*

TM: I believe it is important, mainly because it provides a sound they can make that doesn't use their throat. In addition, it makes high pitches not seem high, because falsetto gives the sensation of air blowing downward, thereby relaxing the throat.

RR: *Who are some of your biggest influences?*

TM: My biggest influences today are the great conductors who are still conducting like [James] Levine, [Daniel] Barenboim, and [James] Conlon. When I hear what they are looking for, I try to make certain that my students are doing those things. I feel that being interesting to conductors and directors is important to career development. Therefore, you have to be prepared, have impeccable rhythm, and sing right in the center of the pitch. My personal, biggest influences might be Wayne Dyer, Deepak Chopra, Bill and Hillary Clinton, Roger Federer, Janet Baker, Cecilia Bartoli, Bryn Terfel, Placido Domingo, Barbra Streisand, Seth Riggs, Richard Marzollo, Virginia Zeani, Mary Henderson Buckley, and Vera Rosza.

RR: *What do you think are the top attributes of a successful, young professional singer?*

TM: Intelligence, the ability to find joy in the work and process, imagination, and balance.

RR: *What changes do you typically make to the singers' voices that come to you?*

TM: Pitch, rhythm, and word accuracy, along with vocal clarity and freedom.

RR: *Do you feel that you are more successful with certain voice types?*

TM: Frankly, I feel that I am more successful with men, simply because my personality does not seem to disturb them. They seem to be used to sports coaches who provoke them in a similar fashion as I do and do not react emotionally. Sometimes women react to my demanding personality very emotionally, when I am only trying to give them a good result.

RR: *How do you know if a singer needs to change Fach?*

TM: I suspect a singer is in the wrong *Fach* when I observe over a period of time that the voice is chronically stressed, even when the student is complying with my instructions.

RR: *How do you select repertoire for each singer?*

TM: I imagine who the singer standing in front of me reminds me of and review that established artist's repertoire and then choose appropriate repertoire accordingly. When it is a young singer, I assign music that will develop their voice in the right direction. That always includes *bel canto,* whether it is an art song or aria. When people are in school, I am pretty intent on assigning them specific repertoire. Once they are in graduate school, I attempt to make it more collaborative. With professionals, I make strong suggestions but also support them in what they want to do and help them do it to the best of their ability.

RR: *What do you recommend that singers use for sensory feedback?*

TM: With respect to how they hear themselves or how they hear their sound? I feel that it is a pretty bad idea to gauge your singing from how it sounds or feels. Every day you are singing in a different acoustic and feeling differences in your resonance as you experience body variations resulting from sleep deprivation, allergies, colds, or menstrual periods. Making a judgment on a past perception can be a bad idea. I always say, "just do the action rather than sing the reaction."

RR: *How much time do you recommend your students sing per day?*

TM: No more than three hours per day.

RR: *How do you describe the intake and use of the breath to singers?*

TM: I teach three types of breath with my students. The first comes from a paper written by Hermanus Baer in 1974 that talks about breathing through a straw, dropping the diaphragm, filling the lungs, and maintaining a sense of drinking the sound. I call this the straw breath. Additionally, I teach the nose breath. I recommend drawing the breath to the third eye through the nose and sighing the breath down throughout the phrase for light mechanism, Mozart, and fast passages. Lastly, the one I call the 'beautiful' breath could be paralleled with the Italian phrase '*portare la voce*' [carry the voice].

RR: *How do you describe the sense of placement/resonance to singers?*

TM: I really do not talk about placement. Rather, I ask them to make certain that the vowels are right next to each other, and then I make certain that they are connected to their chest voice for the brilliance of the vowel.

RR: *What sources would you recommend to every singer?*

TM: I ask all my singers to read Caruso's doctor's ideas about singing [P.M. Marafioti, *Caruso's Method of Voice Production*], Hermanus Baer's treatise on breath, the books written by Richard Miller, Martha Graham's ideas on the artist, *Fight Fear and Win* by Don Greene, and pick any concept that helps them stay emotionally and physically in balance. This is not always easy for an artist; we have enormous highs and lows.

RR: *How do you recommend that singers deal with disappointments?*

TM: Basically, I tell them what my hero Roger Federer says about disappointment. His rule is to allow himself twenty-four hours of grief, disappointment, and even anger. When the twenty-four hours have passed, he must let go of all of his disappointment and negative thoughts and use all of his energy to go forward positively.

RR: *How do you feel about current trends?*

TM: I think the trend is good-looking people, with good bodies and big voices that record well. I do not think you have any choice about that, regardless of how you feel about the trend. You have to help your students stay current in the most organic way for each individual.

RR: *If you could unlock one mystery about the voice, what would it be?*

TM: I do not think there is any mystery about voice. There is a mystery about each human being. If you can unlock the person, you can free the voice.

Parting Thoughts

As Trish said in her interview, she has an unorthodox style and a great desire for her students to succeed. Personally, I didn't find anything about her teaching to be unorthodox. She is very clear about what she wants, efficiently instructs the student, and doesn't let them get away with anything less than one hundred percent of their best. She thoroughly understands how the many facets of technique intersect and influence singing outcomes. Her eyes and ears are so very finely tuned that she often knows what the singer is going to do before doing it. What also is apparent to an observer is the deep bond she has with her singers. There was always a mutual respect and positive mood in the studio. Nothing said to the student was taken personally. It was about business. Trish speaks her mind and gets results. The singers I heard that day were professionals and all actively performing at a high level.

Trish often talks to the singers as they sing so they can correct themselves in the moment. She also stops them frequently. She will not allow the student to finish a phrase that was begun poorly. One of her favorite directives is "tell me," to elicit the singers' ideas about and reactions to what they are doing. By making the singers verbalize their thoughts, they can better understand their bodies and mental processes. At times, this meant verbalizing what they were doing well, and at other times what they were doing ineffectively. Trish is insistent that her students understand all aspects of their technique and mental game. She refuses to let anyone slide.

She uses targeted top-down exercises to help students understand the need for consistent connection to high resonances while not losing the connection to the chest register. However, she does not want singers to make a major shift as they enter the middle and lower voices. The singer must perform these exercises without any upward motion in the body or upward mental concept in the mind. Trish does not believe in "up." Notes do not go up or down; they are on a geometric plane. Consequently, no singer I heard had any trouble accessing his or her top register.

Her concept of avoiding consonants in the chest voice was enlightening to me. I had never thought about it in such a way, but as I listened, I noticed what Trish heard and how it affected the sound. The singer she was working with was so studious about the consonants that they were pulling the sound down and adding weight to the tone each time she entered her chest register. The heaviness would then disrupt her vocal balance as she reentered her head register. When the singer adopted the idea of using consonants with more of a head voice orientation, her registration became more balanced, as did her sound.

One of the singers I observed that day sang impressively in every style, including pop, musical theater, and opera. She was able to cross over easily while managing to maintain clear, uncomplicated technical concepts. Trish used some exercises that involved "snorting" and "oinking" sounds with her that proved to be very useful for soft palate awareness and highlighted the concept of creating relaxation in the backspace. In addition to these primary goals, I have also used snorting sounds with students to help them relax the palate, tongue, and lower abdominals during a breath intake or to help younger students take a more intentional, aware in-breath.

In several lessons, Trish used the term, "You look marvelous." For those of you who were not watching Saturday Night Live in the 1980's, this is a reference to Billy Crystal's parody sketch of Fernando Lamas called, "Fernando's Hideaway," which always included the catchphrase, "You look marvelous." It is worth finding an example of this on Youtube.com so you can view Crystal's facial position as he says this line: a slight opening of the jaw, small embouchure around the mouth, and an opening of the cheeks and face. In other words: *Singer's Position-101*. If you make that face, the space in the mouth and palate are prepared very well and not over-extended.

Lesson Highlights

Alignment

Releasing Arms and Shoulders

If you have rigid shoulder blades and a rigid place between your shoulder and your elbow, the larynx will also be rigid. This is why one often sees pictures of Callas with her arms folded across her torso.

Elongating and Freeing the Spine

It is imperative that we become aware of our spine and to maintain the appropriate length without aggravating any point from the top to the bottom. On the upper end, it is as if we are strung up like a puppet with the spine finding its length from the top downward. On the other end of the spine, in the region of the L5 [vertebra] and sacrum, you could find a release by imaging the mouth of a balloon attached there and filling it with air. I call this the butt-balloon.

Breath Support/Control

"Kicking the Diaphragm" and its Relationship to Tongue Tension

Don't kick your diaphragm, not only because it is vulgar to the voice, but because it's bad for your health. You can get reflux or a hernia from that behavior. You think it's supporting the sound, but it's not. It causes subglottal pressure that pushes under your throat and feels like a spasm. Then your tongue reacts to try to stop that spasm from coming up. If you never create that spasm to begin with, your tongue won't react like that way. Find your *appoggio* and exercise it.

Drowning Minions

Pavarotti used to say that he had a beach ball that he leaned down into when he sang. But I say, "You are a king or a queen drowning your minions while you are looking down at them."

Resonance

Chiaroscuro

The important thing for resonance is to have a bright word in a dark tube. The bright word in my opinion comes from chest resonance and the darkness is keeping the sound in your tube/body.

Registration

Consonants when Singing in the Female Chest Register

No matter how much chest voice you're using, never sing consonants in chest voice, ever. Use a head connection in your consonants. Only use the front or middle part of your tongue, never the back part of your tongue.

Mixing the Registers in the Female Lower Range

You must always have some degree of chest in your head—sometimes a rope and sometimes a thread. A thread would be more elegant. Never mistake chest voice for dumping down into your throat.

Articulation

Consonants and Vowels

In general, put a consonant through /u/. Do not let a consonant spread the vowel.

Using a Walnut to Assist Tongue Positioning

Put this whole walnut in your mouth and hold it in the back of your mouth on your tongue. Push your tongue up. Now sing /a/ right under the walnut. Don't let your tongue go down; push the walnut up. Push it farther back and open your mouth. One speaks under the walnut, but the sound occurs above, behind and under the walnut. Do not allow the walnut to move when the pitch changes.[8]

Exercises

Exercise 1: (used with all voice types)

Instructions: This exercise goes fast and straight up into the top of the voice. Don't jump in your body. Find the slim air. As soon as you enter the *passaggio,* the velocity of the air increases. Keep body movement to a minimum. Find the constant energy. Don't think up. Find your minions and push them down.

Exercise 2: (used with a soprano)

Instructions: Don't grab the /i/.

Exercise 3: (used with a soprano)

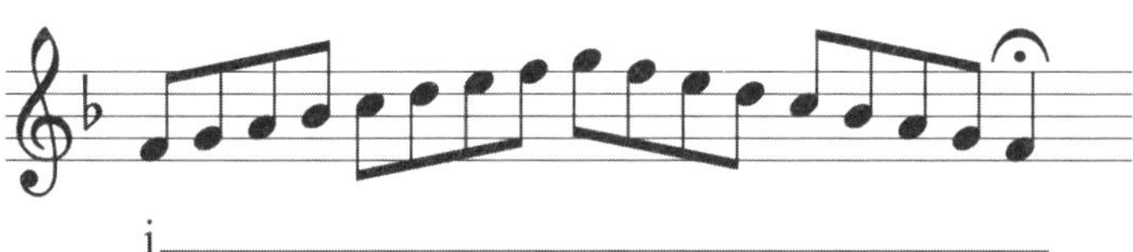

Instructions: Keep your /ŋ/. Find the *appoggio* and maintain that throughout the exercise. Do not accent any note of the range. Keep your body open (meaning the chest away from the back).

---

[8] Publisher's note: please be careful—possible choking hazard

Exercise 4: (used with a soprano)

Exercise 5: (used with women)

Instructions: Start high in the range and quietly. Put the air first and follow the air. Look at your minions. Cry it out your nose. Nothing happens in the throat. Nothing. Zero! Nothing happens in the tongue! Soft tongue. (With a mezzo soprano) Do this exercise very quickly and do not sing louder as you descend.

Exercise 6: (used with a tenor and a bass)

Instructions: Use falsetto. Don't drop it. (With a bass baritone) This exercise starts in falsetto. As soon as you are comfortable, mix in a thread of your real singing voice (not falsetto).

EVERETT MCCORVEY

Dr. Everett McCorvey is a native of Montgomery, Alabama. He earned his Doctor of Musical Arts, Master of Music, and Bachelor of Music degrees from the University of Alabama. He has served on the voice faculty at the University of Kentucky CFA School of Music since 1991, where he currently is Director of Opera and holds the Lexington Opera Society Endowed Chair in Opera Studies. He conducts two professional choirs: the American Spiritual Ensemble, a group he founded in 1997 that celebrates the American Negro Spirituals, and is Artistic Director of the National Chorale of New York City, a choir dedicated to the preservation and performance of the great classical choral works.

As a tenor soloist, he has enjoyed critical acclaim for his performances in many prestigious venues around the globe, including the Metropolitan Opera, the Kennedy Center, Aspen Music Festival, Blossom Music Festival, Whitewater Opera Company, Radio City Music Hall, Birmingham Opera Theater, *Teatro Comunale* in Florence, Italy, Queen Elizabeth Hall in London, England, as well as performances throughout Spain, the Czech and Slovak Republics, Austria, Japan, China, Brazil, Poland, Portugal, and Hungary. He is tenor soloist on two commercial recordings conducted by Maestro Julius Williams: *Sym-*

phonic Brotherhood (1994) featuring the Bohuslav Martinů Philharmonic Orchestra performing the symphonic works of African-American Composers, and *The American Soloist* (2004), featuring the Dvořák Symphony in Prague, Czech Republic, highlighting new American works. He also has appeared in television movies and feature films, including *The Long Walk Home*.

Dr. McCorvey is vice-chairman of the Kentucky Arts Council and serves on the board of the National Association of State Arts Agencies. He is also a member of the Alltech World Equestrian Games Federation Board, which produced the Alltech FEI World Equestrian Games in 2010, the largest equestrian event in the history of the United States. He was recently elected as a faculty representative to the UK Board of Trustees and awarded the Kentucky Star for Literary Arts in recognition of his myriad accomplishments in the field of vocal performance.

Dr. McCorvey is a teacher and vocal advisor to many singers in the profession. In 1998, the Kentucky Advocates for Higher Education named him the recipient of the prestigious Acorn Award, which goes only to one professor in the state of Kentucky who exemplifies excellence, innovation and creativity in teaching and research. Dr. McCorvey also was the recipient of an outstanding faculty award from the University of Kentucky Lyman T. Johnson Alumni Association for 1998 and was selected to receive the Outstanding Alumni Award in the Arts from the Society for the Fine Arts at the University of Alabama, his alma mater, in February of 1999.

The Interview

EM: "This," I say to all of my students, "is not a quick fix." When students begin their study with me, I will warn them that it will be three years before they begin to see any real change. Of course, they will see some changes earlier, but the real changes begin to happen after about three years of study.

RR: *Why do you think that is?*

EM: I think part of it is that there has to be muscle development, muscle atrophy, and muscle coordination. The muscles that have been engaged are not the right muscles for singing. We have to allow time for those muscles to weaken while we give time for the right muscles and muscle coordination to strengthen. I just seem to find that in my approach to teaching voice, it takes about three years to see major results. I'm okay with this and I encourage the students to be okay with it as well. I spend a lot of time working on and helping them to understand breath management, trying to relax the tongue, and working on laryngeal positioning. For me, learning a significant amount of repertoire comes after a technical foundation has been laid. If you're a good musician and you're getting good musical training in theory, history and piano, learning the songs will be easier than learning vocal technique, especially at the beginning of a singer's development.

RR: *How do you talk about breath with new students?*

EM: A large part of my philosophy of teaching is based on management of the breath. I feel that if you can manage the breath, the voice will then know what to do. I have found that if the teacher takes those first two or three years to work on the breath, the student will develop a much better long-term approach to singing. That's one of the reasons why I start every lesson with lip trills. This energizes the body with breath.

I also work with students on relaxing the swallowing muscles. We work on relaxing the tongue as much as possible and also allowing the larynx—without forcing—to sit into a low position in the throat. This helps to keep the epiglottis open so you can have free movement of breath and sound waves through the throat. When the swallowing muscles are engaged and the tongue is tense, the larynx and the epiglottis think you're about to swallow. I have students place their thumb right underneath the chin where the digastric muscles are and swallow. They can feel if the tongue hardens. If the tongue hardens while attempting to sing or speak, the throat thinks that you are about to swallow. So, the larynx rises, and the epiglottis closes over the larynx so the food can go into the esophagus. Imagine this action happening while you are trying to sing! This can cause great tension. That is why the tongue and the digastric muscles need to be soft underneath the chin. Control of the tongue is something that I feel we have to work on our entire lives.

I am also constantly working with students to help them understand the role of the diaphragm. Singers are very confused about this. Their understanding of where the diaphragm is located in their body is typically too low. The diaphragm is higher in the body than one may think. I help them find the diaphragm by identifying a point a few inches below where the rib cage reaches the sternum.[9] Sometimes I ask them to gently cough or laugh so they can feel it engage. There is also the "six inches exercise" where you lie on the floor and raise your feet six inches. That engages the core musculature. Most people realize that the diaphragm is higher in their bodies than they thought after they do this exercise. That exercise also helps them to engage the muscles correctly for singing. Activating the core is very important in singing and in health.

A new student in my studio may only get to sing one or two songs in the first semester. Many universities have a first semester requirement of six or seven songs. I feel that if we as voice teachers are doing our job, we will do well to get to one or two songs in that first semester. That first semester should be about learning about the singer, helping the singer learn about him/herself, helping the singer to learn about you and your approach to singing, and learning about the core of the body and the importance of breath management.

Teachers and students also must get accustomed to each other's language about singing. If I say to students that they are *pressurizing* the sound or I inform them that *the glottis is not open*, they need time to understand what I mean. We need time

---

[9] Publisher's note: The location described is the epigastric region, not the actual diaphragm. Activity that is felt in this area can be the result of diaphragmatic contraction *or* contraction of the rectus and transverse abdominis muscles.

together just to learn each other's language for singing. I mentioned to a tenor student today that the tone needed more *cover*. Well, the student and I spent the first two years just learning what the term *cover* meant. We need time to do these sorts of things. With this particular student, we didn't do much with the upper voice at all during the first year, because I wanted to work on the middle voice. We can approach the top voice more effectively now that he understands the middle voice and also what the term *cover* means to him in the high voice.

RR: *But a baritone could do that in one year!*

EM: That's it—yes, those darn tenors. For most tenors, we have to *build* the high voice. That's a real challenge. During the first year I may assign a student a few selections from of the *Twenty-Four Italian Songs and Arias* book and work on them with lip trills and tongue hums. Everyone in my studio works on lip trills at the beginning of each lesson. With lip trills, I can see where the student is vocally and technically on that day. I also want to see if the breath is flowing through the body. If it's not, then we spend some time getting the breath to flow so the muscles around the larynx and tongue can relax.

RR: *Where do you want them to feel the breath intake?*

EM: I want them to feel an expansion in the bottom of their ribs on each side and in the mid-front area. I teach breathing in two different phases: in the middle voice, we talk about *breath flow* and in the top voice we talk about *breath support*. What is flow? Flow is feeling the inhalation expansion under the ribs when you take a breath and then allowing that expansion to decrease as you are singing. Similar to what happens when you blow into a balloon, it expands and then becomes smaller as the air leaves the balloon. In the middle voice, when you finish a phrase, the body should be less expanded. I want the body to understand that the voice is working because of the flow of the breath. In singing the upper voice, above the *passaggio*, I teach that we have to support the voice with the breath by *resisting* the body's desire to allow the breath to deflate. The feeling is like singing while continuing to inhale. This is the feeling of support.

In my younger days when I first started teaching, I told every student to take a breath and just flex outward. After some time, I realized that this breathing technique made the students too rigid and it made it difficult for their voices to carry well in big spaces. My voice teacher, Edward White, would tell his students to hold a baby and notice how the baby took a breath and how it cried and how its body created tones. If you do this, you will notice that the baby's body is in an active mode as it utters sound. You can feel the diaphragm area moving and the entire middle of their bodies engaging as they laugh, cry, whimper or coo. Early in my teaching and singing when I tried to feel this on my own body, I didn't feel that movement, so I started working with myself to make sure I felt movement in the body from the diaphragm area every time I uttered a word. After I understood this concept, I started working on this with my students. I soon found that as they had a better understanding of how the breath worked in their bodies, their voices started sounding fuller and could fill big halls in a healthy, non-pressed manner.

RR: *You also talked about the heroic position with students.*

EM: It's like bellows when you're trying to get a fire going. If the sternum collapses, you can't control that puff of breath going out. The sternum also presses down on the trachea and inhibits the easy flow of breath through the trachea into the throat. I believe that the sternum should be high. I'll encourage students to take a breath in their chest at first, even though we know this is an incorrect position, then I tell them keep the shoulders low as if they're holding bowling balls in each hand and to let the breath go without changing the position of the chest. I ask them to sing from that position and never allow the sternum to collapse. If the sternum collapses, it will inadvertently send too much breath through the throat and singers lose control of their breath—we work on projecting the sternum upward at the end of the breath. The reality is that the sternum is not moving, but it's also not collapsing. That gives me full access to my breath and full range of choices of how I use the breath.

RR: *The first young man who sang today used falsetto several times. Do you frequently work with falsetto in your teaching?*

EM: My definition of head voice is *a supported falsetto.* Falsetto is an unsupported head voice. I work a lot with the head voice because I think that incorporating falsetto in the head voice is the key to beautiful singing, long careers, and sustained vocal health; the head voice can be very hard to find, however, especially in young singers. Young girls have a very undeveloped head voice because of the mutational chink that inhibits vocal fold approximation. Most young girls want to sing in chest voice. When they get to college or when they start studying voice, they realize for the first time that they must exercise the head voice. They don't like the sound at the beginning because it's breathy and doesn't have any color. We just need to encourage them to stick with it. Eventually they start making beautiful sounds.

I work head voice to help men sing in the high register. Singers, especially men, need to understand the difference between head voice and falsetto. Accessing the head voice when approaching the top keeps singers from squeezing and over-pressurizing the voice. If they spend about one year using head register as a part of regular vocalization and can easily switch between the head and chest registers, the two registers begin to blend. *Messa di voce* exercises are a great way to help blend the head and chest registers and help to give all singers a much easier access to the top of the voice. After that is accomplished, I will typically begin to discuss vowel modification in both the male and female voices. Vowel modification is needed because the airflow is more intense and thinner as a singer ascends the scale. At a point near the *passaggio* the larynx often begins to ascend as the singer climbs the scale. If the larynx does this, it is out of position and will most likely cause constriction in the larynx and the neck, resulting in a spread and constricted tone at the top of the voice.

When the larynx is up and out of position, the epiglottis also is closing, which creates even more constriction in the pharyngeal and laryngeal areas. To help, I work with students on modifying the vowel as they ascend to the top. If the vowel is an /a/, I encourage the singer to use the sound /ʌ/, as in "cup," or ask for an /a/ influenced by /ʌ/. I have tenors sing a pure /a/ up to about F^4 before modifying to more of a /ʌ/ position at around F-sharp^4 through the *passaggio*.

For baritones, that modification will happen typically around an E^4. I have had a lot of success with sopranos using the /u/ position when they have to modify. I believe that *all* voices have to modify. Our work is to find out where the voice needs to modify and what vowels should be used. This takes time. Is it /ʌ/? Is it /u/? Or is it /U/, as in took? A lot of people will teach /æ/ as in cat. I have not had as much success with teaching this sound, perhaps because I wasn't taught that way. I've had a couple of students, especially students with big or thick voices, who find that /æ/ helps to get the right resonance and assists the upper voice, but they are few. The problem that I have with the/æ/ is that as singers age, the voice becomes less warm and the they lose their top.

I think that as teachers, we need to have five to seven ways to address one problem. As I will remark to the students, they only have to know *one* way to solve a problem. We have to have many *ways* to approach a vocal problem in a student!

RR: *What do you really want to see or hear in a singer?*

EM: What I really want to see and hear, but is too often missing, is an understanding of the breath. Singers are not breathing. They do not understand how the breath works in their bodies. I call singers *vocal athletes*. Approaching singing from an athletic point of view means that the singer and the teacher must understand the muscles in the core of the body and how they work in supporting healthy singing. Breath management seems easier for people who are short or who have more compact torsos. It's much harder for taller people because they're singing from the mouth, but all of the magic that makes the singing happen is powered in the core of the body. Taller people seem to take a longer time to understand how the core of the body works.

I go back to my discussion about babies. Babies cry all day. They don't get hoarse. They never lose their voice unless they have a cold, and that is because they are using the core of their body to find the strength and to make sound. We need to know each muscle group's duty in helping us to achieve that balance of breath. When the student understands the responsibility of the core of the body, then the process of singing becomes much easier.

And let's mention the tongue! Most of the tongue tension I see in singing students stems from how we use our language. I'm from Alabama—we have a very pronounced drawl.

RR: *I'm from Texas.*

EM: There you are. There's the Texas dialect as well. That plays a part in how tense or how relaxed the tongue is. That's why we all assign Italian songs, because we don't harden the tongue when singing Italian as much as we do in English. Lack of breath support and breath management also creates tongue tension, especially when we run out of breath at the end of a phrase. When this happens, the tongue typically tenses to help us get to the end of the phrase.

However, if you look at the tongue positions used by Pavarotti, Leontyne Price, and some of the great singers of the past, it's not positioned—it's relaxed and just lies there. It's beautiful! The tongue does not need to be engaged in order to sustain the sound when good breath management and support are employed. I think that tenors and sopranos have to be a lot more honest about relaxing the tongue than baritones, basses, and mezzos, because they really have to work to sing above the *passaggio* on a regular basis.

RR: *What do young, aspiring singers need to know as they prepare for a career?*

EM: They must have *a passion for practice*. Everybody likes the limelight and all of the accoutrements that come with it, but it will be very difficult to have a career if a singer does not have a passion for practice. People who develop really good practice routines tend to have much better and longer careers.

RR: *How do you instruct your students to vocalize? Should they do it every day?*

EM: I try to create exercises that students can do anywhere. Because we are in an academic setting, a student can just go upstairs to a practice room to warm up and vocalize in preparation for a big audition or concert, but in New York, or any big city, practice rooms are harder to find!

Singers need exercises that they can do on the subway, in the hall, in the bathroom, walking down the street, or in their hotel room so that they can get their voices ready in a short period of time. For beginning students, I think that they should develop a very good thirty-minute routine per day in their first semester. That is sufficient. Their practice time will increase as they grow and understand what they're supposed to do.

Singing doesn't just happen in practice rooms. It's using your voice for three or four hours a day singing with an orchestra or engaging in rehearsals. It's working on theory and sight singing; it's practicing scales and vocalises. I instruct my students to have their bodies in a vertical position for at least three hours before singing and then to give their voices an eight-hour time window. If you're going to sing a three-hour opera that begins at 8:00 p.m., don't start warming up your voice before 3:00 p.m. so your voice will still be fresh at 11:00 p.m. You don't have to get up in the morning at 9:00 a.m. and warm up the voice when you don't sing until 8:00 that night. I certainly will do lip trills and some humming during the day, but not full out singing. I think that being quiet during the day is of utmost importance when preparing for a big sing.

No whispering—that's worse—just being quiet and reading, reviewing your score, and listening to music. If you've had a very difficult or long rehearsal period and you start to feel some tension or discomfort in the voice, sometimes a day of not talking will take care of the problem. Hydration is always important, of course.

RR: *Today I heard you do some very similar exercises with different students. Do you use these exercises with all of your students?*

EM: Yes, I will start with those exercises because they give me an indication of where the students are and what they may need for that day. Today you noticed that I went a different way with one student than I had planned, because as I was doing the structured warmups I heard some laryngeal elevation in his singing. I felt that I needed to address it.

RR: *You also talked about the corners of their mouths.*

EM: Yes. I tend to want singers to keep the mouth more vertical. I call it the fish mouth. Not over-opened but vertical as opposed to horizontal. I tend to teach that the outer corners of the mouth should not be wider than the perimeter of the nose because I have found is that it's harder to raise the palate when you are spreading the vowel. You can also get more dome in the palate and better access to head voice with more vertical singing.

However, if a soprano is singing a D^6 and needs to spread a little bit to find the right sound, that's fine with me. I don't want her spreading on a G^5 or an A^5 because I think it brings too much weight into the sound and cuts off access to the top. I think that's what every singer has to figure out as she gets to know her own voice. I think spreading too low in the range is how people begin to develop a wobble and other vibrato imbalances.

RR: *Would you say that there's a voice type that you've been most successful with?*

EM: Probably tenors and sopranos. Part of that is because I had to figure out my own tenor voice, which helped me figure out how to sing, access the top, and develop an understanding of the high voice. I think I can do that very well with tenors. I feel that one of my other gifts is the ability to hear the head voice in the female sound. For the understanding of my own technique, I have to thank my teacher, Edward White, who taught at the University of Alabama. I also have to thank Marlena Malas, who has had a big influence on my teaching. During the summers, I would travel to Chautauqua and just watch her teach. She has an incredible ear and has had so much success with her students. Watching her teach and listening to the sound that she developed in students helped me understand the type of sound that the market was looking for. Marlena and Barbara Doscher are both amazing teachers. Barbara has passed on, but I was so happy to have had the opportunity to watch her teach as well.

RR: *She had a very strong influence on me also.*

EM: Really? Wow. You know, I still consider myself a student and will always consider myself a student of the voice. It has always been very interesting to me to learn what people are listening for in auditions and learn the type of voice that the market is looking for. When I go to the Met, Chicago Lyric, or wherever, I'm always listening for the sound that the current market likes. And then I try to identify students who have the potential to have a marketable sound so I can help them develop their potential. I have come across many cases where the voice simply does not fit the mold. This is okay however. Every singer should celebrate his or her own uniqueness! Some singers may not possess a Metropolitan Opera quality voice, but have a very special sound and the ability to sing with ease. What more could we ask for? I would rather reach the age of seventy, seventy-five, or eighty and still be able to sing, rather than chase a particular sound that may only last for a few years. I'd rather teach a technique that allows lifelong singing. I don't go for a cookie-cutter sound. I try to find the uniqueness in every voice and celebrate that. What the industry wants changes with time anyway.

Another point that I would like to make is that we are not training the dramatic voices like we used to. We have fewer of them now because training that kind of voice takes a lot longer. How do you sustain a dramatic singer's dream from the age of twenty-four to forty-five? How do you tell young dramatic twenty-four-year old singers that their voices will not mature until they are close to forty, and that everybody will be afraid to touch them because they are still too young to sing dramatic repertoire? I think the industry really needs programs that will support dramatic voices by giving them the time to mature, sing, work, learn, and live in a protected musical environment. Otherwise, they lose their joy or desire to sing because of the lack of opportunities. I don't have the answer to solving that problem—perhaps we need long-term young artist programs for dramatic singers.

RR: *We talked about positivity in teaching earlier today. Would you speak more about that?*

EM: Sure. I like to teach in a very positive manner. I think that singing is one of the most personal and most disarming things that we do. Singers are vulnerable. Singers need to understand themselves as individuals to be successful in this business. I have found that I can say what I need to say without going to a negative place. If I need to "set fire" to a student, I can certainly do that too, but typically I choose the positive approach.

I don't believe in beating on students mentally or approaching them with statements like, "You are a failure" or "You will never have a career!" I don't believe in sending students out of every lesson crying. That's just a mind trip that the teacher is on. Unfortunately, some voice teachers gain power over students by demoralizing them both in lessons and in public. I don't like this at all and I don't think that it is needed in order to develop a great singer. I think it's more important to positively engage and support our students. The profession is difficult enough as it is. The market is oversaturated. I will typically say to new students, "If you can do anything else, do it. But, if you *must* sing, then do it. Come to the profession with that level of commitment—I sing because I must." That is the level of commitment that is needed in order to sustain you in this business as it is structured today. If I must beat on students and scream at them or make them cry in order to motivate them to be the best that they can be, then my real assessment is that they might not have what it takes to be successful in the business. What's going to happen to them in five or six years when I'm no longer here to challenge them to work? Will someone else do that for them or will they just go by the wayside? I think that students and singers have to be *self-motivated*. My job is to help define that motivation in the student. A lot of it has to already be there; students must *want this more than anything else*. They must come to the studio each week ready to work hard and develop the tools they will need to be successful. During their weekly practice, they must work on those tools and bring those new skills back to the next lesson. The motivated students will come in and say, "This is what I've done this week. I have three ways that I can sing this phrase. Help me find which one is right." I am not good with students who come in say, "Teach me." I don't respond well to those students.

RR: *Because they don't demonstrate any imagination?*

EM: Correct. They don't demonstrate any imagination or desire. They just want to come in and have somebody else tell them what to do. They don't want to take responsibility. They want somebody else to take the responsibility.

RR: *Fix me.*

EM: Yes, fix me. That phrase doesn't work for me. My response is, "I will give you the map, but *you* must do the driving."

Parting Thoughts

I met Everett many years ago while judging a competition. He is patient and positive in his lessons while always challenging the student to be better.

The cornerstone of his teaching technique is the concept of breath. His work with the vocal function exercises of Dr. Joseph Stemple and straw exercises really focus on the initiation of the breath and breath flow throughout the phrase. He uses the concept of breath flow along with the mixing of vowels to achieve a balanced tone.

He also uses a careful progression of vocalises with each singer. He begins with light exercises in the middle part of the voice to emphasize using a lot of head voice in that register. Next, he progresses upward in the middle voice while maintaining that light mix. Once he feels a student is ready, he begins to work on a fuller, more connected sound that is usually oriented from the top down. Now, at this point, I would like to add that William Vennard must have been having a bad day when he came up with one of his exercises that I heard Everett give a student. That one was very difficult! In response to the difficulty, Everett followed that exercise with a flexibility exercise to keep the voice limber in order to promote vocal balance.

Lesson Highlights

Alignment/Positioning

Laryngeal Positioning

Make sure your larynx stays in the lower position. Massage the strap muscles to help the larynx stay down without forcing it down. Work the middle voice first. If you can get the middle voice relaxed and the breath flowing without the larynx going up, the upper voice will respond more easily.

Tongue tension

Sometimes it helps to massage the tongue from under the chin while singing to get it to release. When a student is tired and is having trouble supporting the sound with the breath, the tongue tries to come in to help. It's a muscle, so massage can be useful.

Breath Support/Control

Preparing to sing

Take a breath, allow the glottis to close, and go. Accomplish all of your breathing activity in one movement.

Resonance

Resonance and Breath Flow

If the breath is moving and it gets to the resonators, the sound is going to carry. You don't have to worry about whether or not your voice is too small or try to push your sound. You have to think, "Is my breath moving?" If so, the rest will take care of itself.

Exercises

Exercise 1: (used with a tenor and a soprano)

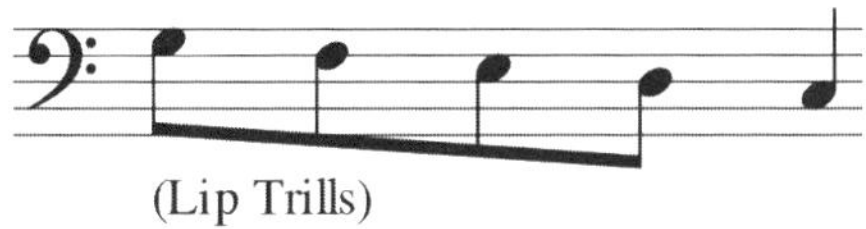

Instructions: Lip trill this pattern. Follow the lip trill with a tongue trill while holding your top lip so the breath can go over the tongue. Now do a "tongue hum" by bringing the tongue to the lipstick part of the teeth, letting the teeth come gently downward, and humming into this position. Check to see whether the tongue is hard or soft by massaging the tongue from under the chin.

Exercise 2: (used with a tenor and a soprano)

Instructions: This exercise is intended to encourage more palatal lift and head voice mixture in the tone.

Exercise 3: (used with a tenor)

Instructions: Use falsetto. Also sing this pattern on an /u/. Do not let the larynx go up.

Exercise 4: (used with a tenor)

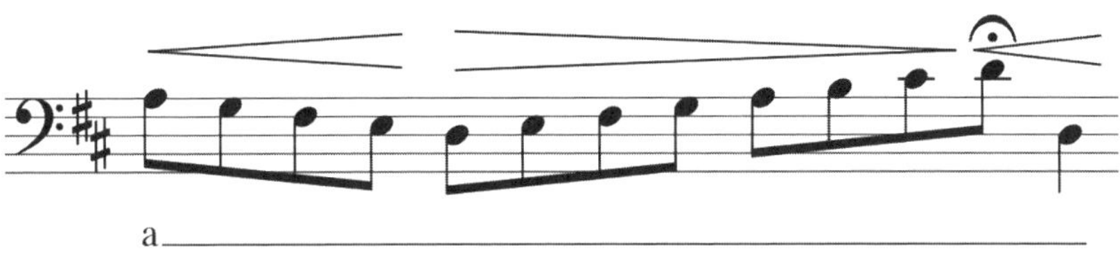

Instructions: [From the writings of Vennard] Sing this exercise in one seamless line with the larynx down and the palate up. Allow your voice to cover as you ascend by letting the /a/ be influenced by /ʌ/, as in "cup." Make sure you don't collapse your sternum as you crescendo. Keep the sternum up. This exercise is a way to get more head voice into the mix.

Exercise 5: (used with a tenor)

Instructions: Start with a /k/. The /k/ should feel as if it's striking the roof of your hard palate right behind the top teeth. Then put that vowel /a/ right there. Hold your nose to see if there is any buzzing. There should not be any buzzing in the nose. You want the energy to strike the palate but not to transfer into a nasal sound.

Exercise 6: (used with a soprano)

Exercise 7: (used with a soprano)

Exercise 8: (used with a soprano)

Pitch glide on /u/

Instructions: Use a little baby sound.

Exercise 9: (used with a soprano)

Instructions: Feel buzzing around the lips and the breath. Don't change from note to note abruptly. Think instead about one note melting into the other like honey going down the side of a glass. Make the pitch changes sloppy and ugly.

Exercise 10: (used with a soprano)

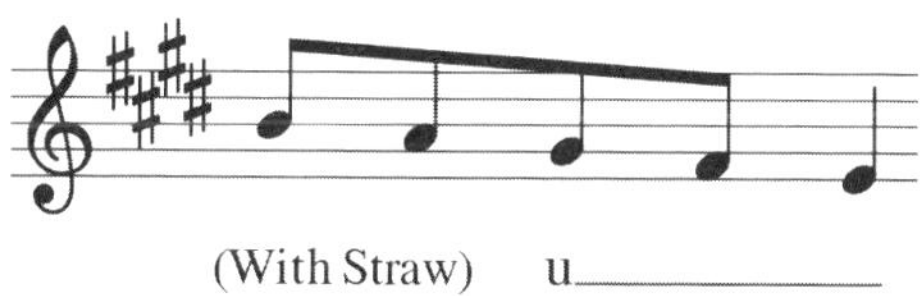

Instructions: Take a breath, blow lightly into the straw, and sing a quiet /u/.

Exercise 11: (used with a soprano)

Instructions: Pull the straw out of your mouth every third repetition and just sing the /u/. No matter how low you go in pitch, keep the placement high. The straw should remind you that the breath generates the tone.

Exercise 12: (used with a soprano)

Instructions: Blow slightly through the straw before singing when you feel like you might be over-pressurizing.

Exercise 13: (used with a soprano)

Instructions: Use the breath to start the tone rather than your tongue. Imagine that you have a little straw that you are singing through. Let the magic happen above the tongue, not from the tongue and below.

HEIDI GRANT MURPHY

Ms. Murphy has appeared with many of the world's finest opera companies and symphony orchestras, notably the Metropolitan Opera, Salzburg Festival, Frankfurt Opera, Netherlands Opera, *Théâtre Royal de la Monnaie, Opera National de Paris,* and Santa Fe Opera. She has been engaged as soloist with the Vienna, New York, Los Angeles, and Buffalo Philharmonics; Cleveland, Philadelphia, and Minnesota Orchestras; and Chicago, Boston, Pittsburgh, San Francisco, San Diego, Atlanta, Saint Louis, Cincinnati, Houston, Nashville, Montreal, National, and Dallas Symphonies. Ms. Murphy has worked with such esteemed conductors as James Levine, Herbert Blomstedt, Christoph Eschenbach, Reinbert de Leeuw, Kurt Masur, Kent Nagano, Seiji Ozawa, Sir Simon Rattle, Leonard Slatkin, Robert Spano, Jeffery Tate, Michael Tilson Thomas, Edo de Waart, Christoph Von Dohnányi, David Zinman, Bernard Haitink, Pinchas Zukerman, and the late Robert Shaw and Lorin Maazel.

Ms. Murphy's nearly twenty-five-year-long career with the Metropolitan Opera has seen her play such signature roles as Susanna in *Le nozze di Figaro,* Sophie in *Der Rosenkavalier,* Palmina in *Die Zauberflöte,* Sister Constance in *Dialogues of the Carmelites,* Servilia in *La clemenza di Tito,* and Nanetta in *Falstaff*. European highlights have included the roles of Anne Truelove in the Netherlands Opera production of *The Rake's Progress,* Celia in *Lucio Silla* at both the Salzburg

Festival and Frankfurt Opera, and Susanna in *Le nozze di Figaro*, Adina in *L'elisir d'amore*, and Sophie in *Der Rosenkavalier* at the *Opera Nationale de Paris*. Over the course of this illustrious career she has been hailed by the *New York Times* for her "bright, focused tone and impressive agility," and by *Opera News*, who said that her "astonishingly pure tone floats with an otherworldly ease," vocal and technical hallmarks for which she continues to be renowned. She has been a featured guest on NPR's Morning Edition and All Things Considered, A&E's Breakfast with the Arts, and BBC Radio 3.

She has recorded for Koch International, New World, the New York Philharmonic's private label, Naxos, Arabesque, PS Classics, Delos, and Deutsche Grammophon. In 2009, her roles as a singer and mother were brought together on a recording especially close to her heart called *Lullabies and Night Songs*, adapted from a 1965 songbook of the same name featuring songs by Alec Wilder and illustrations by Maurice Sendak. *San Francisco Classical Voice* said, "It's hard to imagine a finer singer for this material than Murphy. The beauty of her pure, shining voice and the simplicity of her delivery caress Wilder's music with infinite charm." This recording and several others feature her husband, the renowned pianist, conductor and opera coach Kevin Murphy, demonstrating their longtime musical partnership.

In August 2011, Ms. Murphy was appointed to the faculty of Indiana University's Jacobs School of Music as a professor of practice. In October 2012 Ms. Murphy received an Honorary Doctorate from Western Washington University, where she had pursued a bachelor's degree in music performance. Ms. Murphy resides in Bloomington, Indiana with her husband and children.

The Interview

RR: *Heidi, you have had and are still having an amazing career. I know that it is difficult for women to have children and then resume singing. You have four beautiful children. How did you manage that process?*

HM: For Kevin and me, it was always a given that we were going to have a family. We knew it would never be easy for either one of us in the business we had chosen, but went on to have four children anyway. At first it was all about timing and how to best go about it, and I'm sure some of that helps. But in the end, we realized that as a singer there was never going to be a good time to have a baby—especially as a light lyric soprano. So, I worked hard to get back to form as quickly as I could so that my career and bookings didn't suffer too much. Each time I gave birth to a beautiful little person, I gave myself a few days and then began humming and singing lightly, not asking too much of my poor stretched-out muscles. Then about a week-and-a-half to two weeks later, I would begin to do warm ups for short periods of time. About three or four weeks after, I would go to take a lesson with a trusted friend, Trish McCaffrey, who helped me sing and find my support through my post-birth hormones and jelly-like muscles. Her fantastic ears kept me from overcompensating and going after the feeling I had when supporting before birth. She encouraged me to be patient and to understand the role of all the hormones that come with giving birth and nursing a newborn baby. I had to be patient and listen to my singing instead of feeling how I sang. For nine months of a pregnancy, I had something hard pressing against my core that I became accustomed to using when I sang, and suddenly that feeling was gone. It's pretty scary, and I had to be patient as I worked to get my core muscles back. That doesn't mean that I didn't sing until that point, but I actually began singing professional jobs about a month after giving birth. In hindsight that makes me gasp, but I was able to do it with the help of Trish and my husband.

RR: *What was the most important thing you learned from those experiences?*

HM: Patience and learning not to depend on how my voice feels on any given day. I had to listen more to what was coming out, because if you try to depend on what you traditionally and normally feel in your body, you won't find that sensation in the months after giving birth. For nine months, you've had something hard to press up against when you sing. Then, all of a sudden, it's gone. It always took me six months to get back to my normal support again, no matter how much I exercised.

RR: *I find that most teachers agree about what makes a good breath intake for singing, but lots of variation in how to explain the exhalation/release of breath. How would you describe that process or how do you generally instruct your students?*

HM: I usually tell them that to keep thinking about the continuity of air at the ends of words and phrases. Many students build a lot of pressure and have difficulties releasing phrases, so we work a lot on releasing through the line.

RR: *How you would you describe to them how to accomplish that goal physically?*

HM: I find it's is important to have a balanced approach when talking about anything technical, in this case, the release or exhalation of breath. I find that too much talk about physiology and musculature sometimes gets in the way. It seems that there are two common problems with releasing a phrase: either a singer has too much pressure in the voice and has too much tension in the release that causes an extra-large exhalation, or the vocal production goes flabby and breathy. The issue of too much pressure needs to be addressed for all kinds of reasons, not just for the purposes of releasing the end of a phrase.

Finding the balance of free singing and good breath management is difficult and is one of the biggest issues we deal with as teachers. In regard to releasing the end of a phrase, I like to talk about feeling like you are inhaling off of the phrase—the feeling is going backward, not forward. It starts with the idea that the sound we make comes from setting up a good breath and posture, and then from there allowing the sound to be anchored and spin as opposed to being pushed ahead or pressed. If we are already "supporting" then any added pressure is too much. I like to make my students think of anchoring their sound downward and backward. I want them to create the right tension in the line. A vocal line must have a current in it. It must have the right kind of tension. If you can help them to use their support system the right way and not compensate with the muscles in their neck, jaw, and tongue then you ultimately will be able to help them with a proper release.

I appreciate teachers who talk extensively about physiology and musculature because it can help in understanding how things work. But for me, I have found that being creative and finding the language that works for the singer who is standing in front of me is the most effective tool. If I need to talk about the soft palate, I'll snort. If singers need more overtones and head voice, I'll make them sing like a monkey or make monkey sounds on the text to their aria or song. Sometimes I make them find their old-opera-lady voice, the one who says, "yoo-hoo!" and that gets them to create the right balance of space and clarity. I am not afraid to look silly in order to help them connect with what I am saying. We laugh a lot in our lessons.

RR: *Do you not spend much time on vocalises in a lesson?*

HM: I like to start a lesson with five to ten minutes of conversation before we warm-up. The older students usually have questions about auditions, repertoire, and all kinds of things they have saved up during the week. The younger ones often are just figuring out what it means to be a singer, so we talk about what they need to do or accomplish. Next, we will do about ten minutes of vocalizing. We start with lip trills. I try to let them take their own pace. Some like to do them meticulously slowly, and others like to move through them quickly. What vocalises I use next depend on what the singer's issues are and which way I want to lead him or her. I like to do an exercise that goes up in thirds for an octave alternating /i/ and /a/ vowels starting on /i/, and then skip up to a third above the octave and come down in thirds starting on an /a/ vowel. This helps them understand how to negotiate both of those vowels in the resonating space that works best for them from the bottom range, through the *passaggio,* and into the top. Sometimes we do a vocalise that starts with an octave leap on an /a/, crescendos and decrescendos on top, and then descends through all the notes of the octave back down. I think that's a common exercise that helps to teach breath management and how to decrescendo without getting off the core of the voice.

Next, I usually do an exercise that works on agility and flexibility. It changes depending on the singer. The vocalise can be a five note scale up and back on /i/, then going up the octave plus one note and back down on /a/. We would do this one to the very top of the voice. If the singer is advanced, we'll add another scale after that. I use a variety of warmups like a lot of teachers do, but don't use them as my main teaching tool. I try to teach all of the basics like how to take a proper low breath, chest up, ribcage expanded, shoulders relaxed, et cetera, as we work through repertoire. That is one of the challenges of teaching on the faculty of a music school. Each student has repertoire requirements, whether it's a recital, jury, role, or audition. We have to move through repertoire and don't have the luxury of working on one piece for four weeks, so I try to address technique while working through repertoire and diction.

RR: *Would you tell me more about the octave exercise that you used today?*

HM: I only use it with women and do it carefully so they don't think they are supposed to bring their chest voice up. I do it so they can anchor their middle voice to the resonance of their chest voice. I find it helps their middle voice, and ultimately their top, to feel a connection to their bottom voice. There was a point when I was singing a lot of Mozart and Strauss and then needed to sing the role of Adina in *L'Elisir d'Amore* when I used this exercise to help me find a little more bite to my middle voice. Trish McCaffrey gave that exercise to me. It helped anchor the bottom to the middle and the middle to the top.

RR: *You also talked about finding a longer, taller feeling with some of your students. Does finding this feeling require some jaw opening?*

HM: Yes. Many of these kids sing with a pretty sound, but don't use enough focus or height in the tone. I did that as well until I realized I had a whole bunch of overtones that I wasn't accessing. I like to say to my students that they should set up their voices in a tube that is empty, and in that empty space is where their best sound is with a dark quality. All around that tube is clarity and brightness. Some students find that space best with /u/ vowels, but others find that their tallest vowel is /i/ or /o/. I find that /a/ and /ɛ/ are the hardest vowels to line up. I think that singers have many tools in their tool box, but their best tool is their beautiful voice. They need to find the resonance where their voice works and sounds the best and work to sing proper vowels within that space. It does involve releasing the jaw. It doesn't mean extending the jaw to its fullest capacity, but you have to release the jaw to create a tall space. The goal is to find a space that can allow them to sing with their best, tallest, clearest sound from the bottom of their voices, through the middle, and into the top of their voices. It's particularly tricky with high sopranos. In order to sing the high-pitches they need, they will do whatever it takes. Sometimes they will close down all the space and "chirp" or take all the weight off the voice and "float." I am greatly opposed to both "chirping" and "floating." As the queen of float, I know that high singing, whether sung fortissimo or pianissimo, has to remain connected to the core of the voice. It must remain one voice with the bottom and the middle.

I have to mention as well that when singers know how to keep their voices lined up and functioning in the best resonance, they are free to use all kinds of colors that would have been unachievable before. I used to use all kinds of colors depending on the style of singing I was doing. I used straight tone or very small vibrato, and white colors as well, but they were colors I could use because I knew where my voice functioned the best and stayed there for the most part. I love the sound of an extreme vowel or a wacky vocal sound as long as it's a color that is *chosen* and the singer is secure.

RR: *Some of our students will only meet us halfway when we overstate an idea, but the really responsive students will often take it too far. Sometimes, I have reminded those conscientious students to stay in the middle of the road, rather than going off into the weeds.*

HM: It's true! I am like that, actually, and that's why I didn't study with too many different people. I knew I would be better off with only a few influences over the years. I knew that I would take everything too far.

RR: *Would you talk a little about some of the other people who have influenced you?*

HM: At the beginning, I wasn't a serious vocal student and did everything very naturally. My teacher in undergraduate school was a coloratura soprano, Marianne

Weltman, who was wonderful with the top of the voice. Then I studied at IU [Indiana University] with a Verdi baritone named Norman Phillips, who helped me find a little more color and tallness to my voice. Both teachers taught breath support very well. Obviously, Trish McCaffrey helped me work through some of my most difficult periods vocally. I have to say the two people who had the biggest impact on my singing were my husband, Kevin Murphy, and James Levine, the long-time Artistic Director of the Metropolitan Opera. Kevin has always had great ears for singing, even when he was a piano student. All throughout my singing career he kept me in bounds. I didn't study with many teachers or coaches, so he felt very responsible and didn't let anything go by.

RR: *That can be hard when you're married to each other.*

HM: It is hard. Our collaboration is the best part of who we are as a couple, whether it's raising kids, navigating a crazy life situation, or as singer and coach. Working together professionally has provided some of the worst and most wonderful moments of our relationship. Truly, because as a woman and a wife, I just want him to love everything I do and can't separate my singing from who I am. Because he was one of my few influences, he felt responsible for my vocal health, so he had to say what he thought. It wasn't always easy to hear and I am a stubborn singer with definite expressive ideas. Over the years I have come to see that he was and is pretty much right all the time. In my book, he is the best.

I do have to talk a little about the influence that James Levine had in my professional life. He has always been interested in helping young singers and giving them opportunities. I was lucky to develop a friendship with him early in my time in the Young Artist Program at the Met. He spent a lot of time with me, coached me, and engaged me for many concerts and operas around the world. It gave me the chance to learn all kinds of things from him. I learned about style, technique, being a good colleague, how to teach but not teach, and how to say what you want by leading. He was able to get what he wanted out of singers without having to tell them specifically what he wanted them to do. He was a great teacher.

RR: *Did he talk to you about your singing when you coached with him?*

HM: Oh yes, he was quite straightforward with me. I remember a time when we were doing a piano run-through of *Falstaff* in the basement of the Met and I was singing the role of Nanetta. I was not reacting to the acoustic in the room well and was trying to control my sound too much. I must have been doing something funny with my mouth, because as he was conducting and watching me, he just tapped his mouth with his fingers and I realized I was full of tension in my mouth. I tried to release, and it improved. I also remember a coaching we had on a role I eventually sang a lot with him, Oscar in *Un Ballo in Maschera*. That role has two arias that tend to be relentless in the *passaggio* and I was having trouble singing an /a/ in that area of my voice. He gave me the assignment to work it out and find a way to sing an /a/ in my *passaggio*. I worked hard on that and when I came back for my next coaching it was much better. He appreciated the progress. I think he was tickled and we connected through that little bit of success. I am the same way as a teacher.

If somebody listens to what I say, goes away and really works through it, and comes back improved, it is thrilling to me.

RR: *Do you remember what you did differently with those F^5s?*

HM: I think at the time I was trying to sing /a/ through my *passaggio* with my lips all tied up. He probably heard that I had no trouble with /i/, and I think that is why he told me to find my /a/ through my /i/. I wish I could remember more specifically what he told me to do, but I worked with those two vowels and it really helped. Trying to impress James Levine is a good motivator!

RR: *Matching resonances?*

HM: Yes, though I'm sure I didn't understand that's what I was doing at the time. I just remember that each time I worked with him, I learned. I loved when he would sit at the piano and play for our coaching. When he played, it all made sense. I remember working on *Idomeneo* with him for an upcoming recording, which I was asked to do on short notice and had three weeks to learn the role. I was in Dresden and had no score. This was before IMSLP, so my manager faxed me the arias and I went from there.

RR: *You learned it cold? You didn't know it at all?*

HM: I had never even heard the opera! Sometimes we do crazy things. It came out pretty well. It's not usually the best idea to record something you've never heard, much less sung. In any case I learned it and took it to Jimmy. When I went for my first coaching with him, I had never sung accompanied recitative, and we all know how tricky those are. Jimmy sat down at the piano and told me to just listen. He played and sang those difficult recitatives and they just made sense. Everything just sounds right and easy when he plays. As I said, he is an innate teacher. Kevin is a lot like Jimmy in those ways. I'm sure he learned some of it from the Maestro.

RR: *What do you think are the most important two or three traits for a singer to possess?*

HM: I think the most important trait a singer can possess is the ability to communicate the text that you are singing with openness and honesty so that your audience is moved in some way. It is a quality that is not all that common and is hard to teach, but necessary. I thought everyone did that because I jumped right from my first year of Master's work to the Metropolitan Opera Company by winning their competition. I missed the whole process of working through your Master's and doing auditions for young artist programs. Instead, I received my education from the best singers in the world. But It's not just opera singers who can teach us to do that. One of the best communicators was Ella Fitzgerald. She could sing a line like no one else and paint text so it gave you goose bumps. Tony Bennett is in his nineties and can still do that.

Ultimately, part of what I try really hard to do with these kids is to get them to connect to the text in a real way. Another trait that I obviously think is necessary is the ability to sing well technically. I actually have a couple of students who are so musical that it gets in their way and I have to remind them that their best tool is their voice. That's where all the technical work comes in. Finally, I think the most successful singers are those who are good with languages. Not everyone is, and those who aren't must work really hard. When you hear singers sing in their native language, you can most often connect to that performance easily. But because we don't get to sing in our native language all the time, the trick is for them to find the same connection to whatever language they are singing.

RR: *How do you think a new or prospective singer who works with you in a lesson would describe your teaching?*

HM: I would say that when singers study with me, my main goal is to help them love the music and singing. If they don't, I'm certainly not going to have a good time. I want them to have a really positive experience, but it's not always going to be one. I can get frustrated when students just won't go where I want them to go or trust what I am asking them to do. But that's rare. I want them to love what they are doing and to trust me. Having said that, one of my favorite teachers on the planet is Trish McCaffrey. There is no safety there. It is all dangerous, scary, fabulous, and she gets better results than anybody I know, because she goes right for the jugular without any buffer. That just isn't me.

The things I focus on most tend to be text-oriented and making sure that the voice is lined up, top to bottom. It's hard to sum it up neatly. Ultimately, I want them to say something and love it, because not all of them are going to have a career. Some of them will, but not all of them. They need to come away from this huge, scary school without letting it push their love for what they do right out of them. I don't want that. No matter what they end up doing, I want them to still love singing.

RR: *I met a guy once who described himself as a dream crusher.*

HM: That's what happens all the time. I'm sure you've had that experience many times. Do you tell them at some point? Or do you let it become abundantly clear?

RR: *A little of both, I think. As I suspect you will agree, being honest doesn't have to equal being mean. I think that you let those things play out while giving them a really clear picture of where they are in the gene pool, so to speak. I help them educate themselves about their voice types and the market they are interested in entering by having them listen to similar voices, learning about their career paths, and asking themselves if they want that kind of life. And, if not, get them thinking about other avenues.*

HM: We all have to have that discussion with students, probably sooner rather than later. It's so difficult.

RR: *We don't want to scar them.*

HM: Especially when they're so young.

RR: *How do you choose repertoire for your singers?*

HM: I consider the color of the voice, range, age, and development, and get a sense of the person. You can't give a chirpy piece to someone who isn't chirpy, unless your purpose is to help her with flexibility—and there is a place for those kinds of assignments. Singers need a mix of repertoire that includes selections they can master immediately and some that are challenging and look to the future. They will need a variety when singing recitals.

RR: *Do you ever have people come to you who seem to be between Fachs or in the wrong Fach?*

TM: I haven't yet had to change someone's *Fach*. I have taken opportunities to push boundaries a little to see what works for them or where they might end up vocally in the future. They need to sing what works for them now, while still keeping an eye on the future. I have a student with a big, beautiful voice who sings things like Donna Anna right now, but has the possibility of moving into bigger repertoire in the future. She doesn't have the control or maturity yet. It's a balancing act to assign her repertoire that she can sing and be inspired by right now with some things that can push her a bit, but safely. I think it was Jimmy who said that everybody should be able to sing Mozart. I think he used Birgit Nilsson singing First Lady as an example.

RR: *Singing a Mozartean line teaches singers a lot.*

HM: Definitely. Mozart and Strauss have always been wonderful teaching tools for my voice. Whenever I have been tired vocally, whether rehearsing too much or making a recording, I always found if I sang through a Mozart or Strauss song, my voice felt less stressed and tired.

RR: *Do you have an idea of why that is?*

HM: I think it's because you can't sing a Mozartean line without using a good support system. It forces you to sing well. It's healthy.

RR: *What do you think your three biggest challenges were as a singer?*

HM: I think the biggest challenge I had as a singer was just living a full life and singing at a high level professionally. Because I was fortunate to be nurtured by the Metropolitan Opera at a very young age, I didn't have some of the struggles other young singers have. I had the opportunity at age twenty-two to sing professionally and learn from the best. By twenty-five, I was singing concerts and operas all over the world. When I was twenty-nine, I had my first of four wonderful children. I had to figure out right away how to have a baby and get back out on the road, with baby in tow, while my career was in full swing. I love being a mom, but I also love singing. I had to figure out how to be the kind of mom I wanted to be, live my life the way I wanted to, and still sing at the highest level I could. There was no road map for doing that. It turned out to be difficult, but not impossible. Another major challenge was always to keep my own voice: the inner one and the physical one. Many people have opinions on what we should do—the repertoire, volume, and how we should sing—but I had a very independent spirit when it came to my musicianship and expressiveness and how that coordinated with my style of singing.

RR: *How did you do that? I think an issue we have these days is that everybody starts to sound a little similar.*

HM: I had a very small, trusted group of advisors and influences, and Kevin will tell you just how stubborn I was. I knew what I did well and I insisted on singing with my own musical instincts, even if it was different from the gal who sang it before me. Kevin never let me do something harmful, but he appreciated my independence and helped me to use it properly. The Met played a part by pairing me with gorgeous sopranos who opened my eyes to possibilities. I sang next to Dawn Upshaw, who showed me that you can push boundaries and own your ideas. I admired Barbara Bonney's work ethic and beautiful dome in her upper voice, and I watched as Kathleen Battle focused a note so that it could be heard at the back of the Met. And then, she would go back to her dressing room and practice it some more. These ladies, and others, were all very different and independent singers who showed me it was okay to do things my way—and own it.

RR: *Do you use these experiences as a teacher?*

HM: Absolutely! All the time. I tell students about my experiences and about some of the great singers in their particular *Fach*. I tell them about the work ethic it took to get them there, why they are so good, and much more. I want them to be listeners. I have realized that as I grew as a singer, I didn't study with a long list of teachers and coaches, I but I have been studying voices for a long time. I love good singing, and singing at the Met for so many years has given me the opportunity to listen to some of the greatest singers, and to try to figure out how they do what they do. I was privileged to watch Luciano Pavarotti work his way through his *passaggio*, heard Kiri spin a gorgeous, seemingly effortless line, admire how Kurt Moll sang with a consistently beautiful sound no matter the range, watched Thomas Hampson make singing the "Largo al Factotum" sound easy, even though the sweat on his brow showed the effort it really took. I realize it was a gift to be able to be at the Met at that young age, and I knew to open my ears and listen. I want my students to become singers who watch, listen, and find their own voices.

Parting Thoughts

I was delighted to hear Heidi speak about how much she learned about the voice and our art from watching the greatest singers of our time. I would have loved to have had YouTube when I was growing up. It is a wonderful gift to every singer. We now have access to a whole universe of recordings and a wealth of knowledge that can be gleaned from it. I encourage young singers to understand Heidi's philosophy: she did not copy other singer's sounds, but maintained her individualism and applied the ideas in her own voice. In short, as I tell my students, "Listen to their work; don't copy their sound."

It is immediately evident when you step into the studio that Heidi has an honest, positive personality and a true love for singing and music. This love is infectious to her students and shows in their own singing. Even though she constantly works with them on technique, she always reminds them to find the music and the character within each piece.

One of the major cornerstones of her teaching is finding the core or the thread of the chest voice constantly in the sound. She referred to it in lessons as anchoring the voice so that the voice is energetic and stable. To be sure though, this idea does not mean that she wants a depressed or pharyngeal sound. Her singers sing with freedom, fullness, and clarity; in other words, balance. Even though she doesn't speak in technical terms, she is constantly helping the students to fine-tune their voices so that they find the center of their instruments. This is why she is constantly talking to the students about intonation. As a sign reads in my studio, "Tuning is not optional!"

Lesson Highlights

Breath Support/Control

Inhaling for Singing

Pretend you are going to yawn a tiny bit and let go of your abdominal muscles, even though we all want to hold them in. Let them go, so everything can drop and come in and make sure your chest is up. Then start singing right where you are. Don't clamp down or do anything different.

Phonation

Initiating Tone with Confidence

Whatever you do, start the sound without evaluating it. When your voice starts breathily, it's because you are checking on it as it goes out. Don't check. Set it down. It must happen right when you start. Adjust only with willpower and support. Let everything spin and keep it moving.

Resonance

Placement and Text

As long as it's bright and out front you're okay. If you don't let it out and you don't let it come into a bright place out in the front you'll get stuck, because it's all going to go back and down. Let it anchor and be tall, long, and bright. Let the language be your friend.

Registration

Singing in Challenging Tessituras

(Working with a soprano singing "Ruhe sanft, mein holdes Leben," from Mozart's *Zaide*)

I know you don't like those C-sharps. For some reason, they want to go someplace else. It's okay. You know what? The hard part about this aria is that it sits in the cracks. It sits right between your middle and upper voice in the *passaggio*. It just does. So, you get really high and stacked every chance you get. You have to let it down and re-approach every time you get the opportunity. Otherwise it brings you up, up, up, when we just need to you to release down. Take a deep, low breath and sing. Find your anchor notes so you can always know where you need to be. If you are already worried about the difficult section of the phrase when you begin, even a note that is easy for you may feel difficult. Start by making that first note the best it can be. Don't think about the next thing you are singing. Think about right now.

Exercises

Exercise 1: (used with sopranos)

Instructions: Breathe and keep it easy.

Exercise 2: (used with a soprano)

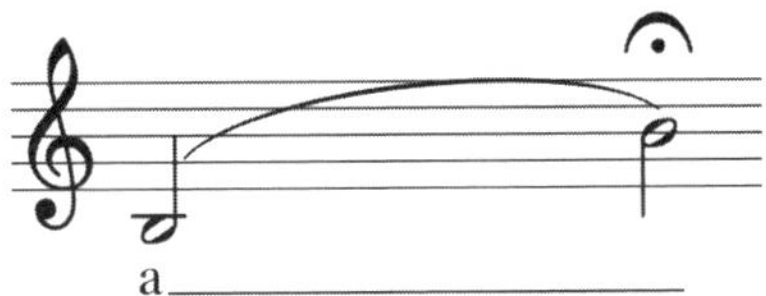

Instructions: Begin in a lower mix with a connection into the middle voice. Do not bring the chest voice into your upper voice. Let go of your tongue. Get the sound out of your throat and bring it out here where we can hear it. Don't press air into it or pull on it. This does not have to be loud. Just put your voice on the breath.

Exercise 3: (used with sopranos)

Instructions: Keep everything in front. Don't worry about the top. If you relax, your voice will already be there. Don't stop the sound on the highest note.

Exercise 4: (used with a soprano)

Exercise 5: (used with a soprano)

Sing lightly on one pitch through the following five Italian vowels: /i, e, a, ɔ, u/. They started in the lower middle voice and ascended into the *secondo passaggio*.

Instructions: Set it up, keep it spinning, and let the vibrato move easily.

Bill Schuman

Bill Schuman is internationally celebrated as one of the world's leading teachers of singing. His students are some of the most important singers in the music world.

A native of Portland, Oregon, Mr. Schuman began his vocal studies under B. Gibner King, the coach of such Met luminaries as Ezio Pinza and Margaret Harshaw. Following his studies with Margaret Woodward at Brigham Young University and with Rita Streich at the Conservatory of Music in Vienna, he became a protégé of the famed vocal pedagogue, Luisa Franceschi Verna, herself the teacher of Zinka Milanov, among others. He finished his studies in New York, studying Italian style and repertoire with Rita Saponaro Patanè. Since beginning his teaching career, Mr. Schuman's success has been completely unique in the Opera world. His students not only are major stars in the great opera houses around the world, but they have won an unprecedented number of international voice competitions and awards. For four years in a row, his students were honored with the Richard Tucker Award, America's most prestigious award for opera singers. Three of his students also were consecutively bestowed the Beverly Sills Award, the Metropolitan Opera's highest award for young singers who have appeared on the Met stage in a principal role.

Over the years he also has maintained his work with non-classical singers, where his students have included some of the biggest stars from the Broadway, Film, TV, and popular music worlds. His non-classical students have included numerous Tony, Grammy, and Emmy award winners, and Academy Award nominees.

Mr. Schuman has been associated with the Metropolitan Opera Young Artist Program, the Curtis Institute of Music, and was personally invited by Placido Domingo to be one of the inaugural teachers at the Washington Opera Young Artist Program. Since 1989, Mr. Schuman has been on the faculty of the Academy of Vocal Arts in Philadelphia, where he has exclusively based his academic career.

Mr. Schuman is in demand worldwide for master classes and lectures. He has been featured in numerous articles and books on the art of singing, and has been the subject of articles in various publications including Opera News and the Wall Street Journal.

In 2008, Mr. Schuman became the youngest voice teacher ever to receive the coveted Lifetime Achievement Award by the Licia Albanese-Puccini Foundation.

The Interview

BS: [Talking about his intensive apprenticeship with the famed vocal pedagogue, Luisa Franceschi] It was a real apprenticeship. Franceschi said, "Now I'm going to teach you how to teach a German head tone instead of an Italian or French head tone."

RR: *So how did she teach the German head tone?*

BS: She showed me an exercise using closed /o/—you have to really close it and almost swallow it down. Italians rarely use it, but these exercises can show you how to build a top voice when there's no top or ability to sing piano. She would show me all these things, including a "glugging" exercise. And I'd say, "Luisa, what's that exercise? Can I make that work for legitimate voices?" So, she said that you use the "go, go, go" sound with a cry in it. It actually uses the tongue to teach the larynx how to float and the tongue to release.

RR: *Is that's why you told someone to have the /g/ below the larynx?*

BS: Yes. The /g/ should be anchored below the throat. Now I'll tell you a classic story. She once said, "This exercise, lip trills, it's a disease—don't ever do that!" She never told me why. So, I asked Margaret Harshaw, who said, "Why would you ever put air at the lips? You don't put air in your mouth." Seth [Riggs] did the lip trills with pop singers to thin out the cords [vocal folds]. Stevie Wonder was doing them. Dan Ferro brought the exercise back to Julliard in the 1980's, so it became the thing to do. It actually thins out the legit voices too much. Speech therapists are using it nowadays. It's a whole new thing. I went to speech therapy. It didn't help. Singing helped my stuttering.

RR: *You have a stutter?*

BS: I have a bad stutter, at times. It was terrible when I was young. The first thing I say in lectures or master classes is, "I'm a stutterer, so if you hear me stutter, it's okay if I make a face or whatever." Singing helped me. But now these speech therapists say, "Raise your speaking voice up." That's the worst thing you could do. Luisa would say, "Get it down, get it down!" But she was the real thing, and she really taught me everything I know about pedagogy. Other people were good coaches and stylists. I met Licia Albanese at a party. When I introduced myself with my last name, Schuman, she said. "You are a German! How do you know how to teach *bel canto*?" I told her that I was a student of Luisa Franceschi. She said, "My friend, Luisa? Oh my God, we spent years together in Milano." They were the women of the Italian school.

Luisa was from Maine. She thought she'd be a Wagnerian soprano like her aunt Lily [Lillian Nordica]. She told me that she wouldn't get on her back for any man in New York, which cost her a couple of jobs. But when she was twenty or twenty-one years old, she sang an audition for somebody who told her, "Go around the corner down to the church. There's a man who's auditioning." She walked in and sang. She was very pretty. The man asked her, "You don't know who I am, do you?" She admitted that she didn't. He said, "I'm Victor Herbert. I'm casting a new show, *Blossom Time*. You're going to star in it." So, she did. She did *Ziegfeld Follies*. She said, "I was the only one in that show who wasn't on my back like the rest of the girls, because I could sing." And then Florence Foster Jenkins became her mentor and debuted her. She said Florence Foster knew everything she was doing. She said, "Don't believe for one minute that she did not know. It was an act for her."

Next, she started singing in Milano and met Luisa Tetrazzini. She became her protégé. That's the reason I do the Melocchi exercises, because Tetrazzini sent her to Melocchi when she was trying to sing *Traviata*. He said to her, "Your voice, it's all head tone. You sing like a perfect bird. If you sing *Traviata*, you need *più cucu* [more cuckoo]." Luisa had been a student of the teaching assistant of the second Lamperti, who taught all head tone. So, she went to Melocchi, who enlarged her voice two or three times and gave her access to a few additional high notes. She was famous for her high notes. She was the real thing, you know? Her master classes were controversial, because she told the students, "You have to go back," rather than asking for forward placement. I heard that from her. I heard that from Vera Rózsa.

Studying with her was intense. I would go for a lesson at 4:00 p.m. and leave at 2:00 a.m. She would make me swim laps. She'd feed me. We'd listen to music. It was incredible! Luisa taught me so much, like how to properly train a Strauss soprano. If you try to train her like an Italian soprano, you'll destroy her voice. It can't function that way. They have to have a dome. They have to go into the sink. Luisa was tough, but never abusive. Mrs. Harshaw was the same way. Old school.

RR: *Yes, Masiello was the very same way. She was tough but did not make it personal.*

BS: I don't know, Robin. I teach on positives, because I find I get better results. It doesn't mean you never concentrate on the bad things, but you do the positives and you go to work, because a singer is such an emotional creature. It's all here [pointing to his head].

I remember working with Lisette Oropesa in her years before singing at the Met. Have you heard Lisette sing? I love her. She is a fabulous vocalist. So, one time I heard a friend say to her, "I don't know about Bill. We do all these scales for a half hour, forty-five minutes, and he only tells me a couple of things when I sing." And Lisette said, "The scales are what he's teaching you. The scales are technique." She's an instrumentalist. She understood. She said, "When he moves the vowel sequences around in the exercises, that's the voice lesson. You go to a coach to work on the music. Bill is building your instrument." I've had so many people that were instrumentalists. They understand scales. But if you stop some students after every mistake, they stop being able to sing.

RR: *Your students have been very successful.*

BS: Mine are doing pretty well, yes. It's tricky being a young artist. With the Met program, the students of mine who have had careers after doing that program have had a very hard time getting respect as mature artists from the Met. They think of them as young artists for years after they finish. When they wanted Angela Meade for that program after the auditions, I said, "Don't you dare. You're coming back to school." She said, "Okay. Fine." She came back to school. Two weeks later, the Met called, "We need you to cover *Ernani* next year." I said, "Do it. Angela, you never would have had that call if you had joined the Lindemann program. They never would have let you be a principal artist." She did it and became a star overnight. The rest is history. It never would have happened if she accepted the young artist program, because of this mentality. Some of these young artist programs take all these kids, strip them down, and destroy many of them emotionally. They give them small parts. Aprile Millo wouldn't do it. She said, "Rosa [Ponselle] didn't sing small parts, and Maria Callas didn't. I'm not going to do it either." And they became furious with her. She was right. She knew how to make herself a celebrity. She understood.

RR: *I think we've been through a twenty-five-year season of very slim, overly narrow voices being the preferred sound. Not every voice needs to be slimmed down drastically.*

BS: Joan Sutherland was a giant with big [vocal] folds—the doctor said they were unbelievably huge. She started out with this beautiful, but fake Wagnerian sound, so slimming her down was the correct thing. But listen, I heard her sing many times. She didn't sing lightly, and she never sang piano. She really sang. *Caballé* is the greatest voice we have in that group of *bel canto* specialists. At the Olympics, she *sang*! I love her. She's real, and she sings. And you know what? All over the world, she's considered the great one. She would have had her career anytime because it's a real voice.

So, I was asked recently by a journalist in D.C. what I thought about our tenors, and I said, "There's a classic tenor sound, with many different colors. But I always thought that tenors quacked like ducks." Tenors are squeaky. Even Caruso, with his dark sound had the quack. Nowadays, there's a trend going toward more of a

German, dark sound. Young singers are listening to that now instead of [Beniamino] Gigli, [Luciano] Pavarotti, [Fritz] Wunderlich, or even [Mario] Lanza. These sounds are not going help them become tenors. They're not.

RR: *I make all of my tenors watch what Giuseppe Giacomini does, which I think is helpful for the guys who don't know how to get to the top of the voice. I tell them to watch and listen to his work, but not to copy his voice. I always say that I had two lessons with John* [former tenor student of RR who later worked with BS]. *During the first one we met each other and vocalized. In the second lesson, I had him doing the Caruso scale:*

We went up through the passaggio. It wasn't working, and then right around F-sharp⁴ or G⁴, I heard it click in. I stopped and said, "Do you know what you just did?" He says, "Yes, I heard it." And I asked, "Can you do that again?" I had him sing it again and said, "Now, do you know what you did?" He asked me, "Is that the way you want me to do it?" I said, "Yes!" He said, "Okay."

BS: That's John. He's a brain.

RR: *So, we just had that lesson for four years, while I kept telling myself, "Just don't screw it up." And people would say to me, "Oh, I don't know, I don't know about that sound when he goes into the top," And I said, "Look, John knows that that's not the final product. However, I want him to know…"*

BS: You're building muscles and building weight.

RR: *Yes! I wanted him to know how to negotiate that part of the voice and not be scared of it. And he knows how to do that. Do you teach male and female students differently?*

BS: Yes, I do, because the women must have a lot more head tone in the sound, and they have different resonating chambers. Men really sing mostly chest-based. Women have to have chest in the sound, but the mezzos have more chest in the sound than the sopranos do. Now, some sopranos are more Germanic, so you have to build more of a German head tone instead of an Italian head tone. You have to try to decide what type of instrument you're working with. For example, if you are working with a [Kiri] te Kanawa-type instrument, trying to train her like an Italian soprano would screw up her voice. I learned that from Vera Rózsa. She was really smart. Kiri was one of the great singers of all time, but there was never an Italian /a/. It was never based on that kind of head tone. So, you have to decide what kind of voice you are dealing with and working to build, while remembering that support is different for men and women. It's harder for women to get the concept of low support because they have sex organs there. Men find it more easily, in my experience.

RR: *How would you describe breath support? How do you help singers develop their concept of support?*

BS: You have to find the way to have the body keep energizing and pressurizing the breath flow without being over-pressurized. You wouldn't believe how active Kiri's body is when she sings. It's unbelievable! It has constant energy and is almost like her tummy is doing a dance. Vera Rózsa taught her that. She was great with body and breath. Vera lost her voice from polio complications and respiratory problems, so she had to rebuild her system. She was big on using the body, and Kiri is living proof of that. She had many, many students, and was the most brilliant teacher of women during the last sixty or seventy years. I loved her. It's interesting, because when you get the voice free and energized, the body starts to kick in. So, it's the chicken or the egg: which comes first? And I have found, through my work, that if you really free the voice, the body starts responding. That's when you can fully start to concentrate on the breath in lessons. If you have your students lie down on the ground for eight months—like a teacher did that I knew back in Los Angeles—the voice never connects or frees.

RR: *I have told students, "When you really find your sound, take an inventory of your body."*

BS: And if you get the freedom and then somehow lose it, you must find that connection again. Sometimes singers lose weight and it changes their bodies enough that the breathing has to be adjusted. Without the fat, they lose track of the weight that they were using to help everything anchor. And then they have to get into their muscles, which is scary. It's hard for them. That's the reason it can take time to adjust technique after a large weight loss.

RR: *That's what happened to Callas.*

BS: When Zinka Milanov was working with my teacher, she lost one hundred pounds in one year, but she lost it slowly. They never let her lose more than two pounds a week. If she lost more than that, they made her eat more. So, the adjustment wasn't as hard for her. It's funny, but the old-school teachers understood more about the physicality of singing. I think some people are afraid of well-supported young voices. Yes, those voices can't do all the delicate stuff yet. They're not supposed to. They're supposed to build the machinery, but people don't like that. If you crack, okay, do it again. It's not a big deal. That's how sports guys learn. Swing! What difference does it make if you strike out or you foul out? You have to. But they create this fear of singing. The Russians don't have that. They dominate our business because they come out and they sing. They sing well because they're fearless.

Where are the great opera singers like Luciano [Pavarotti]? People say, "Oh, you have to close the F^4." But listen to the recordings. He only closed his F^4 when he was older, not when he was young. Now if you listen to [Franco] Corelli, [Richard] Tucker, and [Alfredo] Krauss, you hear more of a mix in the *passaggio*. They were all mixed. Then they turned over. And they all kept their top voices. Young tenors should listen to [Enrico] Caruso and [Richard] Tucker, the guys whose voices kept the top through their whole career. They should listen to it, but they shouldn't do it.

RR: *So, they should keep the F^4 open and mix the F-sharp?*

BS: Yes. Especially when they're young. Of course, there are exceptions. Sometimes tenors can sing the G^4 open, but they need to close earlier to sing things like Mozart. A student asked me the other day, "Why do I need to close more in the *passaggio* when I sing the Duke [*Rigoletto*] than in other repertoire." I asked him, "Is there a difference in tessitura?" He said, "Yes, it feels better this way." When you sing the Duke or other Verdi you're thinking about a dignified tone [demonstrating a darker tone]. When you sing *Bohème*, you want something brighter, so the voice changes. To me there's no rule. Every voice is unique. The good singers are flexible. There are no rules.

RR: *Do you use the term cover at all?*

BS: Yes, but sometimes I will say turn or close instead, just because I think the brain responds better to those words. I also say *cupo* because I think it's helpful. It's all the same. It just depends on the person and the situation. I will say, "Cover that note" once they know what to do when I say it, but I use /u/ to help them find it. The /u/ does it all by itself. So, when they find that, or good /i/ with a low throat, then you can mix. It sounds darker at first, but once they work it out, you get the brilliance too. Once that process is done, I can say "Cover that note. It's too open." But sometimes with young kids you have to find the right thoughts to help them through the process. And then there's *squillo*. Have you read Vennard's book?

RR: *Oh, yes!*

BS: That's the best. He was a true vocal scientist. He wasn't a big teacher, but he was good one. But if you notice what he says about the men's top voices, he said the best tops he ever heard were when the singers were young. They added a little more space, and then a little more space to the open sound until the voice turned over. He noticed that the guys that cover too early in their training seem to put a damper on the voice and never got the real *squillo*. It's very interesting, because if you get a natural tenor, who's just kind of making this open sound on G^4 or A-flat^4 [demonstrates], it kind of stops after that. So, if you vocalize this range with them and help it turn you can bring the B-flat^4, A^4, and A-flat^4 down, which seems to give them more of a feeling of freedom without the manipulation of the cover. I think if you teach a kid cover manipulation too young, it gets very hard.

Right now, I have a tenor who was sent to me by another school who they've asked me to open. And what I'm finding is that it's a good voice, but the throat is moving constantly. Everything is a manipulation for pitch. As you get up the scale more and more, I think, "My God, I have to try to get this kid to not move his throat." He needs to get his throat to just hang low. But every note is like that, with the cover here and the cover there. I said, "Look, I don't want you to sing open, but I don't want you to be afraid to make noise, even if you think it's too open. We'll shade it. It will turn over in a different way, but if you muffle and close it off there can be no *squillo*." He's Lebanese, so his voice is almost like an Italian voice, but it gets dull-sounding. He said to me, "I'm losing because I don't sing from the top." It's not that he doesn't have a top. He just doesn't know how to access the top correctly. I told him, "Listen to rock singers. No one taught them what to do, and they have good high notes. Rock guys can go up and scream high notes." The cantors do it, too. They go up, and no one teaches them how to do it. No, they don't know how to do a proper scale up to it, but they go up to the top. All these other guys have been taught, and they can't go to high notes. So, it's fascinating.

The rock guys can sing. You know, I tell my kids, "Listen to Celine Dion or young Barbra Streisand. They have a lot to teach tenors." Those girls know what they're doing. I mean, have you ever watched Celine physically sing? It's incredible. And she sings in the same range as a tenor does. Her high belts are the same pitches as the tenor high range. Teachers respond, "How can you say that?" because they think belting is dangerous. Well, Streisand is seventy, right? She has lost a couple high notes, but the voice still sounds great. She sounds better than most operatic singers do. Working with Michael Bolton was fascinating because we worked on the range above C^5. He had the mechanism and it was easy for him. It was a little throaty, but he knew how to do it. He instinctively just went up and screamed it.

RR: *You have such a deep knowledge of historical practice. When I watched you teach, you knew how so many great singers handled different phrases in the repertoire. How did you learn all of this?*

BS: My first coach was Gibner King, who was New York's top accompanist. He was Margaret Harshaw's coach and teacher, and Ezio Pinza's exclusive teacher. Then I went to Brigham Young and worked with Margaret Woodward, who was unbelievable. She said, "You have to sing opera. You have the voice." She had been a protégé of Amelita Galli-Curci and discovered Sherrill Milnes. After that, I went to Vienna and studied with different people and then to London to meet Vera Rózsa. I was just twenty. So, I went to Covent Garden and said that I wanted to meet her. They gave me a number for a man named Peter. So, I called Peter, I didn't know that it was Sir Peter Pears. He must have thought I sounded like a cute kid or something, so he gave me her number. When I spoke to her, I said, "I should sing for you. I'm studying in Vienna." And that day I went to sing for her, Joan Sutherland walked out the door as I was going in. I knew that Joan Sutherland was there, but I didn't know that it was her. So, I asked, "Who was that?" Vera said, "Don't ask, darling. Come sing for me."

When I was in Vienna, I went and knocked on [Leonard] Bernstein's hotel door and said, "William Schuman is here to see you." He thought it was William Schuman from Julliard. So, I met him and sang for him. And then I went to Los Angeles, and I worked with someone who might be the most controversial teacher in the world, Seth Riggs. He is the big pop teacher who teaches *speech-level singing*. Seth had taught legit singers before moving to Los Angeles and becoming a teaching star. He is the reason I worked with Michael Jackson, I love Seth. He's a character. Seth taught everyone in Hollywood. When Streisand was working on her Broadway album, she went to him. I learned a lot of the way I teach belt from him. Then I met Connie Cloward, this tremendous mezzo soprano, while I was singing *Messiah*. She told me she was working with Luisa Franceschi, who had helped her with some vocal problems. So, I started working for Luisa and became her protégé. She taught Zinka Milanov, Eugene Conley, George London, Mario Lanza, Dorothy Sarnoff, and Nelson Eddy. I remember her saying to me one night, "I lived long enough to teach you how to teach, to teach you about this art form."

RR: *You mentioned the "Caruso Box" during one of the lessons I observed. Can you tell me more about this?*

BS: There's a famous story about Ponselle and her sister, Carmela, singing together in Vaudeville. Rosa was singing mezzo and Carmella was the soprano. So, Rosa was always afraid of high notes because of her mezzo past. I was always told that Ponselle threw out *Aida* because of the high-Cs. She wrote in her book that she lost her high notes at one time and went to Caruso for advice. And he said, "You've lost the box. You've lost your box." And Caruso told her that you have to make a box up, not down, your throat. She said that this helped her to lift her soft palate and get the space up in the soft palate area. If you open your mouth and sing with the tongue in a relaxed, but slightly elevated position in the back, the Caruso Box is from back there upward. It is another way to describe a very high soft palate. Rosa said that her high notes came back as soon as she found the box and always thanked Caruso for it. You know Robin, the palate is the secret to everything.

You have all these methods. It's so ridiculous. I say, "Okay, show me what you do. What's a German head tone, or an Italian? Show me the difference." They look at me. I say, "Okay, thank you," and walk away. My main teacher, Luisa, taught the classic Italian *bel canto* technique. I use a lot of Melocchi's exercises. A lot of teachers say they teach Melocchi, but they don't know whether the exercises they are doing are his builder exercises or his technique exercises. You have to know what you are trying to do with the exercises. Melocchi was a very good voice teacher.

RR: *I liked what you said about choosing repertoire based on color and other factors. How do you know when someone's singing the wrong repertoire?*

BS: It's hard to describe, because I don't know how to describe how I determine what the color is. I listen and use what I was taught by my elders. For example, the bass student I saw today can sing Verdi, and it's good for him to stretch and open up his voice that way. But there is no way he should sing it professionally because it requires too much thickness in the middle voice for him right now. When you hear a singer who is driving and driving in the middle register, that role is too heavy. Even if they are singing well, the orchestra can be too big for them to be heard. You can just tell. And people have to be honest about that. A real, dramatic voice can sing lyrically and can sing anything big. They don't have to push, because the voice is so big and the resonance is there. It's like prize fighting. If you take the best cruiserweight-boxing champion in the world, there might be a chance that he can run around a super heavyweight, but if his opponent connects the one punch, he's dead.

RR: *I like that comparison.*

BS: That's the problem with singers singing the wrong repertoire in a professional situation. In school, you have more room for error because you're not up there pumping out six or seven shows after six weeks of rehearsals. Say a girl is beautiful and can sing. Her voice is kind of big. She gets hired for big repertoire, screams for two or three years and she's finished. Anna Netrebko sang lyrically for a long time with a full voice. Her voice is big and gorgeous. Oh, it's magnificent! It's the real, real thing. She's beyond sexy. She always had an inner sense of what was right to do. That's why she's still here. Kids don't always know. They blow it up. It's like an athlete; you have to train for a decathlon. Two of the sports are hard for them out of the ten. You have to work on those two sports if they want to win the decathlon. I like comparing sports and singing. It's the same thing.

Individual sports are a better comparison, not team sports, because singing is not a team sport. If you doubt what's coming out of your throat, you're dead. Especially tenors. Tenors have to just throw it out there. But that's like people who stop kids after every three notes. They're never going get the feeling of just singing and letting it ring in their belly. I think the teachers do that because the kids are going to get tight, and they don't know how to get them out of being tight. It is a progression of corrections. You don't stop them and correct every tone. Nobody's perfect. If they were, they'd probably be like an overly light Mozart soprano. You wouldn't want to hear it.

I have some students I think are phenomenal who don't get jobs, and other ones that I think are just okay who do. It's a strange part of the business. I don't understand why. Part of our job as professional teachers is to help students move into careers. It's different from what teachers do in college or when you have the kids who are at a pre-professional stage. They pay us a lot of money in New York to commit and really try to help guide them. You can open doors, but you can't make them walk through when the door's open. But you know you did your best for them.

Parting Thoughts

I met Bill at his studio at the Academy of Vocal Arts (AVA) in Philadelphia. AVA has long been one of the preeminent opera training programs in the world. The singers I heard there were indicative of this type of high profile vocal training program. Despite having students who are impressive singers and beginning excellent careers, Bill spends a good deal of his time diligently working on the basic concepts of singing. Several of my previous students who have worked with Bill have talked about the detail he uses when discussing many aspects of technique.

Bill's lessons are fast-paced with periodic rest periods. He spent time during every lesson talking to the singers about what they have been doing and what they have coming up in their schedule, which seemed to frame the lesson in a focused, practical way. I am always asking my singers what they have learned, which helps them focus on where they are and where they need to be.

As you will see in the exercise section, the vocalises I observed were dominated by a mixture of open vowels sequenced with short consonants like /r/ and /l/, which front and lengthen the tongue. To me, this is one of the basic principles of *bel canto* style: singing pure vowel sounds with minimal amount of physical movement. Singers must understand the minimal adjustments to the breath and the mouth opening as they move from a closed vowel sound to a more open vowel sound or vice versa. This helps them rely more on the breath connection and less on articulations in the pharyngeal area, giving them more vocal freedom and stamina. Additionally, Bill gives each singer a different combination of voice-building and balancing exercises.

I did ask Bill specifically about one exercise, which he used with several of the singers:

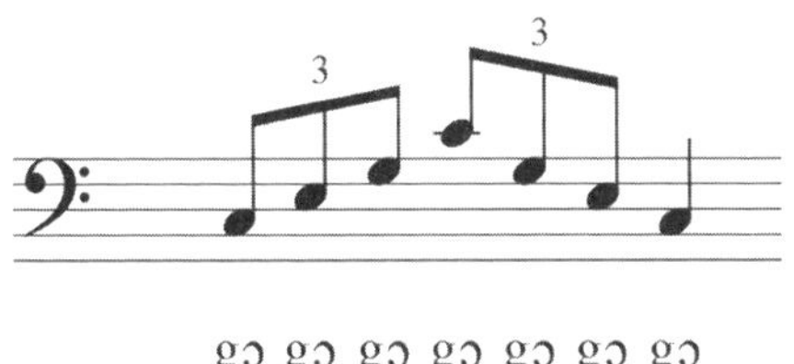

gɔ gɔ gɔ gɔ gɔ gɔ gɔ

He explained to me that the use of the /g/ was to relax the lowest part of the tongue above the larynx, behind the suprasternal notch. This is not an exercise based on beauty of tone. It is about building vocal function.

During the repertoire part of the lessons, Bill never loses sight of fundamental skills like timbre, power and registration. As was demonstrated in the interview, Bill is always aware of both historic and current performance trends and is able to assist singers with finding the most effective choice. He knows how to find the special part of each voice and how to showcase that individuality in both their vocalism and repertoire.

Lesson Highlights

Breath Support/Control

Physicality in the Breath

I'll never forget the first time I met Placido Domingo. I said, "you know, you do something with your body." He said, "You must not have had a good teacher. Learn about your body. It's all about the body." He's right. The tone must sound calm and secure, but the body must be incredibly active. When you go into your body, get into your legs.

Phonation/Breath Connection

What comes first, the chicken or the egg? Until the voice is free, we can do breathing exercises for years and it's not going to do anything. When your voice is getting freer, you realize, "Oh my God, I need to get the air." The body and brain start computing, and when the singer starts physicalizing and using that air they realize, "Oh, that's why I don't use the muscles in my throat." The cords just close and they vibrate.

In a pipe organ, you have to get that air moving, but the pipes don't change or move around. You create your pipe organ and leave it alone. That helps you realize what you have to isolate to get the voice to vibrate.

Breath Support

You have to be open in the body. Feel it in your pelvis; it's that low. Your diaphragm goes down and it goes up. *Basta*! You can't do anything about it. You can control the muscles around the diaphragm. That's it.

It's a tough balance because you want to rest on top of the breath, but you don't want to push out. You need to find the compression like you see in a beach ball.

Phonation

When you really master compression, the body starts helping you instead of fighting against you. You take in the air, but you don't let it rush out. The Italians take air in and lean against the breath. That's your anchor. They knew their pitches by the feeling of the tautness of the cords.

Onset and Offset

(Speaking to a soprano student) You should ask Maestro about his work with [Renata] Scotto on *Adriana Lecouvreur*. He said that she sang "Ecco, Ecco, Ecco, Ecco: respiro appena" for thirty minutes to get it focused and completely coordinated. It's like the first phrase of *Un bel dì*. I need you to really work the attacks over and over again. Your voice depends on the perfection of the attack. All of the books about [Nellie] Melba say that that her voice just appeared, it never started, and her sound seemed to live in the theater after she stopped singing. It's very interesting. She must have really obsessed over that to reach that level of perfection. I think that maybe it looked like she closed her mouth and stopped singing to the audience, but instead ended with a pure head tone with a closed mouth position to give them that effect. If you watch Lilly Pons sing high notes in videos, you'll notice that she closed her mouth and put it all in the back of her head.

Resonance

Placement

(When working with a young bass) On that killer note, the long E-flat[4], I think you have to send the tone straight to the back of your head. Let it just stay there. Thinking about bringing it to your forehead is making you tight. Go backward.

Soft Palate

You know when you're sitting in church getting the giggles and you're trying not to let it show? That's your soft palate! That's it. It's the beginning of a smile. Go smell a beautiful flower. Smile at your girlfriend; it's your palate.

Do we lift the palate and send air up to it, or does it stay up because it's being supported by the air? In the end, it doesn't matter. We physically learn to access it and it becomes a habit. Margaret Price told me that her palate would hurt the next day if she sang "Dove Sono." It would ache. That's how she knew she was in really good voice. She said, "If I wasn't sore, I didn't really have it in the optimal spot." And Marcello [Giordani] says "Oh, God, I have to rest my palate" when he sings the really high stuff. He just wants to shut up and relax everything after.

Tenor Registration

What we're looking for is "a split resonance" (as Luisa called it), rather than wide open resonance. A good balance would be 40% over and 60% down. It's tilted. You never want to flip it all the way over unless you have something really quiet, like in a scene where your character is dying at the end of an opera. But you don't want to really open it unless you're singing runs, and then you keep it open because that kind of singing allows you to do it that way.

(When working with a tenor singing "Ah, mes amis" from *La Fille du Regiment*) Stay inside. Use the breath. Don't move your throat. It's in your body. It's not in your throat.

Repertoire

Verdi versus Bel Canto Repertoire for Young Singers

You know, everyone pushes high notes—everyone in the world. You don't age a voice by pushing high notes. You fatigue and make a voice sound older by pushing in the middle. So, the guys who want to do pure Verdi too early, they're too young to be singing over such thick orchestration in the middle voice. *Bel canto* operas are in the same range, but the orchestra is different. You don't have a lot of horns or brass. You have a lot of strings. So that's why it doesn't cost your cords so much.

Student Repertoire

The repertoire you have to learn as a student at a university is ridiculous. I love *Lieder*, but it has nothing to do with how you get a career as a singer. Nothing. You have to learn to sing. You need to learn to sing composers like Mozart, Donizetti, and Bellini and get your skills ready to try to make a career as a performer. And all these people say, "Oh, you have to do Ned Rorem." Well, I love Ned Rorem songs, but they have nothing to do with anything!

Career Advice

The Right Age to Start Serious, Professional Voice Training

We have taught some really young kids, and that has been a mistake. I think twenty-two or twenty-three is a good age for intense, serious, professional training. That's the perfect age, because they have had some life experience. They've been away from home. They've partied and lived. Singers have to be good singers, but they have to have life experience to portray the drama.

Audition Self-Talk

Just go in and say to yourself, "This is me! If you don't like it, screw you! I'm going to be at the Met in five years. I know it, so get out of my way."

Voice Teaching

On Teaching

Our job as teachers is to release and protect the talent. Teaching is very simple in a way. It is just hard to show students how simple it is to build their instruments and undo all the other stuff. You have to get out of the way and let the talent work. People love to mess with a good vocal instrument. Half of the time you're just pulling off layers of stuff that isn't helping them. Our choral tradition in America is dangerous if you have a big voice because they will always ask you to sing quieter and blend. They shut you up.

Teaching the Fundamentals

José van Dam gave an interview ten years ago in *Opera News*. He said he wanted to start a singing school in Belgium. He said, "I want to go take five to ten kids. I would teach them only three or four things. I would teach them how to breathe properly, open the mouth, lift their soft palates, and just vocalize their vowels. In five years, I'd have great singers." They teach kids too much.

On Being a Student

You have vowels. There are five positions. There is a reason why classical arts are based upon very basic repetitions. When ice skaters do difficult jumps, they are performing a combination of simple movements that you must do with your body. Singers do the same thing: they must repeat basic movements and then learn to get out of the way and let the talent and brain do the work.

Everyone has an instrument to some degree. Every kid in this school has an instrument that will lead them to a career if they are brave and let their voices develop. But they must really learn to function and be able to remember and repeat instruction. It is the same thing in sports. Basketball players practice free throws for hours. They are just repeating the same motion. There's no mystery.

Working with Young Singers with Big Voices

I asked Margaret Harshaw once, "How do you find a Wagnerian?" She said, "You go to an undergraduate choir and you find the thickest, gluiest, wildest voice. Then you take them out of there, work for ten years, and you have a Wagnerian." Those voices don't fit into descriptions early, and these kids get treated like aliens. So, unless you can sing lightly, they make the big voices feel like they are no good, because, "Oh, you can't do this, you can't do that," not knowing that they should be doing other things. They don't allow big voices to be big.

Letting Young Tenors Be Young Tenors

When Michael Fabiano started out, everyone kept telling him that he sang too open. He was twenty-two years old. Thank goodness, he, for some reason, trusted me. He was in the documentary, *The Audition*, about the Metropolitan Opera Auditions. One of the judges was filmed making comments like, "he should be dead." But he's doing great and singing beautifully. I didn't want to take his voice, a big voice, and shut it down. He needed to grow that voice up properly.

Exercises

Exercise 1: (used with a soprano)

Instructions: This is a middle voice exercise.

Exercise 2: (used with a soprano)

Instructions: This is an upper register exercise. Get the palate up immediately after the consonants. Keep the air flowing through.

Exercise 3: (used with a soprano)

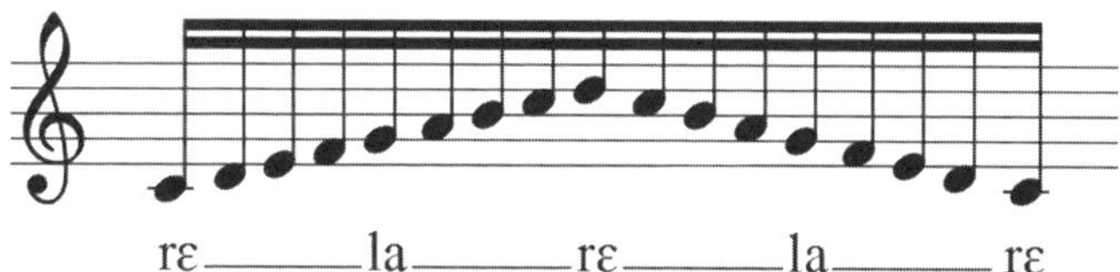

Instructions: Keep the jaw released. Don't help the scale by lifting your body. Use very little tongue movement and close the vowels. Your body needs to keep the air pressure moving.

Exercise 4: (used with a soprano)

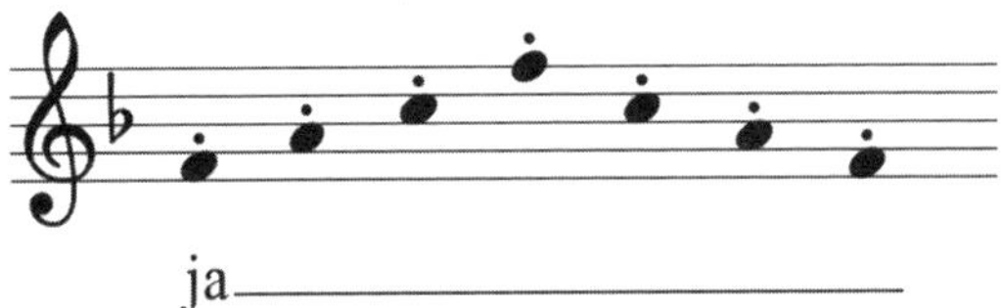

Instructions: Middle to high register exercise. Stay grounded.

Exercise 5: (used with a soprano)

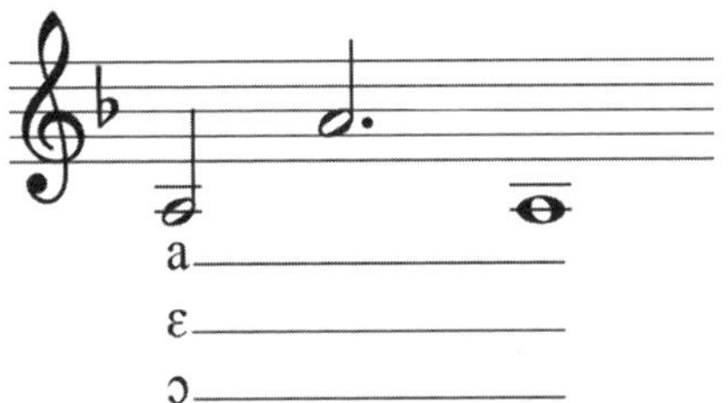

Instructions: Exercise to coordinate lower voice register mixing.

Exercise 6: (used with a soprano)

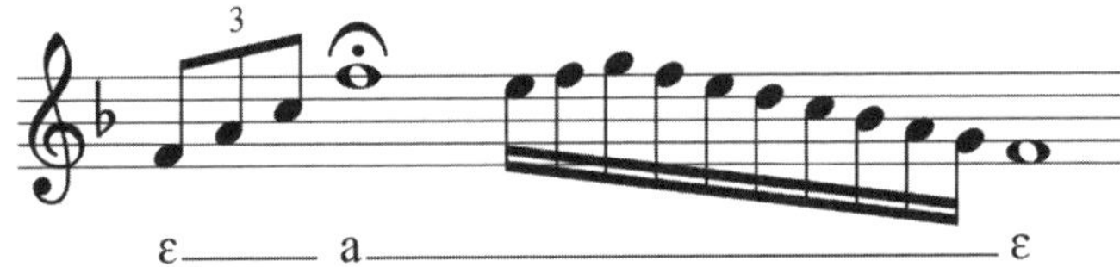

Instructions: Go right to the /a/. Don't find space in the /ɛ/. This is a very fast exercise, so you have to trust.

Exercise 7: (used with a soprano)

Exercise 8: (used with a tenor)

Exercise 9: (used with a tenor)

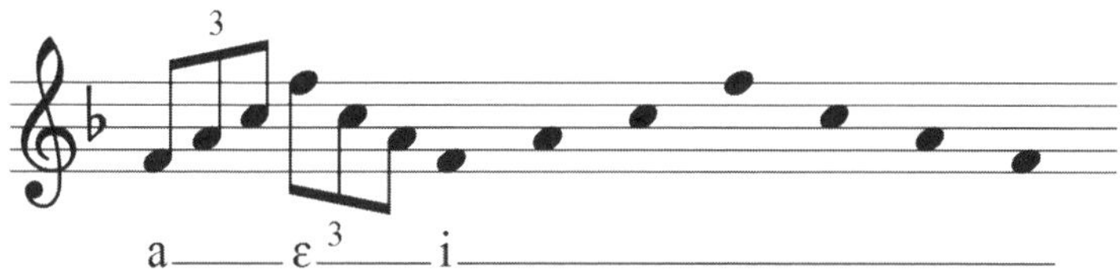

Exercise 10: (used with a tenor and a soprano)

Exercise 11: (used with a tenor)

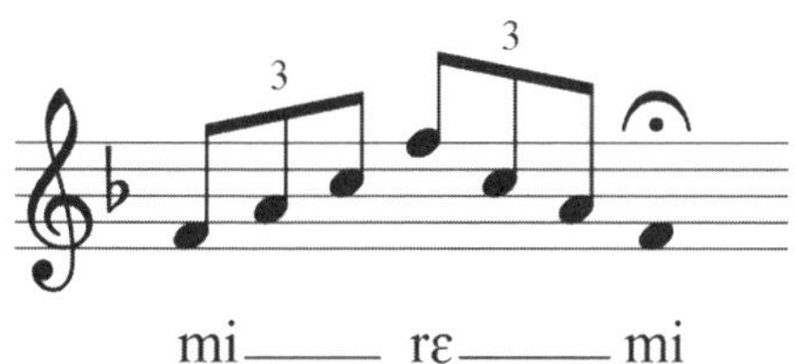

Instructions: Sing it right in the front.

Exercise 12: (used with a tenor)

Instructions: Move that tongue like crazy. Don't be afraid of the /bla/. Use a really nasty sound for the /gɔ/.

Exercise 13: (used with a tenor)

Exercise 14: (used with a tenor)

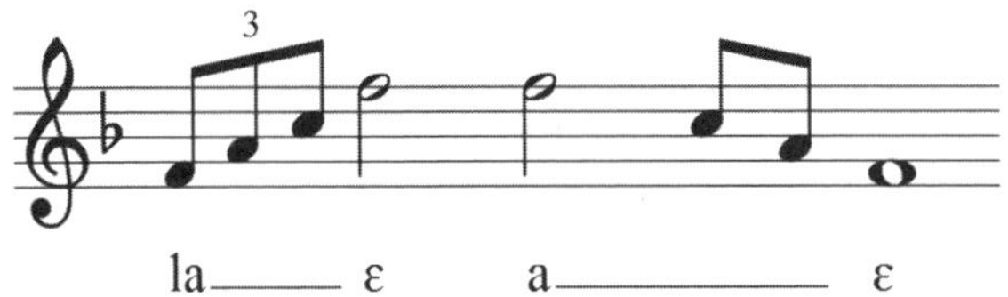

Instructions: Scoop the onset of the /a/ on top a few times and then take it out and keep the onset very suspended.

Exercise 15: (used with a tenor)

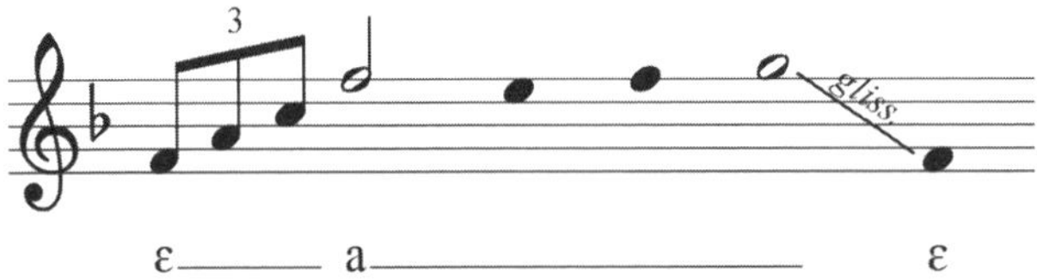

Instructions: Just soar for a second. Feel the anchor. Be aware of how active your breath is. Let it be physical.

Exercise 16: (used with a bass)

Exercise 17: (used with a bass)

Exercise 18: (used with a bass)

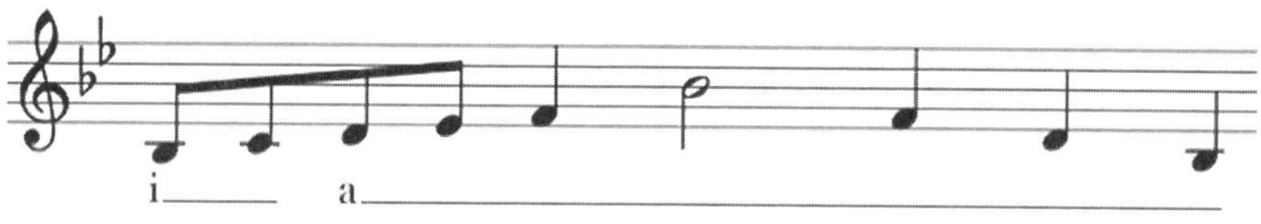

Exercise 19: (used with a bass, a baritone, and with tenors)

Exercise 20: (used with a bass and with tenors)

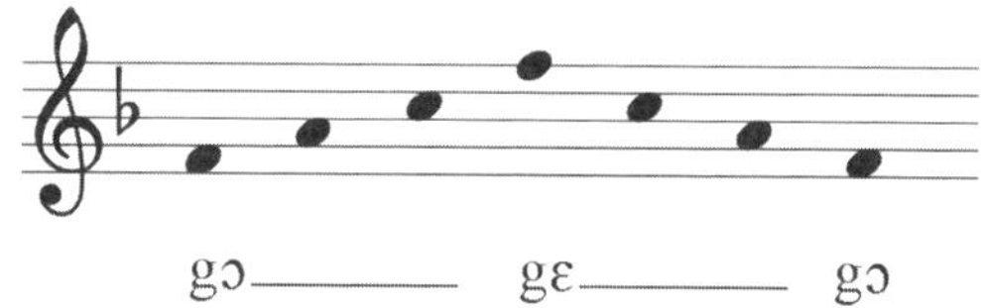

Instructions: Think down the higher you go. It doesn't go up. Drop your mouth. Whatever comes out, comes out. I want simple. Don't make it complicated.

Exercise 21: (used with a bass and a mezzo soprano)

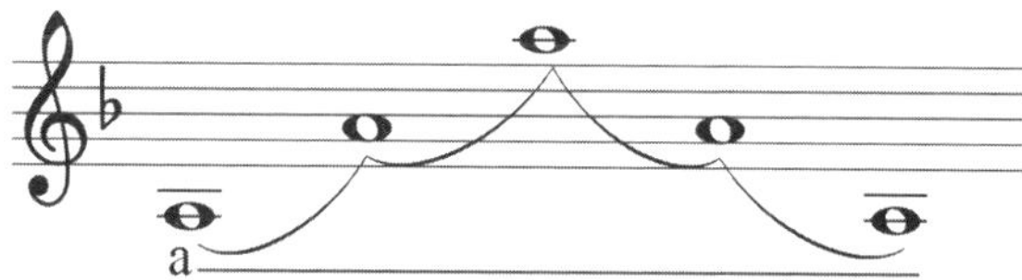

Instructions: Make sure your vowels are right, your body is connected, your breath is working, and just go. It's like you vomit out sound. If you try to control that, you'll never succeed.

Exercise 22: (used with a mezzo soprano)

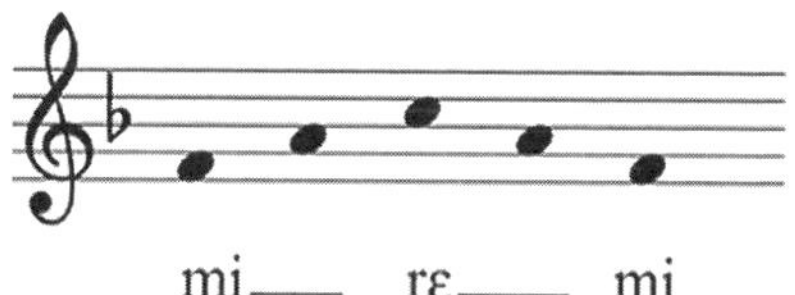

Exercise 23: (used with a mezzo soprano)

Exercise 24: (used with a mezzo soprano and a baritone)

Instructions: Sing a little less strongly as you go up. Feel how the air carries you.

Exercise 25: (used with a mezzo soprano)

Instructions: Go to the top. Lift your palate and make sure you're right on the vowel. Don't add space and then go for the vowel. Go for the vowel. Get the tongue more involved. You can't just sing /rɛ/ in a neutral position. Don't over-support the first /mi/. Sit on it.

Exercise 26: (used with a mezzo soprano)

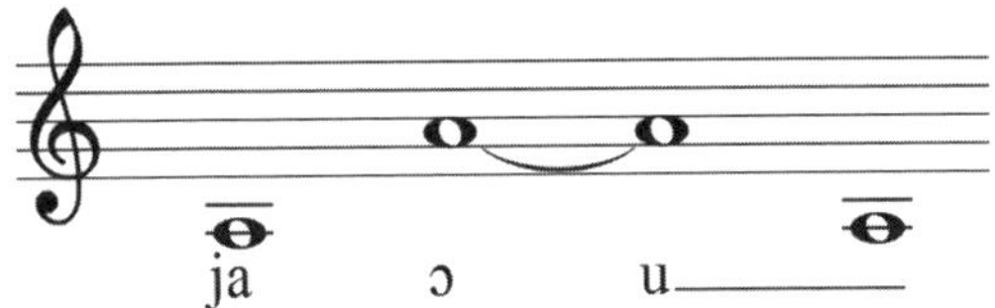

Exercise 27: (used with male singers and a mezzo soprano)

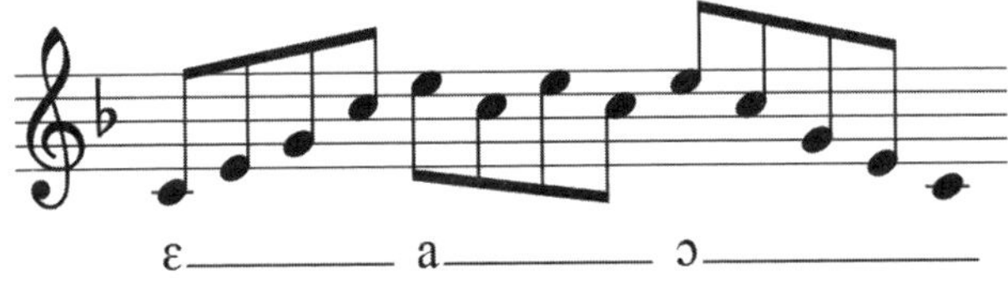

Instructions: Use your body. Always remember the Caruso Box. For high notes, just open the box, and they will appear. Feel the connection.

Exercise 28: (used with male singers and a soprano)

Instructions: Lift your palate. Don't sing lazy. Use an /ɛ/ in the tongue but leave the space of the /a/. Make the tongue form the vowel rather than just closing up your mouth.

Exercise 29: (used with a tenor)

Instructions: Give me a little more Italian /rɛ/. Use your anchor and then turn it. Use the /r/ to keep your anchor all the way down.

Exercise 30: (used with a tenor)

Exercise 31: (used with a tenor)

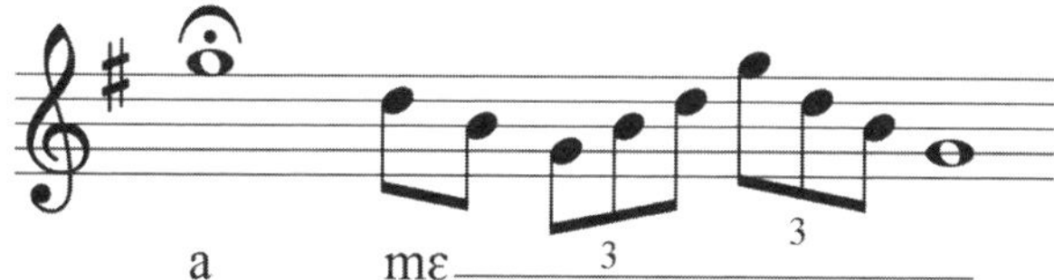

Instructions: Move your air. Don't scoop the onset. Inhale the vowel and the pitch.

Exercise 32: (used with a soprano)

Instructions: Really feel your jaw open. Keep the vowel. Use a nasty, horrible /ɛ/. When you sing it slowly, add a dome /ʌ/ with the vowel as the main shape inside of it. Don't change the vowel when you add the space.

Exercise 33: (used with a soprano)

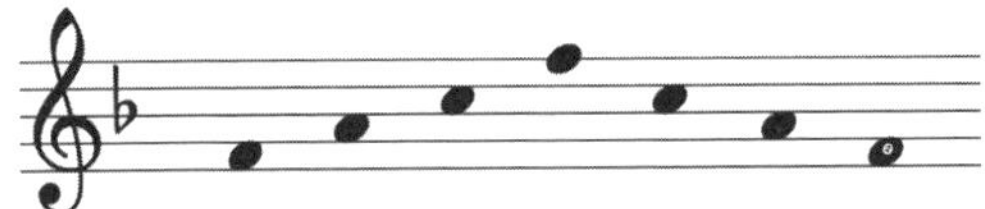

kɛ:i kɛ:i kɛ:i kɛ:i kɛ:i kɛ:i kɛ:i

Instructions. Use the diphthong to let you relax the back of the tongue. Don't stop the air for the /k/.

Exercise 34: (used with a soprano)

Instructions: Sing farther back. Find a deeper position. Keep the support active as you go the small vowel /u/. It's all in the back. Tilt your head back. Make sure the back of your neck is straight and released.

Exercise 35: (used with a soprano)

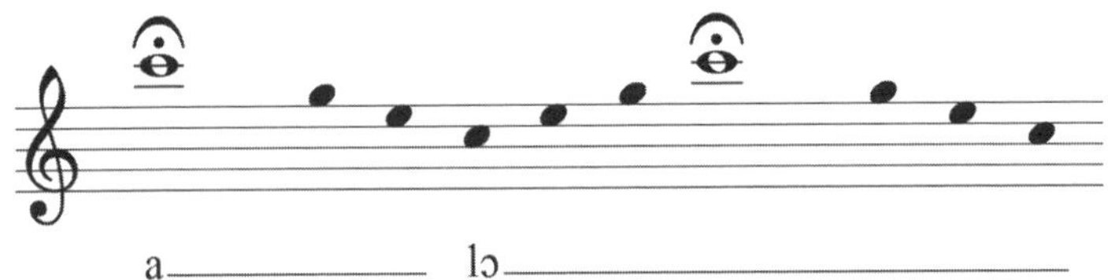

Instructions: Stay low. Use the air and the elevator of breath to take you back up. Don't lead with your throat – it doesn't move. Let the air pressure carry you.

Exercise 36: (used with a soprano)

Instructions: Feel a big /a/. Put your head back. Don't tuck your chin. Go back for the high note.

Exercise 37: (used with a soprano and a bass)

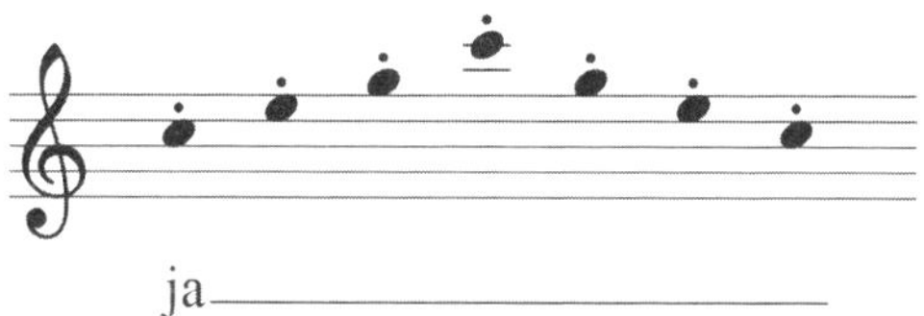

Instructions: (for a soprano) Let the air pressure carry you. Don't reposition anything. I don't want to hear the sound go up into your head. Leave it down here. Don't try to make space in your throat. You almost need to close your throat to sing staccato. Just pop air. (for a bass) You have to allow it to go into your head. Right now, the upper notes are too open because you are semi-belting. Put it inside. Close it. Let it turn over. Go up behind your tongue. Don't go into your mouth. Play with these every day for three minutes. You have to get used to not letting the throat be the ball of the attack; feel how the air does all the work. You have no responsibility for anything but the vowel.

Exercise 38: (used with a soprano)

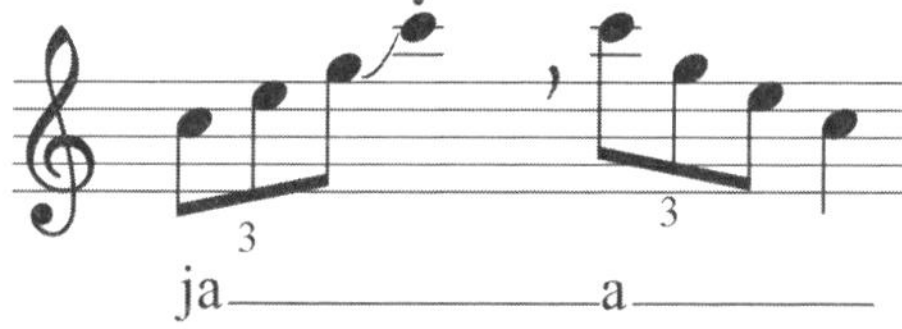

Exercise 39: (used with a soprano)

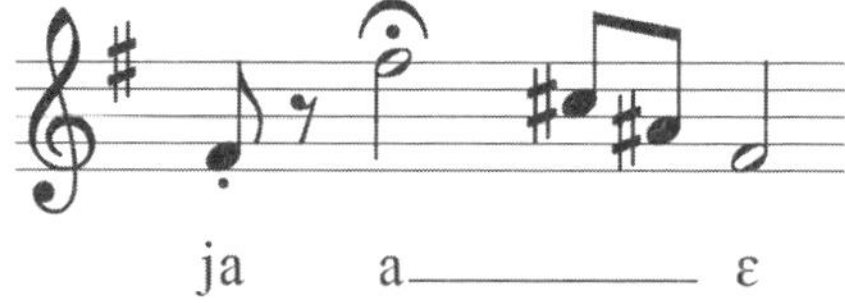

Instruction: I want just the vowel up there. I don't want to hear you mix sound. Thinking of the vowel should be enough to close the cords and hook everything up. Trust the vowel; it's the only thing you can do.

Exercise 40: (used with a baritone)

Exercise 41: (used with a baritone)

Exercise 42: (used with a baritone)

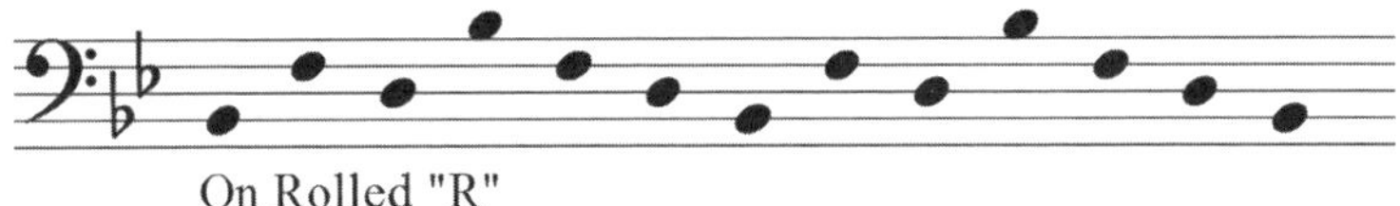

Instructions: Keep flopping that tongue! If you feel that vibrato or a “whoop,” the air pressure is not right. If the air pressure dips at all, it’s going to move that vibration. This is a great exercise to do in the morning during a shower.

Exercise 43: (used with a baritone)

Exercise 44: (used with a bass)

Exercise 45: (used with a bass)

Exercise 46: (used with a bass)

Instructions: Release your head for me. Mix it. Don't close it completely. Let the air leave you.

Exercise 47: (used with a bass)

Exercise 48: (used with a bass)

Exercise 49: (used with a tenor)

Instructions: Use the tip of the tongue for /rɛ/. Keep the vowel open.

Exercise 50: (used with a tenor)

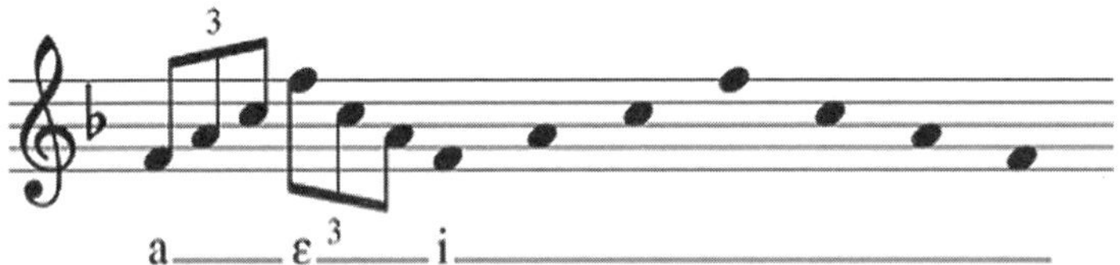

Exercise 51: (used with a tenor)

GEORGE SHIRLEY

Opera singer George Shirley was born on April 18, 1934 in Indianapolis, Indiana, to Irving and Daisy Shirley. By age four, he had begun performing, joining his mother and father as a musical trio within the Indianapolis church community. His musical acumen earned him a scholarship to Wayne State University, where he performed in his first musical drama, *Oedipus Rex,* with the Men's Glee Club in 1955. He graduated that same year, receiving his B.S. in Music Education.

In 1955, Shirley became the first African American high school music teacher in the city of Detroit. A year later, after being drafted into the Army, he became the first African American to sing with the U.S. Army Chorus, where, influenced by fellow choir members, he decided to pursue a career in opera. In 1961, he won first prize in the Metropolitan Opera Auditions, thus becoming the first African American tenor to be awarded a contract with that company, where he performed from 1961 through 1973. He performed major roles in more than twenty operas, often singing with fellow African American opera pioneers Leontyne Price, Martina Arroyo, Reri Grist, and Grace Bumbry. During and after his stint with the Metropolitan Opera, Shirley was a sought around the globe, appearing in productions in London, Italy, San Francisco, Washington D.C., Chicago, Boston and a host of other cities. Shirley also won a Grammy Award for a recording of his performance in Mozart's *Così fan tutte*.

In 1980, Shirley joined the faculty of the University of Maryland as a professor of voice. In 1985, the University honored him with a Distinguished Scholar-Teacher Award. In 1987, he returned to the Detroit area as a professor of voice at the University of Michigan, and five years later, he was named the Joseph Edgar Maddy Distinguished University Professor of Voice. In 2007, Shirley was named the Joseph Edgar Maddy Distinguished University Emeritus Professor of Voice upon his retirement.

On April 29, 2014 Mr. Shirley was honored during the 53rd NATS National Conference with the organization's Lifetime Achievement Award.

The Interview

RR: *You spoke about a support/pressure relationship during the lessons. Would you explain more about that?*

GS: The image that I think best describes the phenomenon of support is a mechanism of pneumatic and hydraulic pressure. I imagine that I have an elevator shaft from the center of my body to my throat. As I sing up the scale, I imagine that the pressure rises with pitch. It's like a rising elevator that pushes air pressure upward starting around the sternum.

RR: *Do you feel it close to the solar plexus?*

GS: I feel it around the solar plexus, because that's where the nerve endings come together. When I'm really emotionally involved in my singing, I can feel all those muscles across my back become firmer. That's where I feel the emotion. It makes my ribcage feel larger without pushing or pulling or squeezing anything to make that happen.

RR: *Which muscles do you feel contracting?*

GS: Put your hands on me. If I sing up the scale [RR comment: as he sang, I felt his abdominals become very taut], I don't do anything consciously to apply pressure anywhere in the support system. It's all mind over matter. It's like a piston pushing pressure up in the center of my body, which I assume is applying the subglottal air pressure that I need. I can feel this sort of tuck itself in a bit [the hypogastric region].

RR: *I felt those muscles come up just a little bit, but this stayed wide here.*

GS: Right. But I didn't do it consciously. It was a result of my thinking about the pressure rising in the shaft I imagine in middle of my body. If I'm getting the physical and vocal response I want in response to this image, then that's what it's about. I call it *pneudraulic* pressure, which is actually a word that describes an instrument that combines both hydraulic and pneumatic principles. When I get kids to imagine and respond to that, it simplifies the process. One school says you need to push down and out. Another school says you need to pull up and in. We get involved in ways that interfere with what will naturally happen in our bodies if we trigger it with our minds.

RR. *Does imagery lead to more natural body function?*

GS: I try to use imagination, which is what I think they did in the old days before they talked about the diaphragm and starting writing treatises on voice. When I went to Glyndebourne in 1966, I went up to London to study with E. Herbert-Caesari, who wrote that whole series of books, including *The Voice of the Mind*. He was trained in the old Italian school, which taught students to work through imagination and mental intention. Nowadays, we try to activate physically what should be activated mentally. We try to activate physically by pushing and pulling, which just interferes with the process. When we sing, we imagine. We imagine the pitches, words, and how to communicate. If we apply that same imaginary power to breath support, it starts to make all the sense in the world.

Herbert-Caesari would begin lessons with rapid scales. He never slowed down, even when we both knew darn well I wasn't hitting all of those notes. What was he after? He was making me think faster, because you can't sing anything any faster than you can think it. He knew that the more successfully I thought, the more technique would catch up with my thoughts and make everything looser, lighter, and easier.

RR: *How long would you work on the scales during the lesson?*

GS: About seven minutes. Then we'd go on to other things. That's the strongest impression that I have of those lessons. His books are amazing. The forward that Gigli wrote really describes the way I was trained. That's what I do and the way I think. Everything we read about the old Italian School singers talks about the phenomenal control they had over their voices. It makes sense that they spent years mastering that way of thinking.

The old teachers knew something. If you sit in front of a monitor during laryngoscopy and think a five-tone scale, what would you see? You'd see your vocal folds making little responses to your thoughts. These old guys knew that the mind controls those little muscles in the larynx even before endoscopy was invented. It's not all physical.

RR: *I also like very much how much you concentrate your work on the ascent into the passaggio. It is very similar to what I read in [Paola] Novikova's writings. Can you tell me more about your approach?*

GS: I simply try to inculcate an understanding of what happens when those registers come together and try to shake hands. It's the weakest part of every human voice. You have to understand how to affect the joining of registers using the support. When the support works properly, then spaces open up. Things happen when you are connected to your pneudraulic support.

The vowel needs to change through the middle voice. That trick is Berton Coffin's, not mine. The rule is that the pitch [GS thumps his cheek while forming the vowel shapes so the pitch changes] governs the space, not the vowel. The vowel has to fit into the space corresponding to that pitch. If I find the pitch and say /a/, only one /a/ is going to come out of that space. Don't change the space to get /a/. That's the vowel for that pitch. Not for a lower pitch [sings a lower pitch]. If I change the pitch the vowel distorts.

RR: *When you demonstrate that principle, I notice that the front of your mouth is not quite as wide open as when you imitate what students usually do.*

GS: Yes, it is in a rounder shape. What is helpful is to think of a small vowel.

RR: *Is it helpful for both males and females?*

GS: I think so. One must take into account the physical attributes of the singer. That's the problem of trying to learn by observing an individual. There are differences in physiology that change the way the concept appears externally. If your concept of the small vowel is right as you ascend, it will come out the right way.

I was invited to a little after-party in a New York City club on the east side where I sat between Giovanni Martinelli and Tito Schipa and listened to these guys trade stories. I used to be five-foot-nine, but they were both shorter. But they had heads, necks, and chests about twice as big as mine, if not more. Schipa's voice was very lyrical and Martinelli's was like a vibrant roar, but they were built the same way. They didn't have to think about diaphragms with that build. They just did it. In this science-based century, there's been so much focus on the muscles involved and what happens when you sing, which is great, but we've gotten away from what these old singers....

RR: *Intrinsically knew?*

GS: Yes. I've taught in Cape Town, South Africa a few times. The quality of voice I heard in the young black singers who came from the townships was the same kind of bright, ringing sound in those Italian singers. Perhaps because they both came from rural areas where they called out over the fields. If you close your eyes and listen to the students at the South African College of Music in Cape Town you can hear it. It is hair-raising.

Pretty Yende came from the South African College of Music. She won first place in the Belvedere Competition in every category several years ago. She became a young artist at La Scala and made her Met debut to great acclaim. She is one of the most phenomenal young singers I've heard in my life. That Italianate [makes a roaring sound] in the voice is there. Many American singers from the south have it too. Then they take a lesson and get so involved in the diaphragm, pushing, pulling, grabbing, and squeezing. There must be a way to teach these students so that they can stand on stage and sing from the soul with a sound that grabs people.

RR: *When you hear a singer for the first time in an audition or a performance, what are you looking for? What must a singer have to be successful in this career?*

GS: Intonation is essential. If you sing out of tune, nobody's going to hire you, even if you have the greatest voice in the world. Sometimes people can sing out of tune because of technical problems, so it's my job to identify whether it can be corrected or not. That can be particularly difficult with young singers. With younger singers, you have to listen for a singing sense, good intonation, and something in the sound that says it's worth developing. If a kid comes in and sings with no imagination or musicality, that's a problem.

RR: *So size, timbre, range?*

GS: Size is less important than the timbre. Range can be developed. If there are six or seven notes in the voice that say, "Wow!" and are in tune, then that's somebody I'd like to spend some time working with to see what's possible.

There was a young lady with a very light, lyric soprano voice who graduated from here over a decade ago. Her voice did not show much operatic potential, but she was very sweet, very musical, and a pleasure to work with. She went to Germany and began to focus on early music. Since then, she has made an impressive career for herself in early music, which fits her voice, her personality, and her intelligence. The voice is not exceptional in the operatic sense. So, it's really hard to sit back and say no from the beginning.

RR: *You talked a lot to students about intonation during the vocalises, especially the half-steps. I remember you said, "Half-steps are a kick in the pants."*

GS: They will kill you. If you don't anticipate them before they happen, the pitch will drop, and then everything else is flat.

RR: *So, when a singer comes to you, what do you think you bring to his or her voice?*

GS: When I hear a voice develop more core, range, or another extension from what the singer initially had, then I know that some of the things I'm trying to get across are taking root. It's the student who does the work. I have to put the ideas out there and see what a student does with them. When it doesn't reach a student, I try to recast that information in a different way. I've had my failures and, thank God, some successes. My way of trying to explain things doesn't always impact the person I'm working with. Sometimes I'll see growth when they go to someone else. Fine. All we want is to see this person advance, because I don't have all of the keys for every individual who comes to me for assistance. I try to learn from every lesson, from every individual with whom I've worked, to expand my storehouse of information and my repertoire of self-expression.

RR: *You have a strong sense of curiosity and creativity that you bring to your teaching.*

GS: Well, thank you. I like the students to enjoy learning. I like to enjoy teaching. I believe that if they feel less threatened by me in this process, they're liable to learn more. It's my job to create what's called a heuristic atmosphere in which they can learn from themselves. In the final analysis, their understanding of something may be different than mine. I say, "Look, you sang those tones so beautifully and effortlessly. If you were to tell me that during that moment you pictured yourself standing in the middle of the room on your head with your head in a bucket of water, I say, 'Cool. Do that! Think that!'" Whatever triggers the right kind of response. It's not monolithic. I'm not going tell you to stop if it's working.

I think the most important teacher I had was Cornelius Reid. Cornelius was the one man who really got me to the point of realizing what was going on inside of the instrument itself. That was of great value to me. He was controversial, no doubt about it. He didn't believe in support, like those Italians I was talking about who said, "I don't really think about it. I just open up and sing." I think this is true for those people for whom the voice works properly. For those of us who have difficulties or who need to have that understanding of the physical processes when we sing, we should be made aware of what's missing until it becomes second nature. Then we no longer need to think about it. Out of all of the teachers I worked with in New York over the years, Cornelius was the one I stayed with the longest.

RR: *He worked a lot with registration, as I recall.*

GS: Yes, that was his whole thing. He would start with isolating the registers, which is anathema to a lot a people. But basically, he just isolated falsetto and chest register and joined them together. I think some singers got into a little trouble because they tried hooting [demonstrates] and didn't allow the subglottal air pressure to work with the instrument. But the "hooty" sound certainly wakes up the top of the voice [demonstrates]. And then it naturally connects the higher you go. Then you come down singing in full voice. But he really didn't talk about support because he didn't really believe in it. I think he found the whole idea of support confusing when he studied voice. It never worked for him, so he just worked on trying to strengthen the mechanism itself without getting to subglottal activity.

RR: *Do you have a system for choosing operatic repertoire for students?*

GS: I don't have a particular system. With art songs, I encourage the students to choose their own material. If they come in with something that's unwise, I'll say no. I want it to be something they choose because they love to sing it.

I have this young tenor with a connected falsetto extension. He can sing a high-F^6 that will blow your socks off. It's easy for him. It's a beautiful sound. He's beginning to link it up now. He comes in with operatic arias like "Nessun dorma." He can sing it, but I told him to bring art songs instead.

He's beginning to link this up in the manner that [Carlo] Bergonzi linked up his top range. Carlo made his operatic debut in 1951 as a baritone. He came back a year later as a tenor, and I asked him once between acts in *Lucia*—I was covering him that night—about whom he had studied with. He said, "*Nessuno. Non c'é maestri per tenore*" [there aren't any teachers for tenors]. "*Io fatto tutto me stesso*" [I did everything myself]. I asked him how he did it. He answered, "The narrow vowels through the *passaggio* and the breath."

I sang with him a lot. I sang Malcom to his Macduff and I had the opportunity to stand close to him and hear him negotiate the break. He didn't have the chest power of Tucker and Corelli and those guys. It was this fully connected and basically falsetto mix. You aren't aware of it when you hear the recordings. You weren't aware of it when you were in the hall. It always traveled to the back. It was a mailed fist in a velvet glove. I could hear him make the change, and it worked beautifully with no break. He would get this plangent, full, warm, but ringing sound. He was a true *tenore di grazia*. He sang in the way tenors sang in Rossini's time before Duprez belted it from the chest. It was flexible. He could do anything he wanted to.

RR: *And Bergonzi did this all on his own?*

GS: That's what he told me. He was a very intelligent guy. That's what this young tenor has. It is exciting as all get out now that he's beginning to join it up. I tell him, "You don't have to over-sing it, just go up there and let it sing. It's going to be loud enough. It's beautiful. It's vibrant. It's bright." He's a *tenore di grazia*.

People don't understand the power of the falsetto. It's part of the voice and it has a function. For those people who can start from a whisper and crescendo into full voice like Gedda and others, that's what they're starting with. It's a sigh. I've never had that kind of facility, and my voice could just never sigh into things. Whenever I'd try to do something at the top that was at all like that, coaches would say, "Oh, no, that's falsetto."

I was put into the cast of *Simon Boccanegra* back in 1964. There's one place at the end during Boccanegra's death scene that Gabriele Adorno sings a big A^4 and decrescendos to a pianissimo. I tried that in a coaching session. I didn't want to sing it forte and I felt it was inappropriate. So, I went to the performance with Colzani and Tebaldi and decided to sing it that way. I felt good about it. Harriet Johnson said I could do anything with my voice the next day in her review. I have an underground recording of that taken off the radio. It's clean as a whistle. I realized that this is what people were trying to keep me away from all those years, but it was there. If I had more faith in that, I could have developed it even more.

I covered Corelli in *Romeo and Juliet* in 1967, during a time when the Met wanted to institute a policy to give the cover cast an orchestra rehearsal. Apparently, it killed the orchestral players, so the policy did not last long. So, for that first orchestra rehearsal, Corelli and Freni were in costume but not made-up. And Jeannette Pilou and I were not in costume. We sang the first act directly after they did. When I came to the aria, I thought, "Hell, I'm going to sing the final B-flat^4 piano, because that's what it is." And I surprised myself. It came out clean and clear and I thought, "Gee." Corelli heard it in his dressing room with the monitors. The next day in the dress rehearsal he sang it forte and then did a diminuendo to nothing. I thought, "That magnificent S.O.B! And he did it that way every time. He had that *voce chiaro* in it. It was an amazing voice.

Parting Thoughts

I was honored to be in the presence of one of the true living legends of our art. George Shirley broke racial barriers and had an impressive fifty-four-year international career, sharing the stage with many of the greatest singers in the world. As a teacher, he has distinguished himself in academic and professional circles. He has a youthful energy and quest for knowledge. Despite having achieved such eminence in our art, he is disarmingly humble and gracious.

His concept of breathing was fascinating to me. I'll be the first to admit that the term *pneudraulic* was new to me. I pondered it greatly on my drive back home and looked up the term as soon as I arrived.

From Dictionary.com:
pneudraulic (adjective)
1. of or relating to a mechanism involving both pneumatic and hydraulic action.
pneu(matic) + (hy)draulic

pneumatic (adjective)
1. of or relating to air, gases, or wind.
2. of or relating to pneumatics.
3. operated by air or by the pressure or exhaustion of air:
4. Zoology. containing air or air cavities.

hydraulic (adjective)
1. operated by, moved by, or employing water or other liquids in motion.
2. operated by the pressure created by forcing water, oil, or another liquid through a comparatively narrow pipe or orifice.
3. of or relating to water or other liquids in motion.

When I specifically asked him about this concept, he had me place my hands on his torso and feel what he was doing as he sang. He does exactly what he says he does; his lower abdominals move in a little, while his solar plexus muscles move up and in. His body is solid, and his singing is still enviable. He draws this map of breathing in his own body very clearly and works on these ideas with each student. However, as he said earlier, he is quite flexible if something else works better for the student. The technique doesn't drive him, his ears do. This is a quandary we face from time to time; we must let go of our technical approaches if something out of the norm works better for a student. When working with unusual or exceptional voices like many great singers likely had in their youth, we have to be willing to follow different paths. George diligently seeks the right answers for each student he works with.

Each student begins the lesson with a light vocalise. The influence of Cornelius Reid can be seen in the way he works with registration. Male and female students work the very top falsetto/whistle register early in the lesson. After that is established, he blends the registers through other exercises. His goal is to have the student's top voice feel like the bottom, and the bottom voice feel like the top. George is patient with students, but is clear and precise about his direction to them. He also allows students to rest between vocalises and during repertoire work through detailed score analysis and fine-tuning diction. He makes every singer speak the texts and understand the correct syllabic stress of every word.

As we discussed, George spends a good deal of time helping the students use their imaginations purposefully. The body can only do what the mind tells it to do. As I say in Carol Vaness' chapter, poor decisions lead to poor mechanics, which leads to poor results. If the brain gives the body clear, positive direction, singers are much more apt to negotiate their lines successfully. George talks about using breath intake and mind preparation to inspire the body to work optimally. I often joke with my students in the style of the book of Proverbs that, "As ye take the breath, so shall ye use it." The body must be prepared by the inhalation of the breath in a manifest way that is proportionately measured for the approaching vocal line.

Lesson Highlights

Breath Support/Control

Intention and Imagination in Breath Function

We tend to forget the motivational part of the breath intake. We want to do so much muscularly that we leave out the boss. The boss is that mass of gray matter that exists between our ears in our cranium that gets everything else to function the way you want it to function. If you imagine that internal pneudraulic pressure inside, it will make everything feel bigger without you trying to make your ribcage bigger in the wrong ways. If you imagine the pressure, you'll feel it. All of those muscles will respond, but they'll do so naturally, without your trying to isolate, pull, or push something. The power of imagination and the connection between the mind and your emotional center is in your solar plexus, where all your nerve endings come together. Your connection to that place is what allows you to express yourself. Breathe in what it is you want to say and what you want to feel. Breathe in what it is you want to accomplish. Chances are you're going to accomplish it.

Phonation

Vocal Onset

Errant onsets are a way of your voice telling you that the pneudraulic pressure and vowel are not right. Make sure you have the right vowel for the pitch. Give yourself enough time to breathe in and relax. Let that action ground you. Take a second after the intake to let your instrument get ready and then speak. Always have the way you want it to feel in your mind before you begin.

Resonance

Vowel Migration

The trick is to never sing the vowel at the bottom of your range that you should sing at the top, and vice versa. You have to allow things to migrate and change so that the lower starting vowel ends up as something else on top.

Articulation

Diction and Legato

Legato is always necessary, even if you are using good pronunciation. Don't sacrifice the line for clean consonants. Use the consonants to tie the legato together. Taste the words and always let the pronunciation communicate a sense of meaning.

Exercises

Exercise 1: (used with a tenor)

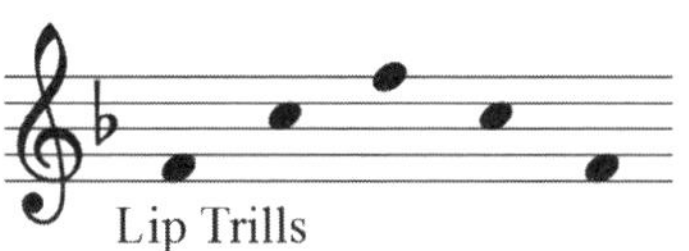

Instructions: Use just enough energy to make it work. Start in an anchored position. Switch into falsetto when you need to. Breathe in with the intention of what you want to do. Anticipate what you need to accomplish.

Exercise 2: (used with a soprano and a tenor)

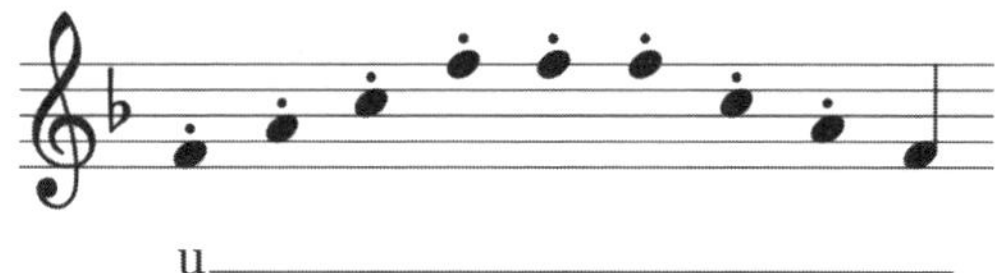

Instructions: Short and crisp falsetto arpeggios ascending in half steps. Let the top note get a little rounder in your mind. Use this through the middle register all of the way up into whistle or falsetto register. When you release a little more, there will be more space in the back.

Exercise 3: (used with a soprano, a tenor, and a baritone)

Instructions: This is an exercise for the middle voice. Be careful to sing the half steps accurately. Think upward as you descend. Get the back-space open before you sing, but don't sing the vowels back there. Make sure that these vowels exist in the front half of your mouth. Use good pneudraulic support

Exercise 4: (used with a soprano, tenor, and baritone)

Instructions: Sing with a legato line and let everything rise and ride on that pressurized breath. It's not pulling or pushing; it's mind over matter. To get the speed, sing every pitch in your mind a split second before it comes out of your mouth.

Exercise 5: (used with a soprano and tenor)

Instructions: *Molto legatissimo*. This exercise is slower in tempo and with deliberate glissandi connecting the notes. Begin lightly in the lower middle voice and continue into the top voice. Feel the internal pressure.

Exercise 6: (used with a soprano and tenor)

Instructions: These two-octave exercises begin on the lowest pitch the student is able to sing without pressing. Each scale pattern rises by half-steps and is performed in one breath.

Exercise 7: (used with a baritone)

Instructions: Make sure the vowel doesn't go back when you do the slide upward. Keep the sense that the vowel stays in front. Make sure the bottom is substantial, not loud, but authoritative.

Exercise 8: (used with a baritone and tenor)

Exercise 9: (used with a baritone and a tenor)

Instructions: Support, make the vowels small and frontal, and go right over the bridge. The airflow should speed up, but it is also imperative that the pneudraulic pressure rises.

Exercise 10: (used with a baritone)

Instructions: Make sure the bottom note is stable.

Exercise 11: (used with a tenor)

Instructions: Keep your toes on the ground.

W. STEPHEN SMITH

MM & Hon. DAH, University of Arkansas; MPA, Oklahoma City University

W. Stephen Smith is currently a professor of voice at Northwestern University's Bienen School of Music. He previously served on the faculties at The Juilliard School, University of Houston, and was Chair of the Voice Department at the Saint Louis Conservatory of Music. Professor Smith also served as a vocal instructor for the Houston Grand Opera Studio from 1990 to 2003 and has held a position on the voice faculty of the Aspen Music Festival and School since 1996. Oxford University Press published his book, *The Naked Voice: A Wholistic Approach to Singing*, in 2007.

Smith's students include many of today's most noted artists, including Christine Brewer, Joyce DiDonato, Eric Owens, and Marietta Simpson. His students have performed principal roles at the world's leading opera houses, including the Metropolitan Opera, Royal Opera House at Covent Garden, Lyric Opera of Chicago, and La Scala, and have won numerous prestigious opera competitions, including the Metropolitan Opera

National Council Auditions at the district, regional and national levels. Apprentice programs where his students have studied and performed include Santa Fe, San Francisco, and Chautauqua Operas, Opera Theater of Saint Louis, and Wolf Trap.

Professor Smith has performed over forty roles in opera and musical theater and has been a soloist with the St. Louis Symphony and the Oklahoma Symphony. He has stage-directed twenty-two different productions and served as music director and conductor for several shows.

INTERVIEW

I had my chance to interview Stephen over dinner after I observed him teach. We started the conversation about one of his students, Joyce DiDonato.

SS: Her reason for singing is always to connect to people and share the music. When she began auditioning, Gayletha Nichols [Executive Director of the Metropolitan Opera National Council Auditions] and I both thought, "There's something pretty special in there."

RR: *Does that go back to the issue of authenticity you were talking about?*

SS: Yes. There was a real sense that she wanted so much to communicate, express, and give to her audience. She didn't have a natural instinct of how to use her voice well yet. But she was an interesting singer in every way, so she got some attention. She had gotten into Santa Fe and AVA, but not everyone was encouraging. It wasn't really until after she sang *Cenerentola* at Merola that people started saying, "Hmm, there is something really special in there."

RR: *One of the things I learned from you through a mutual student is the emphasis on a spoken onset; the idea of not trying to over-manipulate and over-stress muscles before singing really made a difference in my own teaching.*

SS: That's the basic concept: the onsets have to be quick and spontaneous. This over-preparation that singers do to make a particular sound using the muscles around the larynx, pressing the breath, and holding before you start takes a toll on your voice. The whole idea of initiating onset with less pretention, less set, and less entanglement is a big deal.

RR: *So, everybody goes through the exercises you describe in your book?*

SS: Yes.

RR: *Is this what you do in every lesson?*

SS: Mostly. With professional students, we may do things differently based upon their needs. Often a pro may come in and ask to do the exercises so I can keep track of how he or she is doing technically. Sometimes that's all we will do. Joyce [DiDonato] usually will do that for the first lesson or two when she comes in to see me. We just review the exercises to see how they're going, and then move on to repertoire/role work in the next three or four lessons.

RR: *Do you do any kind of other exercises with people?*

SS: I vary them from time to time. I sometimes change the vowel for the onset or use wider intervals for the wobble exercises. Using a fifth instead of a fourth makes the wobble exercise more challenging, but it's the same principle. I occasionally change the order of the vowels to /nu no na ne ni/ rather than /ni ne na no nu/ with some people who have difficulties beginning with a good /i/. They may start with a little less stiffness if they start with an /u/, but usually I try to stay with the system and see if they can do it. If they struggle, I will adjust, because you don't just teach a system. You teach a person. You have to adapt everything to that person, but the principles don't change at all. Everybody is taught exactly the same principles, and all these exercises are applicable to every single voice type and every single person.

RR: *That's what I like best about your system. It's adaptable.*

SS: That's really important. This is an approach that organizes information that has been out there for ages. It's logical, accessible, and straightforward, but it's still the fundamental information that you must communicate to each person. You have to listen very carefully to what students say and how they sing to make sure they are really getting it. Some students say, "Yes, I understand." But if you don't hear the right change in their singing, they really don't understand.

RR: *There's a sign on your wall that says, "He who knows and does not do, does not yet know."*

SS: Exactly. They still don't know. My job is to make it clear. I have to somehow get the idea through to them in a different way. So, I just try another way, and keep evolving and learning from my students.

It's boring to be predictable. I remember the summer before I went to Juilliard I thought, "Oh, my goodness. I'm going to teach at Juilliard. These people think I know what I'm talking about, but I'm just guessing!" So many people pretend that they know, but the fact is that everybody's guessing. Your guesses are better with experience—but they're still guesses. You don't know what's going to be effective with any one person. When I got to New York, I just said to myself that my guesses are as good as anybody else's guesses.

RR: *I notice that you take all the men through the falsetto. Do you find that it is ever counterproductive to their hooked-up, full singing in that range?*

SS: No. It's the particular way in which I teach the falsetto that keeps it from being counterproductive. Stephen Austin did a seminar on registers back in Houston when I was the [NATS] chapter president. I was reticent about it because I try to eliminate the sensation of registers with my approach. I don't like to talk about them in this regard. But it was eye opening because it was based on the *bel canto* pedagogy treatises. He described the subcategories of falsetto, including "open chink falsetto" and "closed chink falsetto."[10] I think a key to understanding falsetto is to remember that the vocal folds are not fully adducted. Only the outside tissue is vibrating, not the vocalis muscles. Singing this way feels a little false, a little off of the voice, a little disconnected. You can also have that kind of falsetto with the

[10] Editor's note: Open chink describes partial glottal closure in which a small opening remains at the posterior. Closed chink describes more complete glottal closure.

chink at the back closed, which makes the sound a little pointed. That's what countertenors commonly do. They're singing falsetto, but they use a closed chink falsetto, which pinches the back of the glottis. That adds a cut and edge in the tone that aids projection. But the problem is that our singing should never be closed chink, because if we completely close the chink, we're actually closing off the sound. When we're talking and using regular phonation, the chink is open. It's not held open or squeezed together. Falsetto with an open chink is the kind of falsetto I'm really working on. Typically, the countertenors using closed chink falsetto don't have longer than a ten-year career.

If you're singing closed chink falsetto, how do you blend into your chest voice? You have to learn how to blend into the chest voice but the chest voice cannot be closed chink. When you're young and everything's flexible, you can blend with the chink held closed. But you only can do that for a limited amount of time. Countertenors using closed chink falsetto develop a big hole in the voice after eight or ten years and their career's over.

RR: *I've never thought of it that way.*

SS: Learning an open chink falsetto makes it easy to blend into the real voice. I say, "Let the air just fall through and don't push it. Let just the edge of the folds vibrate." The sensation of an absence of compression, resistance, or tension is what we want when we sing fully. When you sing fully, you let the air flow through more generously, faster, which will suck the muscles in. The muscles are vibrating, but you're never stiffening them or squeezing them together. The breath flow itself is what makes you sound hooked up and connected. I believe that the way you sound the most hooked-up and connected is to *not* hookup or connect; let the flow of air be what hooks-up and connects the sound throughout the range. Once the vocal folds do come together and vibrate, very little air actually is escaping, but you still have the feeling that it's nothing but the flow of air that's bringing the cords together. So, the majority of the training is this whole concept of being on the air and looking for an open chink falsetto adjustment all the time. You want it to seem like your cords are only vibrating on the outside. Finding that vulnerability, that lack of squeeze, and the more energetic flow of air that results will suck the cords more into the sound. That's what will feel really connected.

RR: *So, the Bernoulli Effect.*

SS: Yes, the Bernoulli Effect. The muscles are vibrating when we talk. Correct, healthy talking has flow already built into it. We are always working for flow phonation, not this compression that we often hear. The more talented and strong the voice and ears are, the more you can sing really badly and still sound great.

Some of the greatest singers in the world, the greatest talents, the greatest legendary singers, don't always technically sing well. They are just amazingly talented because they have a great flow. They have a great ear. They have great passion, and they do a super job as far as communicating the art, but as far as singing technically, healthy, and freely, no. They're not marvels for that at all.

RR: *A lot of them break all the rules.*

SS: I've heard James Conlon say, "The perfect technique is Pavarotti," but perfect technique doesn't exist. You can't say, "This person is perfect. Go listen to him." You have to learn to be objective about everybody.

RR: *What do you look for in singers? What do you think you're drawn to?*

SS: I'm drawn to two things in a student: somebody who really wants to learn to sing better and believes I can help achieve that goal. That's my complete criteria. There are many immensely talented singers who come to me wanting to hear me say that they are talented and fabulous and wonderful. They just want affirmation. A lot of people want me to predict the future for them as a professional singer. I can describe what I hear in the voice quality and what I think a singer needs to do to be successful, but there are too many factors that determine professional success for anyone to predict what will happen. James Levine can say, "Yes, I like you. I'll give you a role at the Met." That can launch a career or possibly ruin a career. Some great singers never get that opportunity. They don't get a venue to show how great they are. I've seen it happen over and over and over again.

Singing artists must believe they have something to share. You only should be a singer if you feel compelled to do so, because you mostly will get criticism and discouragement. If you can be content doing anything else, do something else. But that has nothing to do with whether or not I would teach you. If you are really passionate and you want to learn how to sing, and I have the time, I would be happy to work with you. It's not really about your level of talent, just your desire to improve and willingness to work.

I currently have more people wanting my time than I have time to give. So, I have to make choices. Usually my very frank evaluation of what's not working weeds out a bunch of people. In New York everyone would say, "Don't go to Stephen Smith. Everybody with him has to start all over." I don't take singers where they are and just tweak. I go back to the essence, the foundation, and the principles that most singers have never been given. Many talented singers don't sound like they need foundational principles. It already sounds focused, well supported, balanced, beautiful, and expressive. So, people just tweak little details. But they still must work on the foundational principles of airflow and articulation even when they have no obvious issues with it. The work will serve them in the long term, rather than just relying on a good ear and a good throat.

Joyce DiDonato does almost everything right in the sense that she gives you herself and never holds back anything when she sings. She works hard to give you the character, the music, and herself. She does that as well as anybody I know and has developed the technique to be able to do it.

When she first started singing for agents, she had trouble generating any interest. She was ready to get out there and ready for an agent, so that wasn't the problem. I told her, "You are a kind, gracious person. If you go in and appear to be very self-starting, very ambitious, and go for it, they will think, 'Wow, I can make money off of her without working very hard.' If you go in and are very nice and self- effacing, they will think, 'It's going to be so much work to get her anywhere.'"

They often don't really know who's talented and who's not. They need to get a sense of your ambition.

What you need to do when you audition for an agent is to be businesslike. Your attitude needs to be clear. From the moment you walk through the door, to the time you walk out the door, you have to be thinking to yourself, "I going to be a superstar. Do you want a part of this money, or should I go to somebody else?" If they're not interested, shake the dust off your feet and go elsewhere. Save your really humble self for opera company auditions, because they are looking for kind, generous, well-prepared colleagues. But when you audition for an agent, you have to show your security and confidence.

So, she scheduled several more auditions and followed my advice. Most of them expressed interest in her. She sang the same repertoire for the same level of agents that she'd auditioned for two months earlier, but this time she ended up getting signed.

I think art is a personal expression that impacts somebody who encounters it. Our personal expression is actually pouring ourselves out and emptying ourselves. The sounds are the vehicle by which we are pouring our soul out to the audience. So instead of being about ego, it actually is a totally humbling experience. And if you give singers this gift, they can cherish it, appreciate it, or throw it in the river. But despite the fact that the audience has all those options, your job as an artist and a singer is still to reveal your inner self through the text and music.

Technique is engaging the art. It is teaching you how to pour yourself out. You are doing the job of the art by learning to sing in a freer, more efficient, and more empowered way.

RR: *What are you doing in the upcoming workshop on your book?*

SS: I work with ten singers and ten teachers for a week. The singers are required to have at least three years of college level training. All singers get two lessons from me and attend four master classes, two of which they sing in, and perform one or two opera scenes. Gene Roberts, a former student of mine who is now a college voice teacher and stage director, teaches the acting classes and directs the scenes. The program culminates in a gala opera scenes performance. The voice teachers attend five two-hour seminars during the week, observe all the students' lessons, and come to master classes. I basically do a hands-on kind of demonstration of my method in the seminars. They are required to have read the book by the time they get here.

The singers are like a lab for the teachers, because I accept college-level teachers who are interested in new ideas. They come to learn my approach and my techniques. We always do a concert finale that involves all the teachers and all the singers. The teachers and students participate together during the week and in the final gala performance, which gives them a sense of unity. It's very intense.

RR: *And then you're off to Aspen.*

SS: Yes, I leave the next day to go to Aspen with no time in between. My wife—who's a pianist and plays for a lot of my lessons—encouraged me to do master classes and workshops. Most teachers, to some degree, just simply learn to teach by teaching, just as we learn to sing by singing. But it's hard to learn effectively that way. I think there are a lot of teaching principles that can be passed along. I want everybody who wants to sing to be encouraged to sing. But if we encourage them to major in music, are we saying they can have a career when they clearly aren't going have a career? And can we predict who will and who won't?

RR: *There was a guy in the town where I grew up whose claim to fame was telling people their fortunes. He told HL Hunt [the oil tycoon], "You're going to be rich. You just need to figure out exactly how you're going to do it, and you will be very, very wealthy." HL Hunt was really poor at that time. So, if someone tells you that you're going to be really wealthy, and you go out and you take the risk, does that mean that just saying those words is enough to make you be successful? If he hadn't been told that, would he have still managed to achieve what he achieved?*

SS: Well, there are many failed singers who are bitter about not having a career and try to discourage almost everyone else. I try to teach people how to be self-actualized, empowered, and the most they can be as a singer. If you authentically give yourself to the art, it will sell itself.

Parting Thoughts

I found Stephen to be very open about himself and his beliefs about vocal technique. To get a much deeper understanding about his philosophy, be sure to read his book, *The Naked Voice: A Wholistic Approach to Singing*, published by Oxford Press in 2007. Stephen covers a great deal of material in the book, including physiology, technique, life as a singer, and the singing business. It is an all-encompassing book for every teacher and singer.

Some may be concerned that having everyone do the same exercises in the same sequence could lead singers to a generic sound. Despite this danger, I did not hear similar sounds from his students. Stephen develops each student's individual sound by concentrating on the process rather than pursuing a particular sound.

For me, one of Stephen's most integral ideas is his approach to positioning before singing. I believe this is key for every singer. Before we sing, the body, space, and breath must be prepared. Stephen cautions against unnecessary and static positioning to every singer. However, he also is adamant about providing a balance between positive and negative directives in teaching. If you tell yourself constantly not to do this and not to do that, then what are you going to do? When we drive, even though we don't want to hit the curb, we do not watch the curb. If we do, we will very quickly hit the curb because that is where our focus is. We instead focus on the road ahead and where we want to go. We must balance an awareness of what not to do with a positive mindset. As Stephen said during a lesson, "You cannot commit to inaction if you're going to do anything. You commit to action."

Lesson Highlights

Phonation

Vocal Onset and Offset

You must understand that you cannot onset perfectly every single time. Just feel empowered because you know what is better and what is worse. You can know what you're changing and what you need to do. This can be like biofeedback if you're doing it correctly. If you start on your cords, you have to shut it off that way, and then you're not on the breath. If your onset is on the breath rather than the cords, then you can just move your breath in different ways to get different responses and maintain the vowel. So, it's more than just onset that's important: it's onset, how you sustain, how you off-set, and how you inhale.

Resonance

Lip Protrusion

Bringing the lips forward is a technique for focusing the sound. It works, but it puts pressure on your voice. There are teachers who teach that method to focus and narrow the vowel. If you have been singing wide, it really does make it go to a different place that is more resonant and colorful. The technique works, but in the long term it adds stiffness to the production.

Making Space for Vowels

The issue really has to do with this concept of space. For your voice to sound warm, beautiful, and colorful, it needs to have the sound and the feeling of space. However, you should never *make* space. Every time you try to make space you make it like all of us do: you drop your jaw, lift your soft palate, and depress your tongue. When you sang the exercise on /a/ with the teeth completely together, you couldn't really make space like that, but you could still get the sound and feeling of space because the base of the tongue and the soft palate went up without you physically manipulating them. If you just think about the vowel, the tongue and soft palate go up. Think that vowel with your teeth together. We wouldn't sing an /a/ with our teeth completely together outside of this exercise, however.

The second thing you must do is to allow the cords to be flabby or loose enough so the air can flow through them. If the air flows through the cords, it actualizes the vowel by filling in the spaces. So, if I do a closed /e/ here, there is no space in that vowel or sound. It's all *chiaro*: a clean, clear, bright sound. I'm in a range where it's not killing my throat, but you can tell there's not enough warmth in that. So, when somebody sings that way, most people will say, "No, give it some space. Drop your jaw. Lift your soft palate. Make some room." If I do that, I lose all the *chiaro*. But if I simply release my throat, and let my vocal folds get looser while maintaining that same vowel, it will sound like and feel like I've made space. It's like making space without "making space."

It's the same concept with an /a/. That is the vowel that we drop our jaw the most and have the most space in, which is why we use it a lot. Typically, people will sing an /a/ with either a dark or a wide sound. Both of these sounds will have space as we typically define the idea of "making space," but neither one of them sound like they actually have space. You have to let the tongue go up and release your throat. Just the thought of the /a/ is what makes an /a/ as long as the air flows through your cords and fills the space of the vowel. If you sing the /a/ but tighten your cords the air won't be able to fill the space properly.

Registration

Accessing the High Register

I always say that it's not how high you get that matters, it's how you get high.

Pedagogy

Positive Directives

You can't play tennis by saying, "Don't twist your wrist," or by thinking about your technique. You have to actually hit the ball first. You have to run around the court to get to the ball. While you have to invest in how to do those things, first you must just do them. All singers start by just doing something intuitively to make sound. We imitate a sound and, if it sounds good, we get encouragement to continue. That becomes the unspoken thing that makes you think you know what you're doing, even when you don't. You're just guessing. But that can make teachers think that you actually do know what you're doing, so they start telling you what not to do. Teachers really have to educate singers about what is good and right. I learned that early on. The most profound realization is that if you're committing to an action, there's only a positive commitment to that action. There's no negative commitment to that action.

Objectivity in Voice Study

To be a pro, you have to be objective about your technical work. This can be difficult, because our instrument is who we are. So, everyone starts criticizing us and we try to beat everybody to the punch by criticizing ourselves. Even though on one level this seems humble, it's actually egotistical, because we're trying to prove that we're perfect in front of everybody by beating the critics to the punch. But the real art is showing your ass. It's being vulnerable. You have to let yourself be a failure. You have to let it be the real you. You can't prevent anything bad from happening; just do the right thing. If you do the best you can do at any given moment, it's probably going to be really good. But you can still be objective, even in those good moments. You can know that some aspect or another is not as good as it could be. Owning and claiming that objectivity is actually what gives us security and confidence. It's not ever going to be perfect. That's boring. Who wants it to be perfect? We want it to be a colorful, complete sound that you can engage and use to express yourself. It's never perfect, because nobody is perfect. It's just who we are.

Exercises

Exercise 1: (used with male and female students)
/ni ne na nɔ nu/ first spoken, and then on a single pitch.

Instruction:
(baritone) Keep the jaw neutral. Breathe through the vowel and move your breath to start speaking the tone. Don't "place" or hold any vowels in one spot.
(mezzo soprano) Keep moving both your breath and your vowels. Continue to reiterate or redefine your vowels as you sing the exercises. Don't get locked into a spot. Let the air fall out of you, rather than pushing it out.
(tenor) Avoid taking in too much air and stockpiling it. Just breathe in enough to say what you need to say, and let that flow out of you.

Exercise 2: (used with male and female students)
Siren downward from top falsetto to the lowest range, ending in vocal fry.
Siren upward from vocal fry into lowest range and end in the top range/falsetto.
Repeat using different vowels.

Instructions: Keep intending the vowel sound. Keep moving it, but don't set the position. Only the lips should move between the /a/ and /ɔ/. Rather than surging the air as you ascend, try to keep the breath flow exactly the same throughout the whole siren.

Exercise 3: (used with male and female students)
Free-Flowing Air

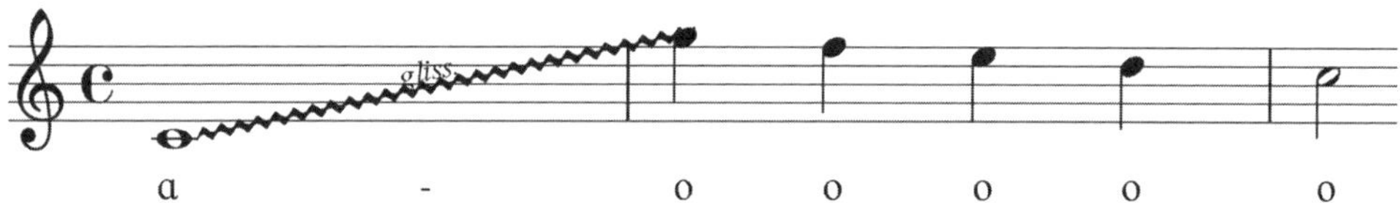

Instructions:
(baritone) Begin in the vocal fry and slide up to falsetto. The descending scale is sung in falsetto. The folds are being stretched longer and thinner without tightness and stiffness or holding back your breath. Keep that sense of flexibility. Keep your tongue high all of the way through. Visualize it going higher so it doesn't drop. Keep it as light as you can.
(mezzo soprano) Don't question yourself as you go toward the top. Don't care about the outcome. Just do it.
(tenor) I think also you're starting with your jaw too wide because you seem to have to close it more as you go through the exercise. Over opening your jaw is causing some

contamination of the way you are positioning your inside structure. Instead, start with your jaw more closed. Belch out the sound.

(soprano) Feel like you're *glissando*-ing between all the notes. Smear from one note into another. That will help keep the air flowing through the phrase. Keep forming, rather than holding, the vowel as you descend.

Exercise 4: (used with male and female students)

Instructions:

(baritone) Picture the arch of the tongue for /i/. It's a little less arched for /e/. The tongue is flatter for /a/; as the front of the tongue comes down, the back gets higher. Just picture that kind of movement as you sing through the sequence. When you go to /u/ and /ɔ/, let the lips assist. Sigh more as you ascend so the air can continue carrying to the tongue.

(mezzo soprano) Let your brain form the /ɔ/ rather than the lips.

(tenor) Keep your breath the same between /e/ and /a/. When you over-open the /e/, you do something with the tongue and soft palate that doesn't allow the /a/ to function as well. If you keep your jaw opening constant, you will have a better shot at letting the breath actualize your vowel. This is very obviously not the way we normally do it, but you have to find a way to sing the /a/ with your teeth completely together. Find a way to feel that opening upward rather than downward.

(soprano) Sing it "blatty,' with that kind of sense of letting it fall through you and out of you with no inhibition. Shape the sound through a narrower alignment.

Exercise 5: (used with male and female students)

Spontaneous Combustion

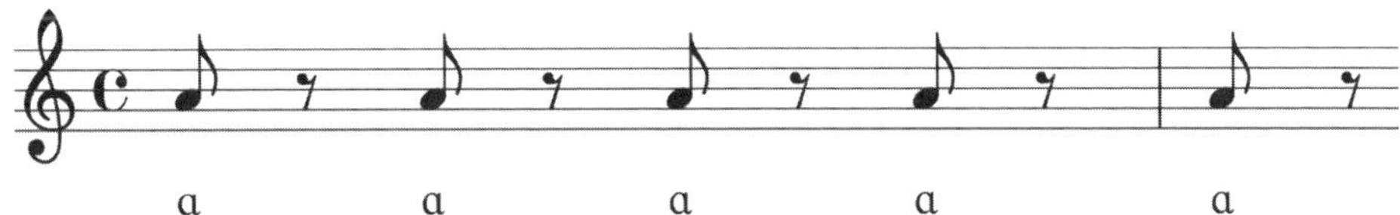

Instructions:

(baritone) Hold each note a little longer with a decrescendo at the end of each note. This is about onset and offset. Remember that you can't really do the onset the right way unless you start on your breath.

(mezzo soprano) Make sure the cords are together. The air flows to a vowel, and magically the cords speak. Every onset should help you sound clear, but it will feel unclear. Trust that your voice will come together.

(tenor) Keep your teeth together for this /a/. This simply forces you to stay on the breath more. The breath is the only thing that you can use if you aren't using your jaw to manipulate your throat. Use your air instead of thinking about the /a/ each time.

(soprano) Think about narrowing the sound more so the larynx can settle. Then it can feel like it takes a pathway through that back route. When you take a wide approach to the sound, the larynx lifts. If you breathe through the /a/, then the onset will have an easier time staying on your breath.

Exercise 6: (used with male and female students)
The Wobble

Instructions: Keep contact with the top pitch. Keep the timbre even on both pitches. Sigh downward, let the air go down, and think of the vowel constantly moving upward to keep the tongue from dropping when you descend to the lower pitch. If you say /a/, you can't really relax your tongue. The tongue has to do something to say /a/. If you are doing this exercise right, the jaw, soft palate, and tongue never change. The only thing that changes is the thickness of the cords as you move from pitch to pitch. Relying on the breath, which stabilizes you. Let the air fully fall out of you, totally uninhibited.

Exercise 7: (used with male and female students)
Getting High

Instructions:

(baritone) This exercise begins in the lower voice and ascends into the top voice, including the falsetto register. Trust your breath and keep thinking an /a/.

(mezzo soprano) Remember that only the lips change between the /a/ and /o/. When you access flute voice, let the voice vibrate the air and disconnect from your cords. Keep the air flowing.

(tenor) Use more upper lip for the /o/. Let it stay vulnerable. Keep defining your vowels. Instead of setting a position when you start, just think of the vowel and the air flow.

(soprano) – Think about more of a sigh as you sing this. As you go over the top, keep reforming your /o/, and imagine your lip moving downward and tongue moving upward.

CAROL VANESS

Carol Vaness earned her B.A. at the California State Polytechnic University in 1970 and her M.A. at the California State University Northridge in 1973. She launched her professional singing career at the New York City Opera, where she appeared regularly from 1979 to 1983. Since then, she has sung on the world's biggest stages and at premier music festivals, collaborated with today's foremost conductors in operatic and symphonic repertoires, appeared on numerous television broadcasts throughout North America and Europe, and compiled a distinguished catalog of recordings.

Her interpretations of Mozart's dramatic heroines, including Fiordiligi in *Così fan tutte*, Donna Anna and Donna Elvira in *Don Giovanni*, Elettra in *Idomeneo*, and Vitellia in *La Clemenza di Tito*, have been hailed as definitive, and she has become especially identifiable with the role of Floria Tosca, which she sang at the Metropolitan Opera in 2004 opposite Pavarotti in the legendary tenor's final operatic performance.

Vaness made her professional debut as Vitellia for the San Francisco Spring Opera and has been acknowledged as the world's leading interpreter of this role. She has appeared as Vitellia at the Met, Paris Opera, Royal Opera, Covent Garden, Chicago Lyric Opera, Gran Teatro del Liceo, the Salzburg Festival, and other leading theaters.

Among her many celebrated television appearances, she has been featured on the "Pavarotti Plus" and "Pavarotti and Friends" telecasts from Lincoln Center, as well as the Richard Tucker Gala and "In Performance at the White House" with members of the New York City Opera.

Her appointment as Music Professor of Voice at Indiana University's Jacobs School of music in 2005 was widely celebrated through both the academic and music communities.

The Interview

Although I have had the opportunity to witness Carol in action with several very talented students through the years, my observations for this chapter were with young artists at the prestigious Castleton Festival in Virginia. The singers I observed were nearing production week, so they all wanted to run through repertoire during the lesson rather than spending time on technical exercises. Therefore, the structure of this chapter will differ from the others to capture the valuable work Carol did with each student with respect to different arias from the standard repertoire.

CV: My first teacher, David, was not particularly wonderful with languages. But I'm pretty good with languages, so that was not a problem for me. I just never found a reason to go to anywhere else, because every time I had a problem or something would happen, I knew I could trust him to keep my voice healthy.

RR: *So, you really only had one voice teacher?*

CV: Yes. David W. Scott from Cal State University, Northridge. In the era when I knew there were famous voice teachers, I just didn't see the need to go elsewhere. It took many years for him to say that something was "great." It's not that he wasn't encouraging. He would just say, "It's coming along. It's coming along, kid. Pretty good. Pretty good." And I'd be thinking, "Yes, he thought I was great!" Of course, he never actually said I was great. I told him once, "You know David? During all these years when I was singing all over the place, you never told me I was great." And he said, "Did I need to?" And I said, "Well, I guess not then."

It's not that I didn't feel that I needed other opinions during my career. I was curious before I sang my last Donna Anna to hear what Margaret Harshaw would have to say about my singing, because I had been doing a lot of heavy repertoire during the ten years since I had last sung the role. My teacher and his wife had gone to Hong Kong during the time I was in Chicago singing with Domingo. So, I drove to Bloomington to see her. It was the first time I ever thought I'd take another lesson with somebody. She was really old by then, but very feisty. I asked her if she would give me a lesson and she said, "Why do you need a lesson from me?" I said, "Well, I would just like you to hear me, and hear what you have to say." She said, "Well, okay. Come on down then." She didn't really say anything about my technique, but advised me to sing "Non mi dir" every day, not because my technique wasn't adequate, but to help me deal with the inevitable nerves everyone has during that scene. I thought that was good advice, but that's really all she said to me. I had a very good time.

RR: *What's the difference to you between Anna and Elvira?*

CV: Probably nerves. I think Donna Elvira's a very easy role because my voice is good with leaps. As long as your voice is good with leaps and you don't over-sing, it's not too taxing. Donna Anna was always a tightrope walk for me. You have to be really precise with Donna Anna. It's not that you don't get into the emotions and the music, but there are really times when all I thought was, "Get rid of your air. Take your air. Get it forward—not too dark." Elvira just hops all over the place, but to sing Anna you just have to be singing every day so your voice stays well-oiled at the top.

RR: *You talk a lot about taking a "reset breath." Do you mean to blow out all of your breath before inhaling?*

CV: No, I recommend blowing out all of the air before singing a particularly long or big phrase. If I make sure I have all my air out, my inhalation can be as wide and full as it can be. For me, a reset breath is something I find more often in the middle of a long progression of shorter phrases. An example of this would be something that needs a constant balance, like "Dove sono." The breaths that come quickly in that aria are just resets for me. I don't really need them for the air. I don't really need a ton of air. I just need to relax my throat for an instant and let go of the tension. If I can find an inhalation at that moment to open my throat and reset my voice, I'm set to go on. When I breathe into the position for the next phrase after the reset, I can continue with the right body and mental focus.

RR: *So, you're always preparing the space for what you need to do next.*

CV: Absolutely. Every single time.

RR: *You talk a lot about the width of the ribs and finding width inside the body.*

CV: I talk about it because I think so many people talk about low breath already. I believe strongly in taking a low breath, but if someone is having difficulties with it, I will often suggest thinking about a wider breath. The instant you find the concept of a wide breath, you effectively get a low breath. Everything gets low if you think wide—at least on my body. I don't have a set rule for anything. I just look at what everyone needs and do what I can do to help this person.

When I work with a student, I ask myself, "What is this person attempting to do? What do she hope to gain? What is the most important thing I can help her with." And I listen to her ideas about what is going on. That kind of discourse is important with a student. When young singers come to me for a lesson, they're probably also getting ninety-nine other opinions. They will take what they like out of it, but sometimes everything they like doesn't necessarily fit together in one package. One thing may feel good for a bit, but then starts to become an issue. I really loved to sing a dark F^4 in the middle. My teacher always used to say, "Carol, that F^4 cannot be so dark." And I would reply, "but it feels so good, David." He would say, "I don't care what it feels like. I'm just telling you, it doesn't match." I don't think our voices should be monotonous, but I think every voice has a tonal range that is wise to use. I would hate to take out all the interesting parts of a student's voice.

I think if you're a good diagnostician, you have to remember that you can diagnose more quickly than you could ever fix those issues. Sometimes you say to someone, "That /i/ is too tight:" but the next time you see her, she is taking that directive to the extreme. And the next thing you know, she's taking in another direction that you never intended. That's why I think it's so hard to travel around and not be with your students.

RR: *I notice a lot of times you point up here on your cheekbones, but you don't lift your cheeks.*

CV: No, I don't want them lifting their cheeks. I want them to feel an inner lift. Some people who do it say, "That feels so much better!" My response to that is always, "Now don't do it too much. Don't overdo it." There are always students who will carry an idea too far.

RR: *Do you work with men the same way you work with women?*

CV: Yes, in the sense that I diagnose what their issues are when I first work with them. While men have *passaggi*, it doesn't seem like they have as many as women. I feel changes on every single note on the way up. Every one of them has a different place.

RR: *Can you explain where you feel those places in your head?*

CV: I don't feel it in my head. I feel it here inside my mouth. I put my B-flat^5 on my hard palate so it can stay rounded. My B-natural^5 feels like it is on my eyeteeth. The C^6 goes in the same direction, just not quite as wide. My A-natural^5 is in a smaller place—much smaller. Most of the time, however, I've tried not to think of my voice as being anywhere.

RR: *What do you think about giving dramatic repertoire to young singers?*

CV: There was a girl who showed up at Indiana University singing *Du bist der Lenz* for the first master classes I did there. I was really surprised they wanted to hire me after that, because I stopped her and said, "Wait a minute! Wait a minute! Don't start. Let me set everything up for you." I pushed the piano back, put the concert grand on the high stick, and said to the pianist, "play as loudly as you can," A couple of the teachers said, "No, no, no! That can't be loud! She's too young." And I said, "But this is Wagner. You need to know what to expect. For whatever reason, you're doing it, you need to know what you're up against, and this isn't even going to be a real test. This is just going to be a little bitty thing with a loud piano." And they said, "That's not fair!" But it was more than fair.

RR: *During your singing career, was there anyone in particular from whom you learned a lot, just by watching?*

CV: Yes. Renata Scotto and Beverly Sills. I watched Renata do *Adriana Lecouvreur*. From her, I learned that you have to be, above all, consistent. You have to go in one hundred percent prepared every day, note-perfect, and be consistently good on some level. You can't have a horrible day. She was always ready to sing, appropriately dressed for each rehearsal, and had a consistency of tone. I learned how to be fearless, or look like you're fearless, from Leontyne Price. I asked her once what I should do with a high-C[6]. She said, "You have a high-C, just throw it up there!" And I replied, "Yes, but I'm nervous." And she said, "Don't let them know that. They don't know it. You'll get very brave very soon. You'll see." She was right. I just started to act like I was being brave, and all of a sudden, I was brave. Then I became fearless enough to sing a B[5] softly. I think I just needed to have someone famous tell me, "Things happen to everybody, but, you know, you just act like it's not going to go wrong."

RR: *It's all about attitude.*

CV: Yes! I learned how to put myself into a character from Beverly Sills. I feel like my generation started to think that getting too much into character would wreck our voices. I had an incident early on when I was twenty-three years old when I sang *Così fan tutte* one day and was asked to rehearse *La Traviata* scenes the next day in a young artist program. I was a little bit sick already and very tired. When the stage director wanted me to sing full out, I said, "I can't sing full. I just sang *Così* yesterday." She started yelling at me, "You are not a professional. You are not a professional if you are not prepared to sing in a rehearsal." So, I became really angry, started singing "Sempre libera," and my vocal fold hemorrhaged on the high-C. Between that and a tonsillectomy, I required a long recovery. I had to relearn how to put two notes together. David actually rebuilt my voice.

RR: *Was this in San Francisco right after you finished school?*

CV: Yes, four months before I sang *Giulio Cesare*. I was really scared, but learned how to stay calm. It made me realize that I had to take care of my voice in a different way. Beverly said to me later, "What you need to learn from this experience is that people cannot make you put your vocal cords together. If something is wrong, do not sing." I say that to every single person. The kids get really tired, and there have been plenty of times when I've had to say, "Look, you have to be quiet. It's not worth losing your entire voice to do one dress rehearsal. Don't do it!" Amazing how many of them will still throw everything into a rehearsal, and for what? There's not always going to be somebody there to pull you aside and caution you to rest, and there often are people there who will want you to continue no matter what. You have to take control and be wise.

RR: *Do you never let students breathe through the nose?*

CV: I do only if I think it's dry enough in the room to make it necessary. I think it's fine to breathe in any way that is not detrimental.

RR: *Do you have specific things that you tell people to do? What would you like them to think about after they inhale?*

CV: Motion. I think their bodies should be ready before they take their breath, and then lightly move as they inhale to make sure the knees aren't locked. They can use the piano a little and lean in or take a step forward. It doesn't have to be much, just enough to unlock everything.

RR: *What do you think they should notice in their lower bodies while they are singing?*

CV: Ideally, they should remain very strong once they have their breath. It's not necessary to have abs of steel—they shouldn't lock up. I think it's good to use your legs to stay flexible. I think the lower part of the body has to be like an earthquake ready machine. Have you heard of those earthquake ready buildings in Los Angeles? They have flexible materials that allow the building to move during an earthquake so it can withstand the motion. I think that's what the lower body should be like.

RR: *What would you say are the top things singers need to do to prepare during their undergraduate or graduate years for auditioning and having a career?*

CV: That's a giant question. They need to be very good with languages. Their diction has to be beautiful. They have to be comfortable on stage. They have to say something with the music. It's not just about how loudly or softly you sing, it's about what you do with being loud, or the words, or what the composer put in the score. If you look at any Verdi or Mozart score and do one-third of what the composer put on the paper, you are doing more than most people do in the world. And then you must find the special quality that you love about your voice. For me, it's clarity and color. I had to love my individual sound and use that clarity and color.

You also need to have a figure. I don't mean every singer needs to be built like Marilyn Monroe or anything, but I think you have to be able to present a good, viable physique in today's world. That's probably the one thing that has really changed over the years. When I started singing, there was an understanding that being a singer meant you probably couldn't get married, have children, have a dog, or own a home in the country and an apartment in the city. Nowadays, singers don't want to give up anything or even spend as much time practicing in front of a mirror, as they should.

I've been coaching a woman for a long time who just made her major operatic debut as Fiordiligi. Now she's singing Donna Elvira in Salzburg. If you had heard her when I first started working with her, you would say, "This girl is not going to make it." But she felt compelled to keep working. She asked herself, "Who's the greatest singer around here? Okay, that's Carol Vaness." She called, introduced herself, and asked to work with me. And now she's out giving interviews telling everyone that she has been studying with me. I'm grateful for that. Lots of singers say that they got where they are all by themselves, but none of us do it ourself. I don't know what I would have done if I had never heard Carol Neblett sing Elettra in Ponnelle's *Idomeneo*. I loved her. I thought, "Wow, she can really sing *D'Oreste, d'Ajace*. That's my goal." You have no idea how many years it took me until I could sing that aria from the beginning until the end. It was long before I made my debut at the Met with that particular role. It is a monster. I knew exactly how I moved at each moment and I can still feel how I sang it. I can feel exactly how I breathe in that aria for every phrase, and can share it now with students. That's what I love about teaching. You have a chance to tell these things to somebody who might now have a really good go at it.

I hear good voices, but seldom an instantly recognizable one. I don't think anybody sounds like this one tenor I am teaching. I think that's the number one thing that I'm very proud of in my voice. The instant you hear two seconds of my voice, you can say, "That's Carol Vaness." The instant you hear Luciano Pavarotti, you know, "That's Luciano." When you hear Placido Domingo, you know it's him. It's the same with Jim Morris or Sam Ramey. We need to have more singers who are instantly recognizable.

RR: *Why do you think they're gone?*

CV: Maybe people haven't been listening to historic recordings as much. There's a reason so many Eastern Europeans are singing and not quite as many Americans. I think, in many ways, American teachers must be cautious to not train out the interesting part of people's voices.

RR: *I think there's a lot of that. There seems to be a trend toward squeezing out a little white, wide sound.*

CV: Yes. I don't understand that. Some voices are just supposed to be warm, dark, and velvet-like. Not everybody, but if your voice is like that, why would you change it? I remember listening to some old recordings of me in college and I thought, "Oh, my God! That fast vibrato and overly dark sound.

RR: *You had a fast vibrato?*

CV: Too fast—it was horrible. It was normal by the time I left grad school. David helped it settle down.

RR: *How did the two of you do that?*

CV: Through breathing. Just breathing. As my vowels got longer, and my breathing became better, my vibrato calmed down. David only taught breathing. He would say, "Get some breath under there! That's too dark! That's not bright enough. That's still not bright enough. That's too bright." And, very early in my studies with him, he told me that I needed to do something more with the music. I auditioned for grad school as a mezzo, singing "O don fatale." I do have a great chest voice. I remember asking my teacher how to handle the F^4's in *Norma*. He said, "Carol you're the one who signed up for the part. What do you think you're going to do with them?" I said, "I think the only way I can really do them is in a mix or in a chest mix." He said, "Then do it in a light high chest and mix it." That's what I did. People thought I was singing it in my chest voice, but I sound like a man in my chest voice. I just floated along in that lighter mix.

RR: *In looking back on your career, who were the primary people who influenced you?*

CV: I trusted Warren Jones. He was my primary coach and dear friend for about thirty-five years. We began working together in the Merola program. Robert Kettleson was my primary coach in Italy and Riccardo Muti's assistant at La Scala and in Salzburg. Then, of course, there was James Levine, who gave me a ton of my phrasing, Riccardo Muti, who gave me beautiful style and passion, and quite a few others. Those are the best in the world and in my life! Never mind the great directors like Sir Peter Hall and Trevor Nunn who made the words so magical! I have been so blessed. They all helped my technique and helped me form ways to teach younger singers.

Parting Thoughts

Carol Vaness truly is a legendary soprano. Her performances are remarkable in every way. As a teacher, she brings the same sort of insight and intensity to her students. In short, she is a *tour de force*.

There were many things to glean from my time with her. During the lessons, she was able to describe what she was hearing, what she would like to hear, and how to effectively get to that desired sound with the students. She did model for the students, but never in a way that was detrimental or without pointing out to them what she specifically wanted them to notice.

I was very happy to engage Carol in the discussion about the use of a reset breath, which is a valuable tool for any singer. The use of this kind of breath can prepare the body and energy to sing challenging musical lines. Barbara Doscher once told me, "Three things must always be prepared, Robin: the body, the space, and the breath must *always* be prepared before you sing."

All of this work on the breath helps her singers to pace their voices and measure their energy: after years at the top of her field, singing in the greatest houses with the greatest artists, she acutely understands this aspect of singing. It is not about power all the time, but about knowing when and how to use it that allows for the best release of the voice from the singer.

I thought that Carol's work in the middle section of "O du mein holder Abendstern" was very insightful [as can be seen in the lesson transcript posted at voxped.com/GTOGS]. This is a tricky spot because it lies right at the seam of the *passaggio* for the majority of baritones. The entire section is marked *pianissimo*. When I sang this in my younger years, it used to bother me that some notes around the upper *passaggio* would turn over and others, on the very same pitch, would stay open. It was not until later that I understood that both the vowel and the dynamic intensity determine the point in the scale where those pitches stay open or turn over. For me, the lighter dynamics and the closed vowels go over sooner in the registration. So, for the *pianissimo* dynamic and the closed vowel /u/, it is not unreasonable at all for most baritone voices to want to naturally go over into a *cupo*, or covered, sound.

I also noted Carol's insistence of avoiding glottal onsets in Italian literature. This reminds me of a story from my past, of which I hope you can forgive my inclusion. Back in the early 1980s, I had the distinct pleasure of having Italian Opera classes with the revered coach, Alberta Masiello, which was the highlight of my week. Yes, she was a chain smoker of cigarillos and sipped what I assumed to be scotch throughout classes at her apartment, but I always knew that I was in the room with a person who had incredible knowledge and history. To Miss Masiello, especially when it came to the Italian language, things were either right or wrong. There was no middle ground. She never attacked anyone personally, nor did she curse, but she made her points very clearly. I admired that very much. One night when we were working on *Gianni Schicchi*, a singer used a large glottal attack somewhere during a phrase. Quite uncharacteristically, Miss Masiello, quite evidently upset, erupted into a long Italian discourse. All I could understand in the tirade was something about the German language. Then she took a moment, took a draw on her cigarillo and a sip of her drink, and said, "There will be no glottals. We will begin again." I made a very concrete mental note at that moment: there are no glottal onsets in Italian. Period.

Lesson Highlights

Male Student 1: (baritone)
Tannhäuser: "O du mein holder Abendstern" (Wagner)
Using the physicality of the staging and character to aid technique

You must know what you are going to be doing actively before this aria begins. Are you moving about the stage? If you are singing "Hai già vinta la causa," it's almost imperative that you move, but not in this aria. You must know what the stage director has planned for the aria in this production. If you must be still, you can start thinking about finding an active stance. It doesn't mean you have to go anywhere, just that you must think actively. Think of finding a truly stable position for yourself and an eye focus at your height, rather than down at the floor. Try taking two steps forward as you sing it to see if that gives you more freedom.

We use the word "buoyancy" a great deal. Another term for it is "flexible tension." We need that kind of tension to allow the pitch to stay spinning, vibrant, and interesting. With you, all it takes is a couple of steps while keeping your head up and you find that flexible, buoyant, and continuously moving sound.

Female Student 1: (soprano)
Excerpts from *La Traviata* (Verdi)
Fully Supported Piano Singing

When you start teetering on the edge of going off the voice, your vibrato gets a little faster. That alone isn't a problem. I happen to like that sound here. That is a tool you can use, almost like you would for marking in rehearsals. But for fully supported, quiet singing, you want to keep the core in your voice small as you sing. Never lose it. The vibrato should not affect that small core. Just make sure that you always feel that little buzz running through it.

This does not mean to lower the soft palate or to make a "white" sound. If you keep your soft palate up, everything will stay true and you won't have to worry about ending up in a tricky situation. Then you can just play with the balance of how much breath you use and what color you choose for each vowel. If you have to sing with the soft palate down, it's impossible to determine what you're going need when your voice has to crescendo back to full voice.

Female Student 2: (soprano)

"E Susanna non vien…Dove sono" from *Le nozze di Figaro* (Mozart)

Singing Climactic Sections

Do not sing the second A^5 softly. Just sing both of them beautifully and full. I'm not saying to sing them loud because when we think something needs to be loud we tend to press on the sound rather than work to produce a beautiful tone.

Finding the Center of the Tone in Recitative

In this recitative, you really do need to take enough time to settle into your technique. You have to know as you are singing the first two pages of this recitative: where is my center of the vowel and my voice? When you stress and elongate the accented vowels, each vowel can help you find the center of the sound. For example, when you sing "di gelosia, di sdegno," finding the right tone can even help your position and your support. You need to take a breath before "fammi" and then let the A^5 go into the space, as opposed to thinking, "I'm going to put this A^5 right there!" Take a breath and go without grabbing it.

Using Inhalations to Express and Reset

You can use the kind of breath that expresses what you need to express in the text. I think you could trade some of those sniffing nose inhalations every once in a while, for a big, low reset breath. Breathe through your mouth and think low and wide. As you do that, your body aligns better, rather than lifting around the shoulders. Wider and longer breaths help your intonation a great deal. Truly, it is your reset. Now, feel as if your throat is opening up, release the note, and see what happens without closing anything. It just needs to be released.

Countess Droop

Be careful that you don't fall into the "Countess droop." Too many people think, "This is a droopy person, so I have to sing it droopy," That's just not the case! You have to make sure you're spinning, spinning, spinning the whole time on the breath.

Female Student 3: (soprano)

Sophie excerpts from the *Die Rosekavalier* trio (Strauss)

Singing /i/ in the Upper Register

When you get up to G^5, just relax some of those /i/vowels. If your teeth are locked, that's going to make your /i/ sound very spread. Try taking a breath through your mouth and think, "I want something between my molars. I do not want my teeth to come together." You want to be understood, but you also want to sound pretty. Try not to pull back and close your mouth. Your mouth stays at that "two fingers" space the whole time. I understand that you're trying to keep your jaw down through the *passaggio*, but this isn't enough room. You don't need to lock your jaw. Instead of making a real /i/, think /ɛ/ and remember to bloom. Think gentle and flexible.

Approaching B^5

Think about finding some lift in the B^5 and make it very, very tall. Don't round your mouth. I think it's important that you don't try to carry up a bunch of low voice weight in it. This is one kind of B that you can sing. For Verdi, or something heavier, I go with a wider feeling. It's either one direction or the other.

Female Student 4: (soprano)

"Or sai chi l'onore" from *Don Giovanni* (Mozart)

Finding Places of Rest and Reset

We have to make time to rest and reset in this aria. Let me just show you something right here. Write "calm," and "in two" at the top of your aria score. Regardless of what you see, you must think "two" until you need to think "four."

Whenever you speak of your father, make it as feminine and as easy as you can. Remember, this is your rest. Get a good breath after "rammenta la piaga." The next phrase is low, so you have to work a little harder. Then, get rid of your air on the /f/ of "furor" in *"D'un giusto furor."* Sometimes we forget to get rid of our air in this aria. This is where I do it. At the end of the aria on "vendetta ti chiego," you can either sing those phrases in one breath, or you can breathe. It's really irrelevant. People do them both ways. You have to do what's best for you.

Try to sing them in one breath. If you need a release, get all of the air out and all of the air back in. Air out; air in. Believe it or not, this is exactly how I think when I'm singing. It's all I think about. Here I think [on the lower "vendetta"], "No one's going to hear this." Then I start really singing here ["ti chiego"].

Later in the score, I have written, "Hang on, it's almost over." The breath after the very last "vendetta ti chiego" has to be a total reset. Get rid of any air that's left, but there probably won't be any, and then make sure that you fill right back up. If you get all jacked up through the whole aria, the aria is really hard. Whenever the text is feminine, it's okay to let everything rest for a moment before you come back with the harder emotions and say, "I want vengeance." You have to keep some of it in check. In all of these places we discussed there is a moment to take a good reset breath.

About the Authors

Robin Rice, baritone, is an associate professor of voice at The Ohio State University. He earned the Bachelor of Music degree at Baylor University and the Master of Music and Doctor of Musical Arts degrees from the University of Cincinnati College-Conservatory of Music. A specialist in the French repertoire, Rice became an honored participant under Elly Ameling, Gerard Souzay, and Dalton Baldwin at the Cleveland Art Song Festival. He also won the Carolyn Brice Award in the National Association of Teachers of Singing Artist Award Competition. He has worked with many luminaries such as Maestra Alberta Masiello, Theodore Uppmann, Barbara Honn, Jon Spong, Richard Hughes, Joyce Farwell, Kenneth Griffiths and Tom Jaber.

Dr. Rice has received international acclaim for his teaching. He served as the Master Teacher with Utah's Young Artist Apprentice Programs, San Diego Opera Ensemble, Florida Grand Opera's Young Artist Apprentice Program, Nightingale Opera Theatre Young Artists program, Pensacola Opera AIRS program, and the Indianapolis Opera Resident Artists program. Rice has also taught at many prestigious summer programs such as the Amalfi Coast Music Program in Vietri sul Mare, Italy, the International Asian Opera Workshop in Taipei, Taiwan, the International Asian Opera Project in Kunming, China, the Up North Vocal Institute, and the International Opera Festival in Beijing, China.

In addition, Dr. Rice has given master class at *Instituto Superior de Arte del Teatro Colon* in Buenos Aires, Argentina, Castellina in Chianti Vocal Workshop in Tuscany, Italy, Cullasaja Vocal Workshop in North Carolina, University of Colorado at Boulder, Rice University, Saint Mary's College of Notre Dame, Baylor University, and he has given a series of master classes in Taiwan. He has also appeared as a Master Teacher in Kunming, China and at Beijing University.

Rice's students have performed leading roles in major international opera houses, including the Metropolitan Opera, the Royal Opera House at Covent Garden, *Opéra-Théâtre de Limoges, Teatro Dell'Opera Roma,* Glyndebourne Festival Opera, *Deutsche Oper Berlin, Komische Oper Berlin,* Firenze's *Teatro del Maggio Musicale, Bayerische Staatsoper,* Royal Swedish Opera Stockholm, Kyrenia Opera, Los Angeles Opera, Sarasota Opera, San Diego Opera, Opera Company of Philadelphia, Florida Grand Opera, New Orleans Opera, Ft.

Worth Opera, New York City Opera, and Washington National Opera. Many have won prestigious national and international competitions. His students also have appeared in many apprentice programs, including Santa Fe, San Francisco, Chautauqua Opera, Opera Theater of Saint Louis, Glimmerglass, The Academy of Vocal Arts, and Wolf Trap.

Katherine Osborne is a member of the Voice Faculty at the University of Northern Iowa (UNI) where she teaches studio voice, voice pedagogy, and diction. She previously served on the voice faculties at Ohio Wesleyan University and the Washington National Cathedral. Dr. Osborne has presented research and workshops related to pedagogy, voice science, and singing health at the Voice Foundation Annual International Symposium, International Congress of Voice Teachers in Stockholm, Sweden, Fall Voice Conference, the Voice Forum and Pedagogy Summit at The Ohio State University, and UNI's Vocal Arts Festival. Her article titled "Breaking the Glass Slipper: Recognizing and Retraining the Misclassified Low Female Voice" was published in *VoicePrints: The Journal of the New York Singing Teacher's Association* in 2016. She was honored to receive the 2014 Van Lawrence Fellowship, presented by the Voice Foundation and NATS, and the 2015 Helen Swank Pedagogy Award from OSU.

Dr. Osborne maintains an active performing career in opera, oratorio, and art song. Her performance in Donizetti's *L'ajo nell'imbarazzo* was hailed by The Washington Post as "outstanding...[she] projected a fiery personality and sang graceful coloratura." Recent performances include a series of concerts at the Härnösand Summer Opera Festival in Sweden, where she is a member of the artist teaching faculty. Her training includes a Doctor of Musical Arts degree and Singing Health Specialization from OSU, Master of Voice Pedagogy degree from Westminster Choir College, a Bachelor of Music degree from Stetson University, and a 2010 teaching internship with the National Association of Teachers of Singing (NATS).